Canada
Handbook

The 49th annual handbook
of present conditions
and recent progress

Prepared in the
Publishing Section
Information Division
Statistics Canada

*Published under the authority of the
Minister of Supply and Services Canada*

©Minister of Supply and Services Canada 1981

Available by mail from:

Canadian Government Publishing Centre
Supply and Services Canada
Hull, Quebec, Canada K1A 0S9;

Publications Distribution
Statistics Canada
Ottawa, Canada K1A 0T6;

or through your bookseller.

Catalogue No. CS11-403/1981E   Canada: $6.00
ISBN 0-660-10860-7   Other countries: $7.20
Price subject to change without notice.

Contract No. OKP8-1563
Typesetting: Southam Communications Ltd., Toronto
Contract No. 02KX.45045-1-8197
Printing: Ashton-Potter Limited, Toronto.

Preface

Canada Handbook tells the story of Canada — its people, environment, culture, social and economic development, governments and services. The present 49th edition for 1980-81 provides both historical and up-to-date information on all aspects of Canadian society.

From education to farming, from technology to multiculturalism and from balance of payments to recreation, this book provides information and perspective. Like previous editions, *Canada Handbook*, 1980-81, with its succinct text, excellent photography and informative statistical tables will prove of interest both to those who want a general appreciation of the country as a whole and to those who want more specific insights into particular aspects. The book makes interesting reading wherever it is opened.

Many persons and departments have participated in this work, including contributors from the private sector, from several Statistics Canada divisions and from other federal and provincial departments. The planning and production is due to Margaret Smith, Editor, assisted by Patricia Harris and other members of the staff of Statistics Canada's Information Division. This partnership has done a fine job in portraying our country in text and colour photographs.

Martin B. Wilk
Martin B. Wilk
Chief Statistician of Canada

April 1981

APR - 7 1982   75423

Contents

The Environment

Regional Geography of Canada

Canada can be divided into smaller units to help comprehend the similarities and differences from place to place across its vast area. The defining of these regions should be based on distinguishing characteristics of selected criteria. Regional geography is not a collection of miscellaneous information about a region. It entails the selection, arrangement and interpretation of facts to present a viewpoint about an area which can be called geographical; emphasis will be on the distributional aspects of phenomena. Just as in history, for example, facts are selected to illustrate events in a period of time, so in geography there should be a selection of facts which characterize areas. Every valley and every village has its own unique geographical character; in theory, a study of each of these small units should lead to understanding of the geographical patterns of larger regions, and finally to Canada as a whole.

Geography describes and explains as much of the totality of a regional landscape as possible. This landscape is made up of both the natural (physical) environment and the distribution patterns of man-made features. Large areas of Canada have

Geographical Regions of Canada

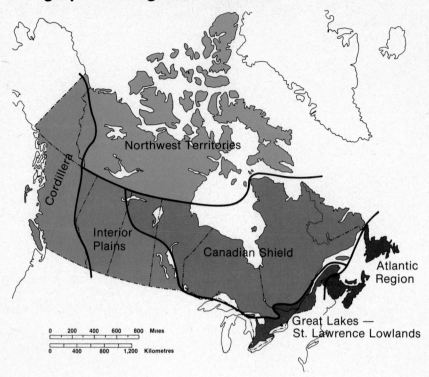

similarities in certain elements of their landscapes; by grouping these selected similarities into regional units the "character" of a region may be described and its differences from other regions clarified. Many people have a "regional conscious-ness" which tells them intuitively that their local area differs in certain aspects from some distinctive characteristics of nearby or far-off regions. As people travel more throughout Canada, they realize the similarities that may be seen from place to place; thus comparing similarities in regions is equally as important as defining differences. The purpose of regional geography is to assist, along with other disciplines, toward the goal of understanding as much as possible about Canada in whole and in part.

Canadians need more specific regional and locative terms than the frequently used "eastern", "western" or "northern" which means different things to different people depending on where they are at the time. Kirkland Lake is probably "northern" to most people in Ontario, but it is the same latitude as Vancouver which considers itself to be "southern".

The mountain peaks of Alberta tower over the blue and green mosaic of the rushing water and majestic trees below.

→

The silent beauty of winter in New Brunswick.

In this article Canada has been divided into six regions. The regions are generally well known to Canadians and, therefore, have the advantages of local familiarity and national recognition. The criteria for defining these regions differ; some are landform areas, whereas others are political units. Following are summaries of the characteristics and definitions of these six regions of Canada.

The Atlantic Provinces are mainly a political region including the Maritime provinces and the island of Newfoundland. The Labrador section of Newfoundland may be considered part of the Canadian Shield region, an area with which it has similar environmental and resource-use characteristics. The Atlantic provinces have been known to Canada statistically for their lower incomes, and their less expanding economy. Fragmentation of the economy and dispersal of population are two of the distinctive geographical characteristics.

The Great Lakes–St. Lawrence Lowlands are bounded on the north by the geological and landform escarpment of the Canadian Shield which is quite visible in the landscape. This landform feature separates the high intensity agricultural and urban characteristics of the Lowlands from the forested and sparsely populated Shield. The Lowlands have the highest densities of industry, commerce and population in Canada; the region is the "heartland" of the nation. There are cultural differences between parts of the region in relation to the prevalence of either the English or French language, suggesting division into at least two sub-regions based on human criteria.

The Canadian Shield is another landform region, defined on the basis of its exposed ancient Precambrian rock base. Its physical environmental characteristics of bare rocks, forests and lakes are quite distinct from the Lowlands. Because it is a huge area, covering about half of the mainland of Canada, there is environmental diversity within this region, but there are also large areas of similarity. The southern part of the Canadian Shield is known for its vast natural resources which are functionally linked to the heartland region. The northwestern part of the Shield has a different surface environment and different human use and is included as part of the Northwest Territories, a region defined by political criteria.

The Interior Plains are sharply bounded on the west by the high wall of the Rocky Mountains, but on the east the geological and landform edge of the Shield is often hidden beneath former glacial lake deposition or by coniferous forest. The plains are the largest area of nearly level land in Canada; their human use is characterized by the large grain farms in the southern parts. Only a small part of the plains is covered with prairie grassland, despite contrary popular opinion. Although all of the Prairie provinces might be discussed as a political region, the environmental, economic and human characteristics of the Shield sections of northern Manitoba and northern Saskatchewan are very different from the plains.

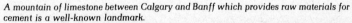

A mountain of limestone between Calgary and Banff which provides raw materials for cement is a well-known landmark.

The Cordillera is a mountainous region which coincides closely, but not entirely with the political limits of British Columbia and Yukon. The level section of northeastern British Columbia is part of the Interior Plains, emphasizing its differences from the rest of British Columbia. The geography of the Cordillera is characterized by great contrasts within small areas in the physical environment and in population densities. The resource-based economy is similar to that of the Atlantic provinces, but on a different scale. In a regionalization of Canada it is debatable whether the Yukon should be part of the mountainous Cordillera or should be studied for its "northern" characteristics with the Northwest Territories.

The Northwest Territories are a political region with no landform or other environmental uniformity; the population is small and dispersed. A decision concerning its regional boundaries raises several geographical questions. Will the people and economy of the Mackenzie Valley be better understood by emphasizing their similarities with the northern Interior Plains, or by thinking of the Territories as a political unit separated from Southern Canada by the sparsely populated northern parts of the provinces? Although Keewatin District is part of the Canadian Shield based on geological criteria it is different from the southern Shield geographically because of its treeless environment, arctic climate and its Inuit inhabitants.

Mirrored beauty at Mount Revelstoke National Park, BC.

The splendour of Quebec.

The Atlantic Provinces

Fragmentation and dispersal are themes which run through a geographical discussion of the Atlantic provinces. By many economic and statistical measurements of Canadian regional development the Atlantic provinces are at the lower rank among the provinces. The internal environmental variety, the separation of economic activities, and the lack of a very large urban centre are geographical characteristics which are lost when statistics are aggregated into regional totals for the four provinces.

The Atlantic provinces region differs from the rest of the country in several physical characteristics. Its low hills and mountains and rugged, indented coasts are different landform types than those of the St. Lawrence Lowlands. East Coast landforms separated people into small patches of settlement in the past. The maritime climate is not the same as that of the rest of Eastern Canada and it differs from the maritime climate of the West Coast. Although trees are similar to those growing elsewhere in Eastern Canada, the way in which they are areally associated requires classification as a separate vegetation region. Resource-based primary occupations are more important in the Atlantic region than they are in southern Ontario and Quebec, but eastern resource-use activities often result in single-industry towns which are dispersed around the coasts. There are few areas of high concentrations of people. Although the individual farms, villages, towns and cities are often similar in form and function to other settlements in Canada their geographical dispersal into small areas, strips and dispersed centres gives the region a different geography of settlement and human use.

Distribution patterns are not static in any region; they change over time. The geography of agriculture and fishing in the Atlantic provinces illustrates these changing areal patterns. Most of the former part-time and subsistence farms, associated with rural poverty, and located on the poorer soils, steeper slopes and away from main roads have been abandoned; the distribution of commercial farms is now much more closely associated with improved roads and access to the larger cities. The past regional character of agriculture in the Maritimes did not stem from its type of farm or general land use, but was distinguished by the shape of its farmland strips and its areal dispersal.

Fishing activity is also changing from dispersal to concentration. In Newfoundland mainly, and to a lesser extent in Nova Scotia, the small fishing "outports" or villages were dispersed along the coast in sheltered bays, near headlands, or on islands. Because each family wanted space for drying flakes, separate wharves, and adjoining gardens — all with shore location — these fishing villages developed distinct dispersed housing. The visual form of these villages was different from other resource-based settlements in Canada; those which remain constitute one of the elements in the total landscape which gives regional character to the Atlantic provinces. Fishermen are now concentrating into larger towns near the processing or freezing plants where there are more health, educational and social services. Sometimes, however, this geographical trend has changed the fisheries' rural poverty and low incomes to increased urban unemployment.

The Great Lakes–St. Lawrence Lowlands

The small Lowlands region extending across southern Ontario and southern Quebec holds more than half of Canada's population and produces about three-quarters of the value of its manufactured goods. This densely-populated part of Eastern Canada has more large cities of over 100,000 population than any other similar sized part of the nation. Its excellent agricultural lands help to feed the nation's two largest cities — Montreal and Toronto. The region is the "heartland" of the country, characterized by high densities of urban, industrial and agricultural activities. In the 19th century the Lowlands region had a favourable combination of many elements in the natural environment in an accessible geographical location; it presented an attractive environment for people looking for agricultural land. The region had the largest area of level land with a warm summer climate in Canada, and it was accessible by the St. Lawrence River to settlers entering from the East.

Some of the internal contrasts are the result of cultural differences between French-Canadian and British-origin settlement. The rural landscape of southern Quebec, with its long, narrow farms, often demarked by old rail fences, is distinct within Canada, and contrasts with the rectangular farms and dispersed farmhouses of southern Ontario. The rural villages of Ontario, with their small, compact central business sections and rectangular street patterns contrast with the linear Quebec villages in which residential and commercial uses are often interspersed.

A blaze of autumn's colour in Nova Scotia.

In addition to a prosperous intensive agriculture, a closely-linked urban system has been built. The activities in industry, commerce, transport, service and recreation of more than 12 million people in the Great Lakes–St. Lawrence Lowlands are all closely interrelated areally. A size-hierarchy of hamlets, villages, towns and cities is spaced in geometric patterns across the Lowlands from Quebec City to Windsor. The size and spacing of these urban places is related to the size and population of the hinterland area that each serves. Despite different histories, economies and cultures these cities have many similar internal areal patterns.

Some of the areal relationships between Lowland cities and their nearby rural hinterlands can be illustrated by Montreal. It has had a dominant influence on the areal arrangement of the economy of Quebec. The dairying and market garden agriculture in the surrounding Montreal plain supplies this large urban market. The changes in the rural landscape from the "quaint habitant" farms of the 19th century to the present, well-equipped dairy farms can be attributed directly to the market of Montreal. The city's clothing industry is functionally connected with the many textile and yarn mills in the towns and villages south and east of Montreal. Many of the resource industries of the Canadian Shield are managed from offices rising above Montreal's city centre.

There are similar spatial relationships between cities and hinterlands in southern Ontario. Greater Toronto is the focus of transport lines that serve all of the Ontario Lowlands and bring the natural resources of the southern Canadian Shield and the Interior Plains to the city. The manifestations of these many geographical connections are illustrated by the thousands of management and clerical workers who cluster into the high-rise office buildings of the financial core of Toronto.

The cities around the western end of Lake Ontario are now an urban complex which is not duplicated on the same scale elsewhere in Canada. From Oshawa to Hamilton and spreading east to St. Catharines and Niagara Falls, this part of southern Ontario has unique geographical patterns formed by the coalescing of individual cities. On a smaller scale, the same coalescing of urban activities is taking place in the nearby Grand River Valley from Woodstock to Kitchener and Guelph. The industries of the Grand River sub-region and the Toronto-Hamilton complex are already integrated in many ways; products move from city to city for assembly or further processing or for final consumption. The changing geographical patterns, resulting from changing rural to urban land uses, have given rise to numerous social, economic and local government problems.

The Canadian Shield

The enormous Canadian Shield occupies about half of the mainland of Canada. Although there are significant differences between the northern and southern parts of the region there are also large areas in which there is much similarity. The Shield is defined as the area underlain directly by ancient Precambrian rocks. The physical environment of the Shield contrasts strongly with that of the Lowlands south of it. The Shield is a region of forests, lakes and rocks; it is a region of few people, and they are mainly urban dwellers. The southern Shield, sometimes called the "Middle North" by persons in southern Ontario and Quebec, has a resource-based economy; its products — minerals, wood and waterpower — are exported outside of the region or outside of Canada. Interaction and movement between the Shield and the adjoining Lowlands are common, and the regions are interdependent. Many of the raw materials of the Shield move to the Lowlands for processing or consumption; a reverse flow of people comes into the Shield for recreation or holidays.

The geography of natural resource utilization in the Shield has evolved in specific distribution patterns. From the south-central outer edge of the Shield, man and his resource-exploitive activities have spread outward across the outer sections. This semicircular pattern of utilization is now penetrating slowly into the Shield, but vast areas still remain unoccupied. The natural environment in the northern Shield is different, however, and the resource potential there is scanty or lacking; the same type or intensity of resource development and allied settlement cannot be expected in the northern Shield.

Although known in Canada as "a storehouse of minerals", not all of the Shield is mineralized. Mining settlements are both clustered and dispersed; they form an interconnected network of communities in the south-central part of the Shield across the Ontario-Quebec border but they are isolated towns along the eastern and northwestern flanks of the Shield. For example, a functional mining region evolved in northeastern Ontario by 1940, linked by rail, road and power transmission lines.

Rushing River Provincial Park in Ontario.

The availability of railways made it possible to establish pulp and paper mills amid the untapped forests. The area of agriculture expanded in the Clay Belt near these towns as the urban population increased. Most of the mining communities elsewhere in the Canadian Shield were established after 1945 and are examples of the new resource-based, single-industry towns on the "resources frontier" of Canada. Their curving streets and planned separation of work and residence areas are different from the older cities of Southern Canada.

A similar peripheral distribution pattern of pulp and/or paper mills developed on or near the outer edge of the Shield early in this century. Most of the mills were located in an arcing zone between Quebec City and the Upper Ottawa River. The Shield edge westward in northern Manitoba and Saskatchewan does not have a sufficient natural endowment of trees to support a local pulp and paper industry.

The third major natural resource of the Shield, waterpower, also has a peripheral distribution along its outer edge. Fortunately, the outer "fall-line" of the Shield, where outward-flowing rivers tumble over the southern escarpment, is close to the region of greatest need for power — the Lowlands. The evolution of a spatial pattern of hydro-power development can be illustrated in Quebec. The earliest sites were in the south-central edges of the Shield, such as along the St-Maurice River; later plants were built progressively outward to the east and west along the Shield edge, such as on tributaries of the Ottawa River and in the Saguenay Valley. The eastward-evolving pattern of power development was highlighted by the Bersimis River in the 1950s, the Manicouagan-Outardes rivers in the 1960s, and the Churchill River of Labrador in the 1970s. With no other large, outward-flowing rivers from the Shield available for hydro-power development the Quebec government had to turn to La Grande River whose water drops down to James Bay, thus beginning the utilization of an "inner fall-line".

One of the major natural resources of the Shield is its landscapes or scenery. The totality of its natural environment, with its varying combinations of trees, lakes, rivers, hills and animal life appeals to urban people of the adjoining Lowlands and nearby United States. Whereas other natural resources are shipped out of the Shield, scenery, a resource which can be used over and over again, brings people into the region. The south-central edge of the Shield, closest to the high densities of people on the Lowlands, has the greatest use with decreasing intensity of use and accessibility outward along the Shield edges and into the northern interior.

Agriculture is a decreasing activity within the Shield region. The largest areas are on the level land of old glacial lake bottoms in the Clay Belt across the Ontario–Quebec boundary, and on the Lowlands around Lac St-Jean. Whereas farms are a part of the regional landscapes in most parts of Southern Canada, they are a minor element near Shield settlements and are totally lacking over the major portion of the Shield.

Autumn gold in Ontario.

Although the Plains are very flat, landform regions include hills, escarpments, river valleys and low mountains.

The Interior Plains

The words "flat, prairie, wheat and petroleum" might well characterize the environment and resources of the Interior Plains of Canada. Although these words accurately describe certain outstanding parts of the Plains environment and economy, they do not tell of the variety found within the region. It is true that large areas of the Plains are very flat, but the landform regions include hills, escarpments, entrenched river valleys and even low mountains; although prairie grasslands of varying height once covered the southern plains prior to cultivation, now more than half of the region is forested; although wheat became a staple crop for export after the land was subdivided for settlement, other grains were also grown and several new crops now occupy significant acreages; although petroleum was important in diversifying the Plains economy after 1947, other fuels and minerals have become significant in particular parts. Similar to the Canadian Shield the Interior Plains has large areas of generally uniform environmental conditions, but the characteristics and combination of these physical elements are different from those of the Shield.

Large areas of the Plains have generally similar climatic conditions but the variations away from the averages and extremes give a distinct regional character to the Plains climate. Variability of precipitation, for example, is more characteristic of the Interior Plains climate than in any other region of Canada. Vegetation patterns are indicative of areal differences in climate. The original grasslands of the southern Plains indicated the areas of lower precipitation and higher summer temperatures. North of the grasslands small deciduous trees were able to survive where the average precipitation was slightly higher and summers were cooler. Coniferous forests cover the northern Plains where winters are continually cold.

The distribution pattern of types of agriculture coincided fairly closely with the semicircular zones of soils, vegetation and climate until the 1940s. Since then non-environmental factors have had much more influence on the kind of crops grown and their areas of concentration. Crop acreages change from year to year within the region and also within farms as a result of management decisions concerning acreages, changes in foreign markets, consumer preferences and other external factors. An aerial view of the large, rectangular farms with only a few crops, the widely dispersed farmhouses, and the absence of trees except near the farmhouses leaves little doubt that agriculture of the Plains region is different from that elsewhere in Canada.

The internal urban geography of Plains cities is quite similar to that of eastern cities but shades in the urban landscape help to characterize prairie cities. Because they were settled mainly in this century, there are few old buildings compared with eastern cities; narrow streets are rare and wide streets are common; the line between urban and rural land uses is quite sharp and has been more carefully planned and controlled than in eastern cities.

One of the geographical characteristics of the Interior Plains is the geometric spacing of its villages, towns and cities. The size and function of Prairie villages and towns are related to the number of farmers in the surrounding area needing certain urban goods and services. Other specialized items and services, needed less frequently, tend to be located in larger cities where they can serve more people locally and also be available to people from a larger surrounding rural area. In addition, small urban centres show regularity to their spacing which is related to the railway lines and to their function as grain collecting centres. The size gradation of this distribution pattern is breaking down as road transport improves and people can travel farther for their services.

The Cordillera

A mountainous region known as the Cordillera extends along western North America; most of British Columbia and all of Yukon are within the Canadian Cordillera. Great contrasts within small areas are characteristic of the natural environment of this mountainous region. It is a land of urban people; agriculture is entirely lacking over large areas or is confined to certain narrow valleys or flood plains. This urban population is concentrated into one small area in the southwestern corner of British Columbia where 75 per cent of the population lives. Settlements throughout the remainder of the Cordillera are based mainly on the exploitation of a natural resource. This resource-based economy is similar to that in the Canadian Shield and the Atlantic provinces.

The only other parts of Canada with comparable spectacular mountain landforms are Baffin and Ellesmere islands in the northeastern Arctic. Although the Cordilleran mountains seem to be a jumbled mass of peaks when viewed locally, and stretch endlessly to the horizon when seen from the air, they have specific areal patterns and can be classified into smaller sub-regional landform units. The Rocky Mountains, for example, are a specific line of mountain ranges extending from Montana along part of the Alberta–British Columbia border to the broad plain of the Liard River in northeastern British Columbia. The western landform boundary of

Man is dwarfed by the unlimited scope of the Yukon.

the Rockies is the Rocky Mountain Trench, one of the world's longest continuous valleys, extending from Montana to the headwaters of the Liard River in the Yukon.

Contrasts in climate within small areas are characteristic of all mountainous regions and the Canadian Cordillera is no exception. The greatest amounts of precipitation recorded in Canada are one of the distinctive features of some of the west-facing slopes of the Insular and Coast Mountains and only 320 to 480 km (kilometres) eastward, in the southern interior valleys of British Columbia and in southern Yukon, are some of the driest weather stations outside of the Arctic.

The geography of forest utilization indicates that the original density of development was in the southwest and the wood-processing industry is still concentrated there. As forests farther away along the coast were cut, and a log transporting technology developed, the coastal hinterland could be exploited to supply the urban sawmills around Georgia Strait. After 1950, increased world demand, plus improved rail and road transport into the little used forest reserves of the interior, permitted inland expansion of cutting. Areal patterns of dispersal followed by concentration, and corporate integration of processing, were established in the interior forestry industry similar to the patterns which developed on the coast prior to 1940.

The West Coast fishery has different areal patterns than that on the Atlantic Coast. The industry has adapted to the natural habits and migrations of the five main species of salmon. Fish canneries were established at or near the mouths of most rivers all along the coast early in this century, but the greatest concentration was near the Fraser and Skeena rivers which had the largest drainage basins and therefore usually had the most fish production. Fishing technology gradually improved so that larger and faster fishing vessels, with better gear, could harvest a larger area away from the river mouths; thus the need for many small dispersed canneries decreased, and the processing industry concentrated into large canneries near the mouths of the two largest rivers. The lack of coastal settlement for fishing contrasts with the type of fishery settlement in Eastern Canada.

Through more than a century of mining the geographical patterns of development have been consistent. At the turn of this century southeastern British Columbia was one of the important mining areas of Canada while the rest of the province was struggling to create a viable economy. This region is still the main mining region of the Cordillera functioning around the large smelter-refinery at Trail to which a variety of ores can be taken for processing. Although mineralization is apparently widely spread throughout Yukon, the few operating mines are dispersed across the southern part. Having only a few internal transportation lines until recently, potential mines in the Yukon face high transport costs to external markets. The characteristics of mining in the Cordillera are similar to those in the Canadian Shield but the density of development is not as high in the former area.

The recreational use of the spectacular and varied environments of the Cordillera has been similar to that in the Canadian Shield. The empty areas of the Cordillera will have increasing value to visitors as population densities increase in the western part of North America.

The Cordillera has two sub-regions: the coast, with its distinctive climate and urban concentration, and the interior, with its growing resource-oriented settlements. Despite the great latitudinal extent from central British Columbia to northern Yukon, there is a great deal of similarity in the interior environments and in the type and sparsity of settlement. Improved transport is breaking down this coast-interior division and a new set of interconnected areal patterns is evolving in the Cordillera.

The Northwest Territories

This region is defined by political boundaries and lacks the uniformity of certain physical or economic criteria used to describe other regions of Canada. The Northwest Territories is characterized by diversity of its natural environments, lack of developed resources, scanty population and a different type of government. The relative lack of developed natural resources is related both to the internal poor endowment of the natural environment and to external problems of both distance and accessibility.

Within the large area of the Territories there can be two sub-regions: the subarctic Mackenzie River Valley in the west and the arctic area of the islands and north-central mainland. These regions are defined by the 10°C July isotherm; northeast of this line the arctic area has no summer. This climate coincides closely with the northern limit of tree growth; it is also a cultural line separating Indians and Inuit.

The agricultural and forestry uses of this enormous area are minor in the subarctic and entirely lacking in the arctic sections. Not only are summers too cool in the arctic part but its landscape is characterized by bare, glacially-scoured rock

The Territories are underlain by parts of two geological regions: the Precambrian rocks of the Canadian Shield and the flat-lying young sedimentary rocks of the Interior Plains.

where soil is lacking. More favourable summer conditions in the subarctic Mackenzie Valley permit the possibility of agriculture; gardens can be productive, but the lack of large local markets discourages agriculture as an occupation.

This is the only region of Canada in which undomesticated animal resources are a significant element in the local economy. Game resources are still significant to some Mackenzie Valley Indians and for many Inuit the sea remains an important source of food. For both people, however, animals constitute a decreasing percentage of their food intake. Fur-bearing animals became important to the native economy after the white man entered the region early in this century. The treeless Arctic has only the white fox as a fur resource, in contrast to the variety of fur-bearing animals in the forested Mackenzie Valley, where most of the dispersed settlements were originally fur-trading posts.

Mineral resources are the hope that some parts of the Territories will become significant in the Canadian economy. The Territories are underlain by parts of two geological regions: the Precambrian rocks of the Canadian Shield in the eastern mainland and eastern islands, and the flat-lying young sedimentary rocks of the Interior Plains in the western mainland and northwestern islands. The latter rocks have apparently smaller quantities of petroleum and natural gas than is known in the Interior Plains further south. Development of arctic mineral resources has been hampered by difficulties of water transport which must operate in seas that are ice-covered for nine to 12 months of the year.

As in other regions of sparse population in Canada, the total natural environment, or scenery, may attract short-term visitors. The tundra vegetation of the treeless Arctic is unique in Canada; the mountains of Baffin, Devon and Ellesmere islands are the highest in eastern North America and their ice-caps and glaciers present spectacular alpine scenery; ice floes and icebergs could contribute to a different water-travel experience for most people. The vague "lure of the North", and the chance to see a different environment and a different people — the Inuit — may yet be one of the most valuable elements in the arctic resource base.

J. LEWIS ROBINSON

The Climate

Canadians have tended to accept their climate fatalistically. However, the desire to remain both a consumer society and a custodian of ecological values poses a need for skill, efficiency and prudence in using and living with climate. Sustained economic development is essential to providing an increasing population with desired consumer goods and this demands greater efficiencies and effectiveness in the use of our limited resources. On the other hand, the desire for a sustained high environmental quality demands that commerce, industry and social practices be within the restraints imposed by our climatically controlled ecosystem. Failure to do so now for the sake of short-term benefits may require very costly corrective measures in the future, or create irremediable problems.

Climate and the Economy

Climate is both a resource and a liability. As a resource, it provides the heat and moisture that are essential for life; it is a basis for agriculture, it provides warm lakes for swimmers and snow for skiing and it drives ocean currents. Drought, floods and hurricanes are among its hazards; these destroy life, damage property and inconvenience people, often stopping all normal economic activity within a community. Climatic change can drastically alter a regional economy by altering the ecosystems that are fundamental to its way of life.

Economic activity serves social goals and must usually be considered in the light of social desires and needs. Conversely, the need and desire to maintain unique landscapes, to reduce travel time between functional areas or to reduce the cost of public services are basically social, but they have great economic implications. Accordingly, many environmental and social issues are referred to in this article because, like climate, they too shape the Canadian economy and must be considered in the evaluation and use of climatic resources.

Climate as a Resource

It has been pointed out that "in general the centre of active progress in civilization has migrated from relatively unstimulating warm regions with few storms, where the winter is the most comfortable season, to stimulating regions with many storms, where the summer is the most comfortable period".[1] This has been made possible by the development of housing and buildings that provide a suitable indoor climate and of transportation systems that withstand the rigours of temperate-zone winters. That our climate is economically stimulating is attested to by our gross national product compared to those of low-energy-consumption countries of the tropics.

But our weather is much more than stimulating; our heat, cold, rain, snow and wind are exploitable resources. Definition of the nature of climatic resources has been a major occupation over the past century — in the planning of land use (particularly for agriculture), in the development of water supplies and in the

---

[1]Ellsworth Huntington, *Mainsprings of Civilization* (John Wiley and Sons, Inc., New York, 1945).

Petty Harbour, Nfld.

development of drainage and irrigation systems. The trend to optimal productivity through fuller exploitation of climatic energy, light and moisture sources is increasing as natural resource supplies become more stringent.

Renewable resources are the basis of much of Canada's industry; they provide the necessities of life — food, drink and shelter — and earn about one-half of our export dollars. These resources depend primarily on climate. Resource management and use must therefore be based on climatological knowledge and the use of weather forecasts for optimal productivity.

The extraction and use of other resources are also highly climate-dependent. A major use of oil and gas, for example, is to offset cold, snow and heat. Climate-dependent ice fields and weather control the economics of arctic development. Much of our industrial energy is generated from climate-dependent water resources and water is used extensively in processing — for example, up to 22 m³ (cubic metres) to refine one cubic metre of petroleum and 3 000 m³ to make one tonne (metric tonne) of synthetic rubber.

On the other hand, the impact of industry, cities and people on the atmospheric environment places an upper limit to certain types of economic endeavour.

Economic activity must therefore be tailored in the light of an understanding of the environment, man's influence thereon and the capacity of the atmosphere to safely disperse industrial effluents. The interactions of weather, ecology and economy demand understanding.

Climate as a Liability

Climatic hazards stand out in our memory because of their great impact on society and their resulting newsworthiness. Canada, like most countries in temperate and polar regions, has a fluctuating climate that has caused crises from the times of early settlement.

Direct economic losses caused by some of the more notable weather events in Canada are noted in Table 1. Included in the list are events that are recognized historically as major disasters, but for which there was no available estimate of the direct economic effect.

Table 1. Selected weather events, and some losses directly caused by them, 1868-1973

Year	Event	Estimated losses	
		Life	$'000,000
1868	Drought at the Red River Settlement		
1860s	Storms on the Great Lakes		
1885-96	Drought on the Prairies		
1912	Tornado at Regina, Sask.	30	4
1917-21	Drought on the Prairies		
1930-36	Drought on the Prairies		
1935	Snow-storm at Vancouver, BC		
1944	Tornado at Kamsack, Sask.	(2,000 homeless)	2
1945	Low temperatures in Nova Scotia		4
1949	Drought in Ontario		100
1950	Red River flood		100
1953	Tornado at Sarnia, Ont.		5
1954	Hurricane Hazel, Ontario	100	252
1954	Wheat rust on the Prairies		33
1955	Drought in Ontario		85
1957	Hail storm in Saskatchewan		17
1959	Wet weather in Saskatchewan (harvest lost)		12.5
1959	Snow-storm in Ontario		
1967	Snow-storm in Alberta		10
1969	Glaze storm near Quebec City, Que.		30
1967-68	Forest fires — all of Canada		100
1973	Drought in British Columbia		
1973	Glaze storm at Sept-Îles, Que.		10

Losses due to storms are rarely easy to express. The dollar value of cattle lost in a snowstorm may be easy to define within certain limits, but it is difficult to place a dollar value on the weakened state of the remaining herd. The $2.2 million loss in the Quebec City ice storm of 1973 does not disclose the fact that 250,000 people were

The white stillness of winter coats the Laurentians in Quebec.

deprived of electricity, heat and drinking water, that quantities of food were spoilt as freezers stopped operating, or that fire protection facilities were impotent during a period when fire hazard was greatly increased by the use of camp stoves and other makeshift equipment.

Defending Against Loss. People have five, not necessarily mutually exclusive, ways of facing up to weather, namely: "1. passive acceptance; 2. avoidance of areas and actions unfavourable to effective use of resource conditions; 3. current operational and defensive actions based on assessment of meteorological information; 4. modification and direct control of the weather/climate; and 5. structural and mechanical defenses — i.e. capitalizing on climatological knowledge."[2] We do not need to take our losses passively; there are alternatives, one of which is insurance.

Typical of our defensive actions are salting programs for highways, switching from carbon to steel trolleys by transit systems, operation of frost protection devices and evacuation of areas likely to be flooded. These actions are frequently based on weather forecasts, and their basis is climatology. For example, the design of a dam

[2]J.R. Hibbs, "Evaluation of weather and climate by socio-economic sensitivity indices," *Human Dimensions of Weather Modification* (University of Chicago, Department of Geography, Research Paper No. 105, 1966).

and the operational program for a reservoir are based on long-term climatological and related information that assures the operator that the stored waters will serve all reasonable demands during the lifetime of the reservoir, including periods of drought, and will also withstand floods and minimize their effects downstream. Weather forecasts are necessary in the operational phase to ensure that the system functions safely and in the best interests of the public.

The Atmospheric Environment Service of Environment Canada has responded with foresight to changing and increasing societal demand. Its service horizon has been broadened and adapted to meet special needs, both national and regional. New technology has been exploited to improve services and achieve greater efficiency. This has enabled meteorologists to apply their science in the resolution of important socio-economic issues in which weather is a factor.

The Applications of Climatology

Agriculture and Forestry

Agriculture and forestry are among those activities that are highly exposed and sensitive to weather. Weather forecasts and planning information are therefore essential in combating the recognized major hazards, such as drought, frost, hail, excessive rainfall, flood, wind, snow and winterkill, as well as climatically influenced diseases, epidemics and insect infestations. Forest fire losses, per annum, average about $23 million and have been as high as $83 million. Recent major crop losses, based on federal assistance payments, are identified in Table 2; they provide an indication of the potential economic benefits of accurate forecasts.

Table 2. Crop losses as identified by assistance payments

Year	Cause	Location	Estimated loss $'000,000
1945	Low temperatures	Nova Scotia	4.0
1954	Wheat rust	Prairies	33.0
1959	Wet harvest	Prairies	12.5
1964-65	Wet weather	Quebec	1.5
1965	Drought	Eastern Canada	5.5

The production of rapeseed, a $100 million business in 1971, illustrates again the importance of climate in the agricultural economy. Rapeseed crops thrive in the prairie climate of hot, sunny days and cool nights, and production is intensive in this area. To the south, the percentage of oil contained in the seed drops off so that growing it becomes uneconomic as far north as Minneapolis. Delineation of the area where the climate is suitable for such crops has obvious economic value.

The weather must be suitable not only for growing, but also for seeding, cultivating, spraying and harvesting operations. Both weather forecasts and

Cape St James on the southern tip of the Queen Charlotte Islands is manned by three meteorological technicians and is considered a key station by Pacific weather centre forecasters.

climatological statistics have been used extensively by farmers in overcoming problems of unfavourable weather (during haying, for example) or in assessing chances of favourable drying weather as harvest season advances toward winter.

Water Resources

Precipitation is the primary source of surface water supplies and evaporation is the major consumer. Planning, public and political conviction and economic decisions as to the viability of a hydrologic system are therefore frequently dependent on climatology. The magnitude and reliability of supplies is dictated by rainfall and snowfall characteristics. Design flood, irrigation need, urban demand, storm-sewer capacity and culvert size are all functions of climate and the operation of water control systems for flood control and conservation of water in times of drought is often highly dependent on forecasts.

Use of water resources by towns, cities, industry and agriculture, as well as natural losses through evaporation, must be understood in terms of probability and seasonality to enable the design of supply systems that will serve all the reasonable requirements of a community. They are predictable, using meteorological forecasts and information directly and in relation to industrial, social and biological activities.

Resource Development

Development of Canada's resources in hinterland and frontier areas poses major environmental problems in which climatology must play a dominant role. For example, sulphur dioxide releases from refineries in the tar sands of Alberta could

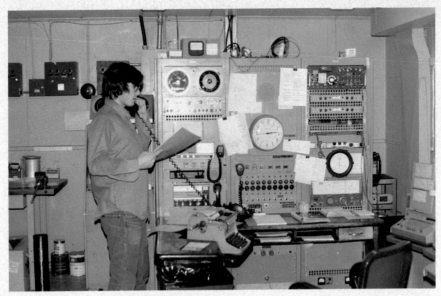
Weather observer at Alert, on the northern tip of the Northwest Territories, sending out the weather report.

destroy vegetation over vast areas of land if improperly controlled; the capacity of the atmosphere to disperse this contaminant is therefore a major concern. Should coal come back into prominence, then the dispersal of sulphur dioxide and particulates could be a major problem. Gasification and cooling towers may release great amounts of thermal energy and moisture into the atmosphere. Safety and security from natural hazards are major factors to be considered in offshore drilling, pipelining (river crossings, for example), the transmission of electrical energy and the operation of nuclear generating stations.

Topoclimatology and air quality studies must play a significant role in the placement of refineries, conversion systems, infrastructures, etc. The marine climatology and weather forecasts are heavily involved in the problems of offshore drilling, shipping in ice-congested waters, oil storage at sea to allow for interruptions of shipments from drilling sites by fog, and the placement of facilities for deep-sea harbours.

Environmental concerns should force greater use of renewable energy resources, which in turn would require much improved interpretation and understanding of the space and time variations of solar energy and wind and of their byproducts, such as waves, currents and thermal gradients.

Land-Use Planning

Resource development, industrialization, the trend to urbanization, growing population, limited resources and moral responsibilities make necessary a rational approach to land use in Canada.

Intensified resource use and exploration are linked with affluence and a desire for urban life. Not only are Canadians leaving the farms for the towns, but they are

Cavendish Beach, PEI.

abandoning the towns to concentrate in a few large industrialized urban centres. It is estimated that, by the year 2000, 20 million Canadians (60 per cent of our population) may live in 15 centres with populations over 300,000, 17 million of these in centres of 1 million or more population.

These trends are of major socio-economic importance, and among the problems created are formidable and complex land-use problems. The potential roles climatology will play in dealing with them are equally numerous and complex. For example, about one-half of Canada's Class I agricultural lands are in Ontario, where urbanization pressures are great. There, the climatic zoning of lands can aid the planner in the conservation of prime areas. Elsewhere, it can provide the farmer with a basis for greater security whenever and wherever the climate is marginal.

Construction

Construction is Canada's largest industry. Highly exposed and weather-sensitive, it qualifies as a prime area for meteorological support. The use of meteorology in the engineering of structures has included the problems of snow loads, wind loads, ice accretion, drainage, rain penetration and weathering of materials. At the same time, the prediction of construction weather — weather for setting concrete, for earthwork and for the operation of cranes — is of major importance to the industry.

Transportation

Aviation has grown exponentially. Airport capacities have in some cases been exceeded soon after their construction, and the noise created by modern aircraft is of increasing concern. To alleviate these growing problems, new airports have been developed in areas removed from the large cities. This has required the determination of locations that have the most favourable take-off and landing weather and whose runway orientations would not cause conflict with established traffic patterns.

Topography-climate relationships are the basis of arctic site selection and are therefore an important factor in northern resource development. Pipelines, ships and tractor trains are an important part of the arctic transportation scene. Their supporting infrastructure requires compressor stations, harbours and towns. In the past, shoreline and inland installations have been blown away or badly damaged by arctic winds; shelter is all-important. On the other hand, unventilated areas pose the hazard of air pollution and ice fog under conditions of persistent cold and airmass inversion. The study of air drainage and wind is, therefore, most important in the collocation of facilities and residential areas.

Tourism and Recreation

For most Canadians recreation is an outdoor activity, and weather dictates whether or not the outdoor experience is enjoyable. Recreation is highly oriented to renewable natural resources and the state of the resources is climate-dependent. In some cases climate is the resource.

Because tourist spending is of great significance to national, provincial and local economies, governments have immediate interests in the development of parks, lodges and other recreation areas. A rational approach to development requires climatological inputs; even the Niagara Falls are unimpressive when they are enshrouded by fog. Methods of getting optimal recreational value on the basis of climate have been developed and climatic studies of national parks have been undertaken to provide a basis for the placing of facilities and roads and for the development of operational programs.

Environmental Impact Assessment

Environmental impact assessments are an essential defence against undesirable environmental effects of man's activities, both deliberate and inadvertent. In undertaking an assessment planners are forced to consider the side effects of their proposals over the short, medium and long ranges, and also of possible alternatives, one of which is not to proceed. A decision is ultimately reached to stop the program or approve the most acceptable alternative in actual or modified form. A surveillance program is also established to ensure desired conditions are met.

The quality of the air and the ability of the atmosphere to carry pollutants to areas where they can damage the environment or buildings, or be injurious to human health, are major concerns of an industrialized society. However, the climatological aspects of assessment do not reside only in air quality. They may start with the evaluation of the engineer's design — will a tower fail under ice and wind loads, for

Spring blossoms at the Central Experimental Farm in Ottawa.

example? Changes in land use such as extending agricultural area, installing pipelines and creating new lakes may also alter climate. Such alterations are usually small in scale, but there is concern that the aggregated sum of a large number of inconsequential projects might be critical. Small changes in temperature, precipitation or fog might not significantly influence a region's climate, but perhaps these conditions could create new extremes that would place an intolerable stress on certain species; or perhaps they are involved in a non-obvious feedback mechanism that would have significant consequences. Broad, positive understanding of interdisciplinary relationships is extremely important in these matters.

There is a need to distinguish between what should be done and what can be done. The potential for applying meteorology in economic decisions is infinite.

Environmental Assessment and Review Process

In addition to undertaking actual environmental assessments, participation in the federal government's Environmental Assessment and Review Process (EARP) is an important aspect of the climatological work of the Atmospheric Environment Service. Participation involves reviewing the climatic portions of environmental impact statements prepared by private industry and federal government departments and agencies for projects subject to EARP regulation. During the review, attention must be paid both to the statement's assessment of existing climatic conditions and to its consideration of possible climatic change during the proposed project's lifetime.

GORDON MCKAY

2

. Public gardens in Edmonton, Alta.
. Botanical gardens in Hamilton, Ont.
. High Park gardens in Toronto, Ont.

. Rain forest on the west coast of British Columbia

The People and Their Heritage

History

Canada developed from colony to nation in the first half of the 20th century, achieving a position as a fully independent state within the British Commonwealth. But at the same time, Canada's dependency on the United States became more critical and the difficult task of maintaining independence from a powerful neighbour more acute. Throughout our history, the twin themes of accommodation and co-operation among the racial elements making up the Canadian population and of defining Canada externally in a manner satisfactory to the people of Canada have affected every aspect of national life.

The territory that is now known as Canada began as a field of settlement in the 17th century. The French were first on the ground, reaching out for the interior of the continent through the St. Lawrence River system. By the 1670s, the English were established on Hudson Bay and the struggle for control of the hinterland had begun. The French pressed north and west, the English south from Hudson Bay and west from their settlements along the Hudson River and in what is now New England. Aided by their Indian allies and abetted by the hostility between Britain and France in Europe, the competitors were fighting to control the resources of the continent, a struggle that Britain would finally win. Before that victory occurred, however, New France had established itself tenaciously along the St. Lawrence and in Acadia.

For its first 50 years of struggle, the French colony was tiny. Settlement proceeded slowly, the missionaries found few converts among the heathen and trade was scanty. By 1663 there were fewer than 2,500 habitants. Their major achievement was that they had survived.

Nonetheless out of that act of survival grew the myths that have shaped French Canada's strong consciousness of its past and of its distinctiveness. There were the heroes, such as Dollard des Ormeaux and his tiny band of compatriots who died defending the colony against the Indians in 1660, and martyrs, such as the Jesuit priests who succumbed to torture while attempting to bring Christianity to the natives. The past was epic.

By the 1740s, worldwide French-English rivalry had brought on the war that would spell the end of New France. The colony had advanced since the mid-17th century, royal government having brought new settlers, trained civil servants and regiments to defend the settlements and their outposts. Nevertheless, against British seapower and the numerically superior forces that could be brought against it, New France was doomed. Quebec City, the major settlement, fell in 1759 to General Wolfe's army and the Treaty of Paris ceded France's major North American possessions to Britain in 1763. North America was now under British control.

Within 20 years, however, the 13 colonies to the south of New France had fought and won their War of Independence, creating the United States of America. Since their seizure of New France, the British had been concerned that the French-speaking habitants might follow where the Americans led. The result was the abandonment of attempts at assimilation and recognition in the Quebec Act of 1774 of the major institutions of the inhabitants — the civil law, the seigneurial system and the Roman Catholic religion. With these assured, Canada resisted blandishments and invasion by the 13 colonies and remained a British possession.

The American Revolution also brought thousands of Loyalists, fleeing the republican institutions of the rebels, into British North America. Settling in Nova Scotia, in what would soon be New Brunswick and the Eastern Townships and in the unsettled regions of Canada north of Lake Ontario, the Loyalists were the country's first substantial group of English-speaking settlers.

Their arrival demanded new political arrangements. Nova Scotia had had a representative assembly since 1758 and this was now to be extended to the Canadas. The Constitutional Act of 1791 divided the old province of Quebec into two colonies, Upper and Lower Canada, each with its own assembly. The colonies began to grow, if not to flourish, and soon a struggle for self-government or, as it was usually known in the Canadas, responsible government, was under way. That was achieved in 1849, but only after rebellions in both Canadas had been crushed with severity in 1837 and the two colonies reunited in 1841; the latter step, suggested by Lord Durham in his famous report, was an attempt to foster the assimilation of the French Canadians.

That failed, as did the political unification of the Canadas. By the mid-19th century the colonies faced mounting costs combined with slowly growing revenues, hardly enough to build the railways and canals necessary for the infrastructure of a modern society. Markets were shrinking, particularly after Britain ended preferential tariffs and

A summer kitchen, a glimpse of early Canadian life, at Upper Canada Village in Ontario.

embarked on a course of free trade. The political picture was marked by bitter sectional conflict and political deadlock, exacerbated by the growing numerical preponderance of the English over the French. Finally, in the 1860s there was a threat from an increasingly hostile United States, just emerging from its Civil War and, many in British North America feared, not averse to reuniting North and South in a victorious war against the scattered British North American colonies. These events, as well as the encouragement provided by a British government that was eager to cut its commitments in North America, resulted in a Canadian decision in 1865 to move toward a federation of all the British colonies — the Canadas, New Brunswick, Nova Scotia, Prince Edward Island and Newfoundland.

That goal was only partially achieved on July 1, 1867, when the Canadas, Nova Scotia and New Brunswick were joined in Confederation by virtue of the British North America Act. The Act, the constitution of the new Dominion of Canada, was the creation of a vigorous group of politicians, including John A. Macdonald, the first Prime Minister of Canada, Georges-Étienne Cartier, George Brown, Leonard Tilley and Charles Tupper. The constitution provided for a centralized federal system, with the national government at Ottawa the dominant force, but leaving to the provinces matters of local concern. French and English were recognized as the official languages within the federal Parliament and courts and in the province of Quebec. The new nation was a parliamentary monarchy, with Parliament of this new nation comprising the Governor General as the representative of the monarch, a House of Commons and an appointive Senate.

The Dominion was incomplete; Prince Edward Island and Newfoundland had declined to join, the great prairies to the west belonged to the Hudson's Bay Company, and British Columbia, beyond the Rocky Mountains on the Pacific Coast, was impossibly remote in a vast land with no efficient transcontinental transportation route. The first step to having the new Dominion live up to its motto (A Mari Usque ad Mare, or From Sea to Sea) was acquisition of the western prairies; a new province of Manitoba was created in 1870 after a brief rebellion led by the able and charismatic Louis Riel was put down. The next year the province of British Columbia was created, with the promise of a railway as a condition, and in 1873 Prince Edward Island joined. The Northwest Territories were formed in 1874, their area encompassing all the lands between Manitoba and British Columbia; in 1885 they were the locale for the second Riel Rebellion, a revolt that failed because the Dominion militia reached the scene with some speed via the Canadian Pacific Railway, whose cross-country line had been completed that year. Twenty years later, the provinces of Alberta and Saskatchewan were organized out of the Northwest Territories, bringing the number of provinces to nine. Finally, in 1949 Newfoundland became the last province to join the union.

But Canada was and had to be more than territory. Policies were needed, national policies. The Conservative government of Sir John A. Macdonald, in power for most of the quarter-century after Confederation, proceeded to create and implement a National Policy. The railway was a major part of it, an essential linking element to tie the scattered inhabitants together. Encouragement of immigration was a second plank, but one that proceeded very slowly until the boom years of the early 20th century started the flood. A third measure, one involving high tariff protection, was believed necessary to encourage the growth of manufacturing in Canada. Only if Canadian industry could be made strong, only if the West could be populated and only if communications could be made swift and sure would Canada stand much chance of resisting the strong attraction of the United States.

Macdonald had laid the foundation of Canadian development, but his policies came to full fruition only under the Liberal Prime Minister, Sir Wilfrid Laurier, the first national leader of French heritage, who governed from 1896 to 1911. Laurier's years were the golden ones, a period when the Prime Minister could say in all seriousness that while the 19th century had belonged to the United States the 20th would belong to Canada.

Despite the prosperity and expansion, the Laurier years saw the continuation and, indeed, the worsening of the cultural and class conflicts that had existed since 1867. The execution of Riel in 1885 strained English-French relations, as did attacks on French and Catholic schools in the West in the 1890s. New conflicts, those between imperialist English Canadians and their more nationalist and isolationist French-speaking compatriots, were fostered by the Boer War and the continuing debate over Canada's place in the British Empire. When Laurier presented Parliament with a reciprocity treaty with the United States in 1911, the ensuing election campaign raised all these issues with a vengeance. The Liberals were defeated roundly and Robert Borden's Conservatives took power.

Fort Walsh, Sask.

It fell to Borden to lead Canada through the Great War of 1914-18, a terrible time for Canada. More than 60,000 Canadians died overseas, while the unity of the country was strained by the conscription issue of 1917. Many Canadians who were not of British background resisted compulsory service and the election of 1917 was fought and won by Borden on this issue. His government, by this time a coalition of English-speaking Conservatives and Liberals, enforced conscription.

Military service also weighed heavily on farmers in Ontario and the West. The war had brought high prices and prosperity after years of tight money, but now the government was taking away the farmer's son. This grievance, added to long-standing complaints about the tariff that favoured the manufacturers, led to the creation of the Progressive Party and to its rise to prominence in the election of 1921.

Organized labour also made gains during the war, but this progress was largely lost after a general strike at Winnipeg in 1919 was broken by the massive intervention of the federal government. Labour was weak for years after, not again reaching for a major role until the Depression and World War II.

The nation as a whole found new opportunities in the changes in the Dominion's status that the Great War had brought. Canada had entered the war as a colony of Britain, but it emerged a near equal, a status that was formalized by the Statute of Westminster in 1931.

For most of the years between the wars, however, Canada took little part in world affairs. The Prime Minister was W.L. Mackenzie King, Laurier's heir and a cautious man. King concentrated on lowering taxes and tariffs. Canada progressed slowly and received a serious setback with the onset of the Depression in 1929.

The Conservatives under R.B. Bennett, who took power in the general election of 1930, faced continuing huge unemployment rolls and declines in trade and gross national product. Canada was in trouble and the people sought for solutions in new political parties. Social Credit won power in the province of Alberta, the Co-operative Commonwealth Federation (CCF) attempted to link labour and farm groups in Ontario and the West, and the Union Nationale led conservative nationalists to victory in Quebec. The Depression also demonstrated that the federal government lacked the constitutional power to deal with a peacetime national emergency and the King government, re-elected in 1935, launched a great inquest into constitutional powers. The Royal Commission on Dominion-Provincial Relations reported in 1940, recommending sweeping changes, but by then Canada was at war and Ottawa already had the power to act expeditiously in wartime.

The war years from 1939 to 1945 were extraordinary ones. The transition to total war under the King government turned Canada into a major military, industrial and financial power. There were a million men in the armed forces, billions of dollars for mutual aid to Canada's allies and full employment in booming munitions plants. There was difficulty over conscription in 1942 and 1944, but this issue left fewer scars than it had in 1917. The government showed similar skill in arranging the transition from war to peace and the economic boom continued unabated through the 1950s.

Mackenzie King stepped down in 1948, to be succeeded by Louis St. Laurent, a Quebec lawyer. The St. Laurent government led Canada into closer military and economic relations with the United States, taking Canada into the North Atlantic Treaty Organization (NATO) and negotiating entry to the North American Air Defence Command.

However, the continuing Canadian economic boom was financed by American money invested in Canada or borrowed in New York, and there was enough concern over these and other trends to result in a victory by the Conservatives under John Diefenbaker in 1957. Diefenbaker's government was in power from 1957 to 1963, a stormy period both domestically and internationally. By the late 1950s economic growth was slowing, unemployment was rising and relations with the US were worsening, in part because of Diefenbaker's reluctance to arm the Canadian Forces with American nuclear weapons. At the same time, Quebec was growing more restive with Confederation, seeking greater provincial autonomy and greater recognition for the French language throughout the country.

Lester Pearson's Liberal government, elected with a minority of the seats in the House of Commons in 1963, set up a Royal Commission on Bilingualism and Biculturalism to examine the whole field of French-English relations. Over the course of the following five years, a period marked by political scandals and social reforms, the Pearson government devoted increasing amounts of time to the question of Quebec.

His strong federalist views were perhaps the major reason for the choice of Pierre Elliott Trudeau as Pearson's successor in 1968, and Trudeau led his party to victory in the general election that year. Two years later, the government imposed the War Measures Act and moved some 10,000 troops into Quebec in response to the kidnapping of a British trade commissioner and the kidnapping and murder of a Quebec Cabinet minister by the Front de Libération du Québec. That strong federal response seemed at the time to end talk of separatism in Quebec and for the next six years other issues dominated the stage.

Daily tasks of pioneer life recreated at Fort William, Ont.

In its first term the Trudeau government made some changes in Canadian foreign policy, reducing the military commitment to NATO and stressing the need to protect and enhance Canadian sovereignty. Economic issues, in particular high unemployment and rising inflation, received much attention and probably were the major reasons behind the losses Trudeau's party suffered in the 1972 election, which left it governing in a minority position. For the next two years it attempted to deal with the economy, with growing problems of energy supply and with the American influence on the economy and Canadian culture. In 1974 the government was returned to office with a comfortable majority.

In the next two years two of the opposition parties changed their leaders. The New Democratic Party, the heir to the CCF, selected Ed Broadbent, an Ontario university professor and the Member of Parliament for Oshawa, Ontario. Early in 1976, the Conservatives chose Joe Clark, a young Alberta MP. Both Clark and Broadbent repeatedly and pointedly stressed economic issues, focusing attention on the wage and

Bluenose II, *a replica of the famous Bluenose, in Halifax harbour.*

price controls introduced by the Liberals in 1975 and the continuing problems of inflation and high unemployment. Controls were beginning to be lifted in 1978, but interest rates, inflation and the cost of living continued to rise, and about one million people were unemployed.

The result was that in the election of 1979, Clark led the Conservative party to victory and formed a minority government. But within months, the Conservatives were beaten in the House of Commons and in an election in 1980 beaten in the country. In one of the most astonishing comebacks in Canadian history, Pierre Trudeau, who had lost the 1979 election and who had in fact declared his intention to give up the leadership of his party, was Prime Minister again.

The major issue he would have to deal with was that of his native province of Quebec. Under the leadership of the able and popular René Lévesque, the Parti Québécois had won a large majority in the National Assembly in the general election of 1976. Pledged to turn Quebec into a sovereign state associated with Canada through a form of common market, Lévesque proposed to follow a two-referendum path to independence. The first was to give his government power to negotiate with Ottawa and the second referendum to allow the people to approve or disapprove the results of those negotiations. The initial referendum, scheduled to occur on May 20, 1980, had finally brought Quebec and Canada to the moment of crisis. Ironically with Pierre Trudeau and a number of powerful Cabinet ministers from Quebec, as well as half the Liberal caucus, Quebec had never been so well represented in Ottawa. What the ultimate result of the votes would be, what the future of Canada, none could predict early in 1980.

J.L. Granatstein

Population

Canada's total population as of June 1, 1979, was estimated to be 23,670,700, an increase of 18.3 per cent over the count of 20,014,880, reported in the 1966 Census. In fact, however, Canada has experienced a declining rate of population growth during this period, the annual increase actually having fallen from 1.6 per cent in the period 1966-71 to 1.0 per cent in 1976-79. Exceptions to this general pattern were Alberta, New Brunswick, Prince Edward Island and Saskatchewan. Alberta's growth rate increased from 2.3 per cent in the period 1966-71 to 3.1 per cent in 1976-79; New Brunswick's growth rate increased from 0.6 per cent to 1.1 per cent and Prince Edward Island's rate increased from 0.6 per cent to 1.3 per cent. Saskatchewan, which experienced a decline of 0.6 per cent in the period 1966-71, showed an increase of 1.3 per cent in 1976-79. The Yukon and the Northwest Territories, which have relatively small populations compared to the provinces experienced very high growth rates in the period 1966-76, but have shown declining growth rates in 1976-79.

Canada's provinces and territories differ markedly with regard to area, population size and population density. Over 80 per cent of the total population is concentrated in Quebec, Ontario, Alberta and British Columbia which have larger land areas than other provinces. Alberta, British Columbia and Ontario were the only provinces whose annual population increases exceeded the national average in the past. Prince Edward Island, Nova Scotia and New Brunswick are the smallest provinces in terms of land area, but have population densities (20.5, 16.0 and 9.7 persons per square kilometre, respectively) well above the national average of 2.6 persons per square kilometre, whereas the Yukon and the Northwest Territories, with vast land areas have markedly low densities of 0.04 and 0.01 persons per square kilometre, respectively.

Births, deaths, immigration and emigration are the components of population change. The high birth rate (an average of 28.0 per thousand in 1951-56) and the high rate of natural increase (an average of 19.6 per thousand in 1951-56) are representative of the rapid growth that occurred in the early post-war period, which peaked to record highs in the mid-1950s (Table 2). Lower rates of growth in succeeding years resulted mainly from the continuous decline of birth rates since the early 1960s. Death rates, though declining slightly, have remained relatively stable compared to other components of growth. Net international migration (the difference between immigration and emigration) during the early and mid-1950s (7.9 per thousand in the period 1951-56 and 5.6 per thousand in 1956-61) has also had a strong influence on Canada's population growth. In recent years this influence has been declining in its significance, contributing about one-third to the total population growth during 1971-76, but only about one-sixth during 1976-79.

In recent years, internal migration has been the most important single factor influencing the geographic distribution of the Canadian population (Table 3). In 1967-69, Ontario and British Columbia were the major provinces to attract most migrants from the other parts of the country. Since the early 1970s, the patterns have changed dramatically. Gains remained consistent in British Columbia while Quebec, Newfoundland and Manitoba experienced consistent losses, but the traditional losers like Prince Edward Island, Nova Scotia, New Brunswick and Saskatchewan recorded gains. Ontario, a traditionally large gainer, recorded loss during this period. Both the Yukon

Table 1. Population distribution and land area, Canada and provinces, 1966, 1971, 1976 and 1979[1]

	Population in thousands				Mean annual percentage change			Land area Square kilometres '000s	Population density[2]
	1966	1971	1976	1979	1966-71	1971-76	1976-79	1979	1979
Canada	20,015	21,568	22,993	23,671	1.6	1.3	1.0	9 205	2.6
Newfoundland	493	522	558	574	1.2	1.3	0.9	372	1.5
Prince Edward Island	109	112	118	123	0.6	1.2	1.3	6	20.5
Nova Scotia	756	789	829	848	0.9	1.0	0.7	53	16.0
New Brunswick	617	635	677	701	0.6	1.3	1.1	72	9.7
Quebec	5,781	6,028	6,234	6,284	0.9	0.7	0.3	1 358	4.6
Ontario	6,961	7,703	8,264	8,503	2.1	1.4	1.0	917	9.3
Manitoba	963	988	1,022	1,032	0.5	0.7	0.3	548	1.9
Saskatchewan	955	926	921	959	-0.6	-0.1	1.3	570	1.7
Alberta	1,463	1,628	1,838	2,012	2.3	2.5	3.1	638	3.2
British Columbia	1,874	2,185	2,467	2,570	3.3	2.5	1.4	893	2.9
Yukon	14	18	22	22	5.7	3.5	-0.4	532	0.04
Northwest Territories	29	35	43	43	4.1	4.1	0.6	3 246	0.01

[1] Based on census data for 1966, 1971, 1976 and estimates for 1979.   [2] Persons per square kilometre.

Table 2. Components of population change, 1951-56, 1956-61, 1961-66, 1966-71, 1971-76 and 1976-79

Date	Births	Deaths	Natural increase	Immigration	Emigration	Net international migration	Total change
	Rate per thousand[1]						%
1951-56	28.0	8.4	19.6	10.4	2.5	7.9	27.5
1956-61	27.5	8.0	19.5	8.8	3.2	5.6	25.1
1961-66	23.5	7.6	15.9	5.6	2.9	2.7	18.6
1966-71	17.8	7.4	10.5	8.6	4.1	4.5	14.9
1971-76	15.8	7.4	8.4	7.6	3.1	4.5	12.8
1976-79[2]	15.3	7.2	8.1	4.7	3.2	1.5	9.6

[1] Mean rate per one thousand people, for each time interval indicated.   [2] Preliminary estimates for post-censal years.

Table 3. Internal migration by province for selected periods (annual averages)[1]
(hundreds of migrants)

	1967-69			1972-74			1977-79		
	In-	Out-migration	Net-	In-	Out-migration	Net-	In-	Out-migration	Net-
Canada..............	3794	3794	—	4102	4102	—	4028	4028	—
Newfoundland	86	117	−32	122	133	−11	103	123	−20
Prince Edward Island..	36	43	−7	47	38	9	43	39	5
Nova Scotia..........	234	255	−22	254	232	22	225	222	3
New Brunswick	186	228	−41	213	188	24	193	180	12
Quebec..............	389	596	−207	384	539	−155	259	632	−373
Ontario..............	1064	835	229	969	1033	−64	981	1003	−22
Manitoba	277	348	−71	300	351	−51	242	348	−105
Saskatchewan........	231	368	−137	246	364	−118	272	254	18
Alberta..............	563	490	73	688	608	80	923	643	279
British Columbia	678	471	206	812	552	260	726	511	215
Yukon.............. ⎫	49	41	8	67	64	3	24	26	−2
Northwest Territories . ⎬							37	47	−10

[1] Calendar years.
— Nil or zero.

and the Northwest Territories also experienced losses. Alberta, which had been attracting migrants since the mid-1960s, recorded the largest gains by the mid-1970s.

Over the years Canada's population has changed from predominantly rural to predominantly urban. According to the 1901 Census, only 37.5 per cent of the total population lived in urban communities; by 1976, 75.5 per cent of the total population were located in urban areas. Of the 5,625,635 persons making up Canada's rural population in 1976, 1,034,560 (18.4 per cent) lived on farms, while 4,591,070 (81.4 per cent) lived in dwellings not situated on farms.

In 1978 over half of Canada's total population resided in 23 census metropolitan areas (CMAs), as shown in Table 4. Each of these major urban agglomerations contains the main labour-force market for a continuous built-up area that has a population of 100,000 or more.

Population estimates for 1978 show that Montreal and Toronto were Canada's largest metropolitan areas, each having over 2.8 million inhabitants, while Vancouver had grown to 1.2 million. In terms of proportionate growth, however, Calgary, Edmonton, Ottawa–Hull and Kitchener have developed most rapidly in recent years, Calgary having increased its total population by about 25 per cent in the period 1971-78 and Edmonton, Ottawa–Hull and Kitchener each by about 17 per cent. In contrast, the populations of Sudbury and Windsor actually declined slightly over this time interval, while the populations of Montreal and Chicoutimi–Jonquière experienced relatively small increases.

The age structure of a population is of vital interest to all levels of government involved in designing social and economic programs for their constituents. Educational planners, for example, have noted a sharp drop in school enrolment rates at the

Table 4. Population of census metropolitan areas (CMAs) 1971, 1976 and 1978[1]

	Population in thousands[2]			Percentage change
	1971	1976	1978	1971-78
Canada..........................	21,568	22,993	23,483	8.9
Total CMAs....................	11,985	12,799	13,053	8.9
Percentage of total population	55.6	55.7	55.6	...
Toronto	2,602	2,803	2,856	9.8
Montreal	2,729	2,802	2,823	3.4
Vancouver.....................	1,082	1,166	1,173	8.4
Ottawa-Hull	620	693	726	17.2
Ontario portion.................	474	521	547	15.4
Quebec portion.................	146	172	179	22.9
Winnipeg......................	550	578	589	7.1
Edmonton	496	554	581	17.2
Quebec City...................	501	542	554	10.6
Hamilton......................	503	529	536	6.6
Calgary.......................	403	470	504	25.2
St. Catharines-Niagara...........	286	302	306	7.1
Kitchener......................	239	272	280	17.4
London........................	253	270	274	8.3
Halifax........................	251	268	271	8.2
Windsor.......................	249	248	246	−1.0
Victoria	196	218	222	13.6
Sudbury	158	157	155	−1.7
Regina	141	151	160	13.7
St. John's	132	143	146	11.1
Oshawa[3]	120	135	139	15.8
Saskatoon	126	134	139	10.1
Chicoutimi-Jonquière	126	129	130	2.6
Thunder Bay..........:	115	119	121	5.2
Saint John	107	113	117	9.8

[1] Based on census data for 1971, 1976 and preliminary estimates for 1978.
[2] Based on 1976 area.
[3] Not a Census Metropolitan Area in 1971.
... Not applicable.

elementary and secondary school levels as a result of the declining proportions of the population in the younger age groups. Table 5 shows that the proportion of Canada's population under 15 years of age declined from 32.9 per cent in 1966 to 23.5 per cent in 1979, a decline of 9.4 percentage points. This was the result mainly of the declining birth rates in previous years, a fact clearly indicated by the decrease of about 20 per cent in the number of children 0-4 years of age in the period 1966-79.

As the population "bulge" resulting from high birth rates in the 1950s has moved into early adulthood the working age group (15-64 years of age) has increased rapidly. The proportion of the total population between the ages of 15 and 64 years increased from 59.4 per cent in 1966 to 67.2 per cent in 1979. Immigration has a strong influence on the growth of this broad working age group, especially at the younger adult ages. In 1976, for example, about 47 per cent of the population arriving from foreign lands were 20-39 years of age.

The changing proportion of the population in the group aged 65 years and over is of particular interest to those planning facilities for the care of the elderly and

Table 5. Population by age groups, 1966, 1971, 1976 and 1979[1]

Age group	Population in thousands				Percentage distribution			
	1966	1971	1976	1979	1966	1971	1976	1979
Total	20,015	21,568	22,993	23,671	100.0	100.0	100.0	100.0
Under 15	6,592	6,381	5,896	5,570	32.9	29.6	25.6	23.5
0-4	2,197	1,816	1,732	1,763	11.0	8.4	7.5	7.4
5-9	2,301	2,254	1,888	1,799	11.5	10.5	8.2	7.6
10-14	2,093	2,311	2,276	2,008	10.5	10.7	9.9	8.5
15-64	11,884	13,443	15,094	15,896	59.4	62.3	65.7	67.2
15-19	1,838	2,114	2,345	2,382	9.2	9.8	10.2	10.1
20-24	1,461	1,889	2,134	2,291	7.3	8.8	9.3	9.7
25-34	2,483	2,889	3,621	3,933	12.4	13.4	15.7	16.6
35-44	2,543	2,526	2,597	2,759	12.7	11.7	11.3	11.6
45-54	2,078	2,291	2,473	2,473	10.4	10.6	10.8	10.4
55-64	1,480	1,732	1,924	2,059	7.4	8.0	8.4	8.7
65+	1,540	1,744	2,002	2,204	7.7	8.1	8.7	9.3

[1] Based on census data for 1966, 1971, 1976 and preliminary estimates for 1979.

Edmonton, Alta. — Calgary, Edmonton, Ottawa–Hull and Kitchener have developed most rapidly in recent years.

determining future pension needs. This segment of the population has been characterized by rapid growth in recent years. The proportion of the total population 65 years and over increased from 7.7 per cent in 1966 to 9.3 per cent in 1979. Declining birth rates and an increased life expectancy are the two major factors in the growth in the proportion of the aged population.

Of the 18 million persons 15 years of age and over in Canada in 1978, 28.5 per cent were single (never married). This category increased by 779,000 (18.2 per cent) during the period 1971-78. The figures in Table 6 also show that, in 1978, 32 per cent of the adult male population and 25 per cent of the adult female population were single; this differential is caused mainly by the fact that men tend to remain single longer than women. According to the 1978 estimates, for example, 71 per cent of the male population 20-24 years of age were reported as single, compared to 49 per cent of the female population in that age group.

In 1978, 63 per cent of the total population 15 years of age and over were married, the number of married persons having increased by about 15 per cent over the period 1971-78. However, the married portion of the population fell slightly during the same period, from 64.4 per cent in 1971 to 63.0 per cent in 1978; this may be attributed to demographic factors such as the changing age structure and nuptiality patterns.

Table 6. Numerical and percentage distribution of population 15 years of age and over, by marital status, 1971 and 1978[1]

Marital status	Population in thousands					
	1971			1978		
	Total	Male	Female	Total	Male	Female
Total	15,187	7,532	7,656	17,797	8,761	9,036
Single	4,291	2,378	1,913	5,070	2,800	2,270
Married[2]	9,778	4,889	4,889	11,218	5,593	5,625
Widowed	944	191	753	1,087	193	894
Divorced	175	74	101	422	175	247

Marital status	Percentage distribution					
	1971			1978		
	Total	Male	Female	Total	Male	Female
Total	100.0	100.0	100.0	100.0	100.0	100.0
Single	28.2	31.6	25.0	28.5	32.0	25.1
Married[2]	64.4	64.9	63.9	63.0	63.8	62.3
Widowed	6.2	2.5	9.8	6.1	2.2	9.9
Divorced	1.1	1.0	1.3	2.4	2.0	2.7

[1] Based on census data for 1971 and preliminary estimates for 1978.
  (Figures may not add to totals owing to rounding.)
[2] Includes separated persons not having obtained a divorce.

Victoria, BC. Over 80 per cent of the total population is concentrated in Quebec, Ontario, Alberta and British Columbia.

In 1971 there were 175,115 divorced persons in Canada; by 1978 this figure had risen to 421,800, an increase of 141 per cent. While the general trend over the years has been toward higher divorce rates and toward a drop in the age of persons obtaining divorces, the marked increase between 1971 and 1978 may be attributed in part to the adoption of new, comparatively more liberalized, divorce legislation.

One of the most striking features of marital status statistics is the larger proportion of widows over widowers. In 1978, 894,400 women (9.9 per cent of the adult female population) were widowed, in contrast to 193,400 men (2.2 per cent of the adult male population). This wide difference is attributed to the lower levels of mortality among females and to the lower remarriage rates among widows.

The Native Peoples

Indians

As of December 31, 1978, there were 302,749 people registered as Indians under the provisions of the Indian Act of Canada. There were 575 separate Indian bands, as of December 31, 1979, for whom 2,240 reserves had been set aside; the total reserve area was about 2 611 800 ha (hectares). Nearly half of the registered Indians, mainly those living in Ontario and the three Prairie provinces, are entitled to receive treaty payments as a result of treaties between their ancestors and the Crown.

The number of persons of Indian ancestry who are not entitled to be registered under the provisions of the Indian Act is unknown. Included among these people are Indians who have given up their Indian status and band membership through the legal process of enfranchisement, Indian women who have married non-Indians, the Métis and the descendants of persons who received land or money-scrip.

There are 58 different Indian languages or dialects in Canada, belonging to 10 major linguistic groups: Algonkian, Iroquoian, Siouan, Athapaskan, Kootenayan, Salishan, Wakashan, Tsimshian, Haida and Tlingit.

Education. The provision of education services to Indians living on reserves is the responsibility of the federal government, which funds a complete range of education

Native dancing at the Calgary Stampede.

Native west coast artwork
1. Indian mask
2. Totem pole
3. Haida carving

services from four-year-old kindergarten to university, professional or technological education and trade training through the Department of Indian Affairs and Northern Development. More than half the Indian student population attend schools operated by provincial boards; the remaining students attend schools on reserves operated by either the department or the Indian bands.

Since the acceptance of the National Indian Brotherhood paper "Indian Control of Indian Education" in 1973, increasing numbers of Indian bands are assuming control of their schools and other educational programs; out of a total of 575 Indian bands, 94 now manage their own schools. A major aim of government involvement in Indian education has been to facilitate the transfer of educational programs to Indian bands and to develop appropriate curricula in consultation with them. Almost all of the 226 federal schools operated by the department in 1978-79 offered culturally enriched programs. Many provincial schools attended by Indian or Inuit children include language courses or native studies units as part of regular school programs.

Several provinces and universities have designed and conducted special teacher-training courses to encourage Indian people to enter the teaching profession; paraprofessional courses are also conducted to train Indian teacher aides and social counsellors for federal, provincial and band-operated schools. Vocational training, vocational counselling and employment placement programs have been supported by the Department of Indian Affairs and Northern Development in co-operation with the Department of Employment and Immigration. The department has also assumed responsibility for training of elected and appointed officials of Indian bands and Inuit hamlet councils that is specifically related to their official duties.

Local Government. A policy encouraging the development of band self-government on Indian reserves began to evolve in 1965 in response to the expressed wishes of the Indian people to assume greater responsibility for the administration of their own affairs. At that time some 26 Indian bands across Canada assumed responsibility for the administration of specific departmental programs whose budgets totalled $66,000.

Increased interest since then is reflected by the fact that during the fiscal year 1979-80, 519 Indian bands administered a broad range of local programs and services with a total budget of $253.3 million.

Depending on a band's desire to become involved and its management capability, it can assume total program responsibility, manage only a segment or share responsibility with the department.

Economic Development. The operational aspects of economic development have been reviewed, an Advisory Board for the Indian Economic Development Fund has been formed in Ottawa and the objectives of the fund have been reassessed. Sectoral development corporations owned and controlled by Indian people are gaining wider acceptance. As this approach to economic development is relatively new, thorough evaluations during the next few years will be important. The value of Indians maintaining traditional ties with, and economic control over, their lands is a major factor in the development of new policies.

Recognizing the positive values of the Indian culture, the government continues to develop systems and processes that better meet the needs of Indian people and to adopt specific economic development tools geared to their special needs. In this way Indian people will be able to develop their own way of managing their own resources.

The sewing of a sealskin cover for a new kayak.

Inuit

There are about 100,000 Inuit in the world, living throughout the northern circumpolar regions. They inhabit Northern Alaska, the eastern tip of the USSR, Greenland and Northern Canada. (Eskimos are increasingly referred to as Inuit, the plural form of Inuk, meaning person; the Eskimo language is Inuktitut.)

Canada's Inuit number around 23,000. They live in small communities on the Mackenzie Delta, the Arctic islands and the mainland coast of the Northwest Territories, on the Quebec shores of Hudson and Ungava bays, and in Labrador. The communities are situated for the most part on bays, river mouths, inlets or fiords, reflecting a past life that was tied largely to marine harvesting — fishing, gathering and hunting.

Today, while the hunter's life and the special relationship it implies with the land remains central to Inuit identity and self-perception, traditional hunting pursuits are not as important economically as they were in the past. The southern world has invaded northern communities with all its comforts and complications; electricity, oil-fired furnaces and stoves, snowmobiles and trucks, schools, hospitals, films and television have all combined to change northern life. As the social environment changes, so do the people. The problems of southern society move north, often to be amplified in the conducive atmosphere of rapid social change.

The question of Inuit origins has been a subject of considerable speculation among archaeologists for many years. The piecing together of all archaeological evidence points to a beginning somewhere in Northeast Asia near the Bering Sea — probably between 15,000 and 10,000 B.C. — and a succession of ancient arctic cultures extending from eastern Siberia across Alaska and Northern Canada to Greenland has been identified and described by students of Eskimo prehistory. While there is not always concensus on the dating of these cultures and their inter-relationships, there is agreement that a number of distinct arctic cultural phases can be identified; the best known of these are the Dorset and Thule cultures.

The Dorset people lived in the Canadian central Arctic from about 700 B.C. to about 1300 A.D., with an economy based largely on walrus and seal, for which they had developed highly specialized hunting techniques. The Thule culture, which overtook and perhaps assimilated the Dorset people, had a relatively short duration, from about 1200 A.D. to the time of the first European contacts.

Life was hard, the climate brutal, and the hunt was the key to survival. When the game disappeared the people starved, or froze to death as animal oil for the lamp (usually the only source of heat) ran out. The hunt was all-important; the sea provided whales, walrus and seal, while the land supplied caribou and musk oxen. Hunting skills were passed down from father to son.

Early accounts and archaeological research show the Canadian Inuit once ranged farther south than they do now, particularly on the Atlantic seaboard. Traditionally,

Salmon drying in the Yukon.

Young mothers and their babies at Repulse Bay, NWT.

they were mainly a coastal people and fish and sea mammals were their sources of food, fuel and clothing. Centuries ago, however, one group broke away from the others to follow the caribou herds to the interior, where they formed a culture that was much different. They lived on the caribou herds and fish from the inland lakes, made fires from shrubs instead of blubber and rarely visited the sea.

The early explorers of the Canadian Arctic met Inuit from time to time over a period of some 300 years, but had few dealings with them; development in Arctic Canada came at a much later date than in other arctic lands. However, with the arrival of the whaling ships and the fur traders early in the 19th century changes began to take place. Through their dealings with whalers and traders the Inuit began to move into a position of some dependence upon the white man's goods and supplies. The traditional nomadic life was becoming less attractive to them.

By 1923 trading posts had been built along both shores of Hudson Strait, down the east coast of Hudson Bay to Port Harrison and up the west coast of Hudson Bay to Repulse Bay; similar development took place in the western Arctic. Today the Hudson's Bay Company has some 30 posts in arctic regions.

With World War II came a rapid development in air travel, and the building of defence installations and of meteorological and radio stations. During the past two decades the reduction of the Inuit's isolation has proceeded apace.

Many of these people have made a difficult and dramatic transition from nomadic hunters to modern urbanized residents. By such means as the Anik communications satellite, telephone, radio and television transmissions are now beamed into Inuit households. The sled dogs, long-time companions and a necessity to the Inuit, have gone; the motorized toboggan has replaced them. For longer journeys the airplane is the Arctic taxi, and few communities are without airstrips. Modern technology in the form of STOL (short take-off and landing) and jet aircraft have considerably shrunk the vast spaces of the Inuit domain.

The general health of the Inuit has improved remarkably in recent years and life expectancy is far greater than it was only a decade ago. The Inuit, susceptible to European diseases for which they had no tolerance, contracted influenza, tuberculosis and measles which raged through groups and sometimes wiped out entire communities; in recent years these diseases have been contained. Medical help is now available throughout the North, in nursing stations in the communities and in hospitals situated at strategic points. Charter aircraft serve as an air ambulance system for isolated communities.

Various government programs in areas such as education, social affairs, local government and economic development have also contributed to the dramatic change in the Inuit way of life. For example, co-operatives now do a total volume of business of over $25 million annually and to a large extent control the marketing of all Inuit art. Schools have been built in every viable Inuit community, and provide education services up to Grades VIII and IX in most locations. Students attend pre-vocational and senior secondary schools either elsewhere in the Arctic or at locations in Southern Canada. A generous post-secondary financial assistance plan is available from the Northwest Territories government to those students attending university and Vocational/Technical Institutes elsewhere.

Many communities have evolved from having a resident government administrator to becoming incorporated hamlets or villages, managing their own affairs through elected councils. The Council of the Northwest Territories, a provincial-style body, has nine Inuit elected members. An Inuk also represents the Eastern Northwest Territories in the House of Commons and an Inuk sits in the Senate.

The formation and growth of native organizations has been a direct result of an increasing desire on the part of the Inuit to conduct and govern their own affairs. The Inuit Tapirisat of Canada (The Eskimo Brotherhood) is a national organization formed in 1971 that seeks to encourage these objectives and foster growth and development in the Inuit culture. Inuit Tapirisat's Board of Directors is elected at the annual general assembly attended by delegates from all Inuit communities in Canada and, in addition to the national organization, there are six regional Inuit associations that speak for their own specific areas (COPE, the Committee for Original People's Entitlement in the western Arctic; NQIA, the Northern Quebec Inuit Association; LIA, the Labrador Inuit Association; BRIA, the Baffin Region Inuit Association; the Keewatin Inuit Association; and the Kitikmeot Inuit Association in the central Arctic).

These associations speak for Inuit interests in discussions and negotiations with industry and with provincial, territorial and federal governments and, with their special agencies, are increasingly concerned with land claims negotiations and the preservation of the Inuit lifestyle in the face of resource development. These associations are also involved in diverse projects that seek to maintain and preserve Inuit culture and promote social improvements for the Inuit. Such projects have included: formation of the Inuit Cultural Institute; the establishment of legal service centres; the development of a comprehensive Inuit communications system through community radio; an Inuit low-cost housing project; non-renewable resources research programs, the publication of *Inuit Today*, a bi-monthly magazine with Canada-wide distribution; and the establishment of boards and commissions in education, language, law and game management.

The federal government has supported all these endeavours and has provided financial assistance in the form of grants, contributions and interest-free loans from both the departments of Indian and Northern Affairs and the Secretary of State.

With the increased demand, and thus intensified exploration, for oil, gas and minerals in the Arctic, the Department of Indian and Northern Affairs and the Government of the Northwest Territories are involved in creating and making available opportunities for employment of Inuit in the non-renewable resource industries and related support industries. The Inuit Tapirisat of Canada and the various regional associations have been involved in representing Inuit concerns about the impact of development on the northern environment and the Inuit way of life. While the Inuit are not opposed to development, they are uneasy that industrial development will harm the land and the animals on which they depend. The federal and territorial governments are sensitive to these concerns, and land-use regulations have been modified to ensure sound northern development practices.

The development of northern society is perhaps the most controversial and difficult subject area to come to grips with and the hardest to deal with in brief form. The problems that develop in this rapidly evolving society are complex and have no easy answers. More and more it is the Inuit themselves who must analyze the problems and suggest solutions that will build a society compatible with their aims and aspirations.

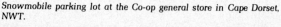

Snowmobile parking lot at the Co-op general store in Cape Dorset, NWT.

Official Languages

Throughout Canada's history the existence of two major linguistic groups has been one of the dynamic forces that shaped the country and contributed much to its unique character. To safeguard this valuable national heritage, the federal government has taken steps to ensure that both English-speaking and French-speaking Canadians have equal opportunities to participate in Canada's future.

In 1963 it appointed a Royal Commission on Bilingualism and Biculturalism to inquire into a wide range of questions relating to language and culture in Canada. Following the publication of the first book of the commission's final report, the federal government proposed an Official Languages Bill, which Parliament adopted in July 1969 and which, accordingly, came into force in September of the same year.

The Act stipulates that "the English and French languages are the official languages of Canada" and that they "possess and enjoy equality of status and equal rights and privileges as to their use in all the institutions of the Parliament and Government of Canada".

The Act states that in the National Capital Region and in other areas where there is sufficient demand federal government services shall be available in both official languages and that a Commissioner of Official Languages reporting directly to Parliament shall ensure compliance with the Act. It should be noted that the Act and indeed federal official languages policy as a whole aims not to make all Canadians "bilingual", but on the contrary to ensure that, wherever they are reasonably concentrated, those who speak English and those who speak French may deal with the federal government in their own languages.

The main responsibility for official languages policies and programs is shared by the Treasury Board Secretariat, the Department of the Secretary of State, the Public Service Commission and the National Capital Commission. In addition, the Commissioner of Official Languages is responsible for ensuring that the official languages are recognized in practice and that the institutions of the Parliament and Government of Canada conduct their business in compliance with the spirit and intent of the Act.

Treasury Board Secretariat

The Treasury Board Secretariat has responsibility for producing general guidelines, for providing overall direction to federal departments, institutions and agencies, including Crown corporations, and for reviewing their implementation of official languages programs. It is also responsible for monitoring the overall progress of the public service toward achievement of official languages objectives and reporting to the government on the status of implementation of official languages policies and programs within the public service.

Official Languages Branch. This branch develops and communicates government policies and programs for the application of the Official Languages Act within departments and agencies of the Government of Canada and in judicial, quasi-judicial or administrative bodies or Crown corporations, and monitors, audits and evaluates their implementation and effectiveness. The branch comprises the Secretariat and the following divisions: Operations Analysis, Policy, and Evaluation and Audit.

The Secretariat provides controls, co-ordination and support services to organizational elements of the branch in the areas of manpower and financial resources, processing of departmental submissions, development and publication of branch operations manuals and monitoring service-wide costs of official languages programs. It includes a documentation and reference centre that provides quick, up-to-date information and reference service on matters relating to the Official Languages Act, government policies and programs, and acts as a distribution and dissemination centre for government policies, circulars and directives.

The Operations Analysis Division is responsible for advising departments on the implementation of official languages programs, including the preparation of annual plans and progress reports. It is also required to analyze plans and other submissions to Treasury Board from departments and, based on its analysis, recommend acceptance, modification or rejection of the submissions. It serves as the Official Languages Branch's principal contact point with departments and agencies, and as such provides a means of communication both to and from departments. It participates in policy analysis and interpretation, particularly from the perspective of program operations in the various departments.

The Policy Division is responsible for the systematic interpretation of the Treasury Board's official languages policies, the analysis of major issues arising in the application of these policies in departments, the formulation of proposed amendments or revisions to the policies as required and the preparation of major reviews and assessments of the impact of policies. These functions include participation in the analysis of annual departmental plans to determine their consistency with current official languages policies.

The division also maintains extensive liaison with other branches of the Treasury Board Secretariat and other central agencies in order to ensure co-ordination between official languages policies and other related personnel or language policies.

The Evaluation and Audit Division is responsible for defining appropriate indicators of program performance, analyzing data collected through the information system and the observations of other reporting media, analysts and audit teams, conducting special studies and determining trends and program effectiveness. The division is also responsible for planning and establishing the systems and procedures which are required to give effect to the government's policies and to evaluate the effectiveness of their implementation.

Department of the Secretary of State

The Department of the Secretary of State has a general responsibility for encouraging and assisting the development of the official languages in education, in provincial and municipal administrations and in the public and private sector; and a responsibility through its Translation Bureau, for translation, interpretation and terminology. The department also has a program of support for minority official language groups; this program is concerned with the linguistic and cultural development of official language communities in areas where they are established as minorities.

Language Programs Branch. A series of programs devoted to the development of the official languages is administered by the Language Programs Branch. Its federal-provincial program for official languages in education is intended to increase the opportunities for Canadians to be educated in the minority official language in each province or territory and to acquire a knowledge of their second official language. Financial aid, offered to the provinces under the terms of a federal-provincial agreement, is based on student enrolment, time spent in language instruction and costs per student. Provision is also made for various individual bursaries and awards, for contributions to language-training institutions and teachers' colleges and for special projects funded on a cost-shared basis. Limited assistance is made available to institutions and organizations to promote the compilation and dissemination of information on the second official language teaching and learning and on the minority language education.

Financial assistance to increase the opportunities for adult immigrants to acquire a knowledge of citizenship and of one of the official languages is also provided to provinces and territories under the terms of federal-provincial agreements. Such support is based on the teaching costs of providing instruction and on the costs of the text books.

In the private and the non-federal public sectors various programs have been developed to encourage the adoption of improved methods for acquiring and using both official languages in dealing with issues and problems related to the provision of services in both English and French. These include technical advice to business and industry, provincial and municipal administrations, educational institutions, medical establishments and social service organizations, and financial assistance to voluntary associations for interpretation and translation.

Official Language Minority Groups Directorate. This directorate was set up to promote the social and cultural life of the francophone and anglophone communities in their own language in the provinces where they are in a minority and thus to favour their successful development.

The official language minority communities have various organizations in each province that relate to some facet or other of social, educational, cultural and economic life. The programs are designed to meet the needs of these organizations and their members by fostering projects that fall within the mandate of the directorate.

The Translation Bureau. The Translation Bureau has been assigned the task of helping the Canadian government and the federal administration communicate effectively in all languages both within the public service and in their cultural, scientific, economic and diplomatic relations at home and abroad. It provides the language services required for the effective operation of Parliament, the government and its agencies, mainly with regard to official languages policy. With their co-operation, the Translation Bureau determines their various needs and takes action to meet them. In addition to providing translation services to federal departments and agencies, it ensures interpretation and translation of the proceedings of the House of Commons, the Senate and their committees, as well as at national and international conferences in which the government participates. The Translation Bureau is responsible for supplying and updating the Canadian government's terminology bank and for standardizing, in both official languages, the vocabulary used in the various administrative sectors of the government; it also participates with Canadian and foreign institutions in specialized assignments conducted in all relevant languages and areas of study, though more specifically in Canada's official languages.

Commissioner of Official Languages

The Commissioner of Official Languages is appointed by Parliament to oversee the application of the Official Languages Act, which declares that "The English and French languages are the official languages of Canada for all purposes of the Parliament and Government of Canada . . .". It is the duty of the commissioner to take all actions within his authority to ensure "recognition of the status of each of the official languages and compliance with the spirit and intent of this Act in the administration of the affairs of the institutions of the Parliament and Government of Canada . . .". The commissioner conducts investigations either on his own initiative or pursuant to any complaint made to him and makes recommendations to the departments or agencies concerned as provided for in the Act. He also reports each year directly to Parliament.

The commissioner is appointed for a seven-year term and exercises three main functions: language ombudsman for individuals or groups; linguistic auditor general vis-à-vis the federal administration; and the advocate of language reform throughout the country.

The Official Languages Act requires all federal institutions to communicate with and provide services to both English-speaking and French-speaking members of the public in the official language of their choice except where demand for service in both languages is so irregular that bilingual services are not warranted. Wherever possible federal public servants should also have the opportunity to work in their preferred official language and this is understood to involve fair participation of both major language groups in the federal public service.

Multiculturalism

According to the 1971 Census, 44.6 per cent of Canada's population were of British origin, 28.7 per cent were French and the remaining 26.7 per cent were of other language origins. The government's multiculturalism policy, announced in October

Ukrainian dancing.

1971, was a response to recommendations of the report of the Royal Commission on Bilingualism and Biculturalism. The policy promised support to programs aimed at retaining, developing and sharing these cultures on a larger scale and programs which encourage mutual appreciation and understanding among all Canadians.

In November 1972 the position of Minister Responsible for Multiculturalism was created to administer the policy, and in May 1973 the Canadian Consultative Council on Multiculturalism (CCCM) was established to provide a focus for consultation by the minister on matters relating to implementation of multiculturalism policy. Provincial, national and executive meetings have since been held regularly in order to review policy and evaluate multiculturalism programs. Extensive consultations have taken place between the CCCM and many local cultural community and youth groups in all regions of the country.

Multiculturalism Programs

Implementation of the government's multiculturalism policy is carried out by the Multiculturalism Directorate of the Department of the Secretary of State and by several federal cultural agencies. It implements a number of programs, which include the following.

The Ethnic Studies Program supports scholarly research and academic courses of study in the field of the humanities and social sciences relating to important aspects of cultural pluralism in Canada. Universities are assisted in obtaining visiting professors and lecturers. The Canadian Ethnic Studies Advisory Committee advises the Ethnic Studies Program on these matters.

Pipe band on parade in Toronto.

The Cultural Resources Development Section encourages the development of resources and the exchange of information about the multicultural nature of Canadian society. The purpose is to display the cultural diversity of the country to all Canadians, particularly through the education systems, media relations activities, the Ethnic History Project and support for the performing arts and for the writing and translation of works of creative literature.

The Multiculturalism Directorate also provides assistance to a wide range of activities initiated by voluntary groups, to enable them not only to maintain and develop their cultural heritage but also to share it with others. Support is provided for the operation of supplementary cultural-linguistic courses, for the training of instructors and for the development of teaching aids for use in ancestral-language schools, intercultural communications, group development, cultural integration of immigrants, etc. By liaising through its national, regional and local offices with groups, individuals and organizations representing Canada's ethno-cultural groups, the department continues to assist them to achieve full participation in society.

Dancing on Canada Day in Ottawa.

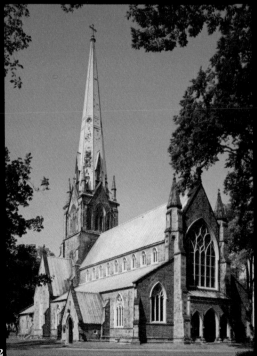

Canadian Churches

1. Our Lady of Fatima, Roman Catholic church in Renfrew, Ont.
2. Christ Church Cathedral, Anglican, in Fredericton, N.B.
3. Christ Church at Millarville, Alta., erected in 1895 and still in use.
4. Christ Lutheran Church, Neudorf, Sask., built in 1914.
5. Greek Orthodox Church in St. Catharines, Ont.

2

4

Arts and Culture

During the 1980s, the arts in Canada will encounter one of the most challenging decades in the course of their development. The veritable explosion in creative activity in the early 1970s was supported by greater interest in the protection of Canada's cultural heritage and an increased recognition and demand for Canadian cultural products on the part of both national and international audiences. Canadian artists in all fields have endeavoured to carry this exciting momentum into the 80s. Unfortunately, the levels of public demand and financial support from all sources have not necessarily kept pace, in part as a result of the economic constraints which we are currently experiencing in all sectors of national activity.

The Economic Picture

The performing arts are inherently financially dependent. They cannot earn enough money even to come close to meeting their expenses, so their existence depends on massive financial transfusions in grants and subsidies. Being dependent on goodwill leaves the performing arts exposed and vulnerable to changing economic winds. Historically, in times of economic retrenchment the arts have been the first to suffer funding cuts. Rising costs and declining subsidies doubly jeopardize the arts.

Rudy Webb as Merlin in the Young People's Theatre production, Arthur, which toured Toronto area schools in spring 1980.

Hugh Webster and Michael Ball in The Black Bonspiel of Wullie MacCrimmon, *a Festival Lennoxville production.*

Earned revenue is the income a performing arts organization generates from its own operations, primarily from box-office sales, but also from such other sources as guarantees and program and beverage sales at performances. Generally the average price of admission to an arts event is reasonable when compared to the inflated costs of other consumer goods. The person who attends a performing arts event is really paying half or less of the cost of production; the rest is subsidized. Average ticket prices in 1978 were: for theatre, $4.00; for music concerts, $5.61; for dance, $4.87; and for opera, $8.63.

Costs in the arts are escalating, as in all sectors of the economy. In the performing arts expenses are rising faster than revenues. In 1978 the average cost per theatre performance was $2,396. For a music concert it was $10,288, for dance $7,800 and for opera $20,273. The income earned by theatre companies represented 51 per cent of total revenue. Opera earned 53 per cent of its revenue. Both music and dance failed to earn half of their total revenue; music 44 per cent and dance 43 per cent. The balance of total revenues was made up of grants and subsidies.

Grants and subsidies come from two main sources, the public sector (governments) and the private sector. On average, grants represented more than half (52 per cent) of the total revenue of performing arts organizations in 1978.

Governments at all levels are the major benefactors. In 1978, 78 per cent of all subsidies to the performing arts flowed from the public funds. Of these 41 per cent were federal, 27 per cent provincial and 10 per cent municipal. The remaining 22 per cent came from the private sector.

Main sources of private funds are foundations, corporations, individuals, fund raising campaigns by volunteer committees, bequests and endowments, bank interest and returns on investments. Nationally, the greatest private sector support in 1978 was from individual citizens, followed closely by corporations.

The federal government has committed itself to a major study of future directions for the development of culture in Canada. Provincial governments, major municipalities, interested organizations and members of the general public have all indicated their support for this undertaking and their willingness to participate in the exercise. Issues involved include: increased incentives to encourage financial support for artists and the arts in general from a wider variety of sources; a more effective promotion and distribution of cultural products across this vast country and abroad; and the need to exploit more fully the significant role which the arts can play as a mechanism for increasing both inter-regional understanding and the appreciation of different cultural traditions and aspirations in order to reflect the diversities of the Canadian mosaic.

Philippe Vita and Manon Levac in Diallele, *a production of Groupe Nouvelle Aire.*

Jack Ackroyd, Sharon Bakker and Dan MacDonald in The Birds, a production of Theatre Calgary.

The Canada Council

The Canada Council makes grants available to professional artists and organizations involved in areas such as the visual arts (including photography, film, crafts and video), writing, publishing, translation, music, theatre and dance. Currently, the Council supports the following programs with grants:

Individual Artists. Grants are available to professional artists for activities in the fields of arts-related architecture, arts administration, arts criticism, creative writing, dance, film, music, photography, theatre, video, painting, sculpture and fine crafts. Individual grants range from $19,000 (available only to senior artists) to small sums for project costs and related travel. In 1979-80 professional artists such as Gratien Gelinas, Irving Layton, Yvon Thériault and Joyce Wieland received grants. Grants for international representation and foreign exchanges are also administered by the arts award service of the Council.

Music. The Council awards the major portion of its budget in this area to professional orchestras, string quartets, chamber music groups, professional choral groups, opera companies, music organizations and schools. Funding was received in 1979-80 by the following: the Toronto Symphony Orchestra ($802,100), the Edmonton Opera ($120,000), and the Tudor Singers from Montreal ($35,000). In addition, the Council has a very small program of assistance to amateur choirs, community music groups and to the publishing and recording of Canadian music.

Theatre. Theatre grants are available to professional companies, festivals, schools and associations in Canada. Operating grants are reserved for well-established

Catherine Lafortune, Josephine Baurac, Betsy Baron (centre), Hélène Grenier and Josée Ledoux in Soaring by Les Grands Ballets Canadiens.

companies, while grants for individual projects and workshop productions are awarded to a limited number of younger companies. Over 160 companies are awarded support each year. In 1979-80 for example the following institutions were funded: Le Théâtre du Nouveau Monde ($465,000), Stratford Festival ($550,000), National Theatre School ($1,020,000) and Rising Tide Theatre Company ($7,000).

Dance. As a result of budgetary restrictions, the Council supports only classical and modern dance and experimental expressions of these two forms, and provides operating funds to a limited number of groups. In 1979-80 only eight companies received operating grants including the following: the National Ballet ($1,198,000), Les Grands Ballets Canadiens ($605,000) and Anna Wyman Dance Theatre ($126,000). In addition, the National Ballet School receives close to $1 million each year. About a dozen dance companies usually receive project grants.

Visual Arts. The visual arts section provides grants for the following: film and video projects, the Art Bank, galleries, museums, and print workshops. A visiting artists program permits post-secondary institutions and visual arts organizations to invite professional Canadian artists for lectures. An artists-in-residence program facilitates the provision of studio space in New York, symposia, and occasional exhibitions of Canadian art abroad, for example, the recent Canadian participation at the "11th Biennale de Paris".

The Art Bank buys existing works of contemporary Canadian art, rents works to public institutions, and occasionally loans them for exhibitions. The Art Bank collection now contains approximately 9,000 works by more than a thousand artists, including Jack Bush, Charles Gagnon and Michael Snow.

Explorations Program. The explorations program provides grants to individuals, groups and organizations for imaginative projects which contribute to Canadian culture. Examples of projects funded are film scripts; craft workshops; biographies; new performing arts projects; exhibits of photographs, slides and other art forms; popular writing; recordings; film; video and audio experiments; community-based cultural animation projects; and local and regional histories. In recent years, the

Council has helped to finance a computer culture exhibition, a project depicting Canada's past through old photographs, and a new gallery of experimental music.

Cultural Tours. The Canada Council's touring office, which aims to ensure access by the widest possible audience to Canadian performers and to develop Canadian expertise in the promotion and management of tours by performing artists, offers grants to Canadian artists and groups to develop and strengthen regional touring circuits. During 1979-80 the National Ballet toured in several Canadian provinces and the Orford String Quartet toured nationally. Some support is also given to foreign companies touring in Canada as part of a cultural exchange. For example, the Peking Opera toured some of Canada's major cities in 1979-80. An apprenticeship program enables individuals to work with people experienced in the management of artists and the management of tours.

Through the program, Concerts Canada, the touring office provides incentive grants and communications grants to managers of Canadian performing artists. The touring office also publishes practical directories for performing artists and sponsors.

The Anna Wyman dance troupe recently performed in China on a three-week tour.

Ray Jewers and Derek Ralston in Savages *at the National Arts Centre.*

Writing and Publishing. Block grants are available to majority Canadian-owned publishing houses to offset publication deficits on a complete program of Canadian books during a calendar year. For publishing houses that have not yet reached the level of development required for block grants, project grants for the publication of specific manuscripts are available. Grants are also offered to Canadian publishers for the translation of works by Canadian authors from one official language to the other.

The Council also purchases Canadian books from majority Canadian-owned publishing houses for free distribution in this country and abroad. It collaborates with associations and publishers to facilitate promotion tours by Canadian authors and the publication of literary and arts periodicals. The Council also provides some support to a limited number of writers-in-residence and a national professional association of writers and publishers.

The National Arts Centre

The National Arts Centre (NAC), located in Ottawa, has three main halls. The Opera, with 2,300 seats, was designed primarily for opera and ballet, with a full-size orchestra pit and the most advanced sound, lighting and other technical equipment available. Its stage is one of the largest in the world, measuring 58 by 34 metres, and the Opera's facilities can handle the most complicated changes required by the largest touring companies. The 950-seat Theatre is ideal for Greek, Elizabethan or contemporary plays, and its stage can easily be adjusted from the conventional rectangular style to the thrust stage style used for Shakespearean drama. Like the Opera, it is fully equipped for television, simultaneous translation and film projection, and its technical facilities are among the best available. The Studio is a hexagonal room which can seat up to 350 persons in a variety of seating plans. This hexagonal room is used for theatre productions, conferences and cabarets.

The 46-member National Arts Centre Orchestra performs some 40 concerts a year in the centre and many more each year on tours in Canada and abroad. Music programming includes about 70 concerts a year, featuring distinguished soloists and guest orchestras from Canada and around the world.

There are more than 400 performances of live theatre a year at the centre. Some of the plays are produced by the theatre department and others represent Canada's regional theatre or come from outside the country. The theatre department tours Canada with productions from the subscription series and also forms small companies which perform in high schools and elsewhere, offering professional theatre in English and French to communities which would not otherwise have the opportunity to enjoy it. Workshops for students and teachers are among the other services offered.

The dance and variety department brings in some 100 different shows a year, including ballet, musical shows and comedy. A number of Canadian dance companies appear on a regular basis at the NAC; dance and variety programming offers a showcase for performers from every part of the country. Altogether, there are about 900 performances annually in the NAC, entertaining almost 800,000 people.

Films

The year 1978-79 witnessed a rapid and profound evolution in the scope and nature of the Canadian film industry.

In 1966, there were three feature length theatrical releases produced in Canada. In the decade that followed the creation of the Canadian Film Development Corporation (CFDC) in 1967, the industry began to grow, with the CFDC investing nearly $26 million in some 220 films with budgets totalling $60 million. It was an important and significant time when the seeds were sown for the creation of a strong and competitive industry.

Production jumped dramatically during 1979-80 when the CFDC provided financial assistance of $5.6 million in 27 films — 17 English, 10 French — with budgets totalling $50 million. In addition, several other features, with combined budgets estimated at $13 million, were produced without any CFDC participation.

While this tremendous growth stems from many factors, the Corporation's new investment, development and promotion activities have been central to the increased activity. Other factors include: the emergence of a group of strong, innovative producers; the tax incentive offered by the capital cost allowance; the development of new sources of financing through public offerings by recognized brokerage firms; and the co-production treaties Canada has with the United Kingdom, France, Italy, the Federal Republic of Germany and Israel.

Reproduction of historic detail requires concentration at the provincial museum in Edmonton, Alta.

Museums and Galleries

Over the past decade, Canada has witnessed a dramatic increase in museum activity. There are now about 1,500 museums and art galleries in operation across the country, and approximately 50 major institutions have a combined annual attendance of nearly 10 million visitors. The number of museum workers has also increased enormously and training programs in museology have expanded. Since 1972 extensive financial support has flowed from all levels of government, indicating strong public interest in the preservation of Canada's natural, historic and artistic heritage.

An important member of the museum community is the Canadian Museums Association, with its head office in Ottawa. Through its publications, seminars, conferences and museological resource centre, the association promotes professional practices among museum employees across the country.

The National Museums of Canada

In 1968 the National Museums Act incorporated the four national museums under one administration as the National Museums of Canada. The four national museums are the National Gallery of Canada, the National Museum of Man (including the Canadian War Museum), the National Museum of Natural Sciences and the National Museum of Science and Technology (including the National Aeronautical Collection).

As a result of federal government deliberations a new national museum policy was announced in March 1972 and the National Museums of Canada was given the responsibility of implementing it. Based on the concepts of democratization and decentralization of Canada's cultural heritage, the national museum policy emphasized access by all Canadians to their national heritage and its preservation. Under this policy, a series of national programs was organized. Other key features of the policy included the establishment of a nationwide network of 25 associate museums, including the four national museums in Ottawa. As well, a network of exhibition centres was set up to meet the needs of communities not served by major museums.

Other national programs include the Canadian Conservation Institute, which provides research, advice and skilled care to protect heritage collections; a computerized national inventory of museum objects; a mobile exhibits program, including a fleet of caravans depicting various regions of Canada, and the Discovery Train, a half-mile of dramatic exhibits of our national and human history; an international exchange program; and a program of technical and financial assistance to

Polar bear diorama at the National Museum of Natural Sciences.

hundreds of qualifying institutions. Publications, audio-visual productions and educational kits serve a wide audience from coast to coast.

The National Gallery of Canada. The function of this gallery since its incorporation in 1913 has been to foster public awareness of the visual arts and to promote an interest in art throughout the country. Under this mandate, the gallery has increased its collections and developed into an art institution worthy of international recognition.

There are more than 23,000 works of art in the National Gallery including paintings, sculptures, prints, drawings, photographs and decorative arts. The historical collections have been built along national and international lines to give Canadians an understanding of the origins and development of their cultural history as expressed through the visual arts. The collection of Canadian art is the most extensive and important collection in existence and is continually being augmented. In addition, there are many Old Masters from the principal European schools from the 14th to the 20th century and growing collections of Asian and contemporary art.

Visitors to the gallery are offered an active program of exhibitions, lectures, films and guided tours. The reference library, which contains more than 67,000 volumes and periodicals on the history of art and related subjects, is open to the public.

The interests of the country as a whole are served by circulating exhibitions, lecture tours, publications, reproductions and films. At the same time, the gallery promotes interest in Canadian art abroad by participating in international exhibitions and by preparing major exhibitions of Canadian art for showing in other countries; it also brings important exhibitions from abroad to be shown in Canada. During 1979-80 the gallery's national program organized and circulated exhibitions, which were seen by over 265,000 people in 30 institutions in 18 cities across Canada.

Exhibits of the colonial period at the Canadian War Museum, the National Museum of Man's second public building.

Refracting telescope at the National Museum of Science and Technology.

The National Museum of Man. This museum collects, preserves, researches, interprets, displays and issues publications on artifacts and data of the cultural and historical heritage of Canada's varied population.

The museum has nine permanent exhibit halls in the Victoria Memorial Museum Building. They include: "Trail of Mankind", an orientation gallery; "Canada Before Cartier", the story of prehistoric Canada; "The Inuit", a study of the people of the North; "People of the Longhouse", a portrait of the Iroquois; "The Buffalo Hunters", a study of the Plains Indians; and "Children of the Raven", on the life of the Northwest Coast Indians. The museum's new permanent exhibits — "A Few Acres of Snow" and "Everyman's Heritage: The Canadian Odyssey" — deal with the history of settlement and social development in Canada and the rich mosaic of cultures brought by settlers.

The museum's work is carried out by seven divisions. The Archaeological Survey of Canada conducts research and archaeological rescue excavations on sites about to be destroyed or damaged by development. The Canadian Centre for Folk Culture Studies has the country's largest archive of folk culture materials. The Canadian Ethnology Service conducts comprehensive research on Canadian native and Métis cultures. The Canadian War Museum, the National Museum of Man's second public building, is involved in research, exhibits and publications on military history, and houses an extensive collection of memorabilia ranging from war art to tanks. The History Division carries out studies of Canadian society and material culture since the beginning of European colonization. The National Programmes Division circulates travelling exhibits across Canada and internationally. The Education and Cultural

Affairs Division produces educational resources, including the "Canada's Visual History" series, films and multi-media "Museum Kits", and provides local programs for schools and the public.

The National Museum of Natural Sciences. The National Museum of Natural Sciences consists of the divisions of botany, invertebrate zoology, vertebrate zoology, mineral sciences, paleobiology and interpretation and extension. A special unit, the Zooarchaeological Identification Centre, identifies and interprets animal remains found in archaeological investigations.

The museum is engaged in many major research projects undertaken by its staff members or associated scientists from universities and other outside organizations. More than four million scientific specimens are maintained in the museum's collections and are available to scientists from all parts of the world. The museum also publishes scientific papers on subjects related to its collections.

Audio-visual presentations, visitor-operated displays, drawings, models and thousands of specimens from the museum's collections are used in six permanent exhibit halls entitled "The Earth", "Life Through the Ages", "Birds of Canada", "Mammals in Canada", "Animal Life" and "Animals in Nature". A new permanent hall, "Plant Life", is expected to be completed in 1981. Temporary exhibits produced by the museum or on loan from other museums and institutions are exhibited in the exhibition hall.

Public lectures, film presentations and special interpretive programs offered by the museum have become increasingly popular with school classes and the general public. Popular publications, a school loans service of educational resource materials and a program of travelling exhibits make our national heritage more accessible to Canadians across the country.

The National Museum of Science and Technology. This museum challenges over half a million visitors each year to climb, push, pull or just view the lively exhibitions built around its collections. An additional 200,000 people annually visit the National Aeronautical Collection at Rockcliffe Airport.

The museum's exhibit halls feature displays of ship models, clocks, communications equipment, a computer exhibit, a chick hatchery, old and new agriculture machinery, printing presses and artifacts of Canada's aviation history. There are numerous examples of milestones in the history of ground transportation, from sleighs and carriages to giant steam locomotives and "horseless carriages". The Physics Hall, with its skill-testing experiments and "seeing puzzles", delights young and old alike. The museum's observatory houses Canada's largest refracting telescope, which is used for star-gazing in evening educational programs.

Educational programs on general or topic oriented subjects for all age groups are conducted by a staff of tour guides. During the summer months a steam train makes a return trip from Ottawa to Wakefield, Quebec, giving its passengers a taste of the sights and sounds of a bygone era.

The museum's work also includes the designing and building of exhibits that are occasionally sent on tour throughout Canada. Artifacts are exchanged with museums in Canada and abroad.

In the National Aeronautical Collection nearly 100 aircraft illustrate the progress of aviation from its early days to present times and the importance of the flying machine in the discovery and development of Canada.

A library of rare books in Toronto, Ont.

Libraries and Archives

Libraries

Libraries have existed in Canada since the early 18th century. Legal, theological, university and society libraries were in existence before 1850; after 1850 business and industrial libraries appeared, along with tax-supported public libraries. The greatest growth for all types of libraries has been in the years since World War II.

Because Canada is a federal state and libraries fall under provincial jurisdiction, there is no unified national system of libraries. The public library systems of the provinces, though varying in detail, are alike in being supported by local and provincial funds (except for the Yukon and the Northwest Territories, which are federally funded) and co-ordinated by a central library agency.

Canadian public libraries are sources of print and non-print materials for the pleasure, information or education of their users. Some are deeply involved in providing information on community services and facilities. A growing number are finding ways to take public library services to those who cannot or do not come to libraries — senior citizens, shut-ins, prisoners and the physically and economically handicapped. People whose mother tongue is neither English nor French find that libraries frequently provide foreign-language materials, often with the assistance of the Multilingual Biblioservice of the National Library, which assembles collections of books in selected languages and offers them to library agencies in the provinces for circulation in their areas.

There are perhaps 10,000 school libraries in Canada, as distinct from unorganized classroom collections. The emphasis in this type of library has shifted from the use of printed materials alone to use of a wider range of information sources, such as films, recordings, tapes, slides and kits. As a result, school libraries have become multi-media "resource centres".

College and university libraries went through a period of rapid expansion in the 1960s and early 1970s, but growth since the mid-1970s has slowed down. University libraries have automated a number of library procedures, especially cataloguing, in order to cope with increasing workloads. They have developed networks for the exchange of bibliographic data and have co-operated in collection rationalization and resource sharing. In these efforts they have had support from the National Library, which has sponsored a number of studies relevant to these concerns (e.g., on the possibility of national bibliographic networks). College libraries are notable for their integration of audio-visual materials into their collections and for innovative measures taken to serve a clientele ranging in age and interests from the high school graduate to the senior citizen.

Special libraries — those serving companies, associations, institutions such as museums and hospitals, and government departments and agencies — number about 1,500. Among them, the government libraries tend to be the largest, especially the provincial legislative libraries. Some federal government libraries are de facto resource libraries in their subject fields for the whole of the country, but in general special libraries serve only authorized users from their sponsoring organizations. Special libraries have been concerned with automation from the viewpoint of reference services.

At the national level, the scientific resource library for Canada is the Canada Institute for Scientific and Technical Information (CISTI), which was formerly the National Science Library. CISTI's services to the scientific research and industrial communities include, in addition to its back-up serials and monograph collection, a computer-based selective dissemination of information (SDI) service, a companion on-line search service (CAN/OLE) and publication of a union list of scientific serials held in Canada.

The National Library of Canada marked its twenty-fifth anniversary in 1978 by an intensive study of its future role and is now seeking to implement the priorities established. The library continues to build its collections in the social sciences and humanities and in Canadiana of all kinds, as well as to discharge many national responsibilities. In accordance with the National Library Act of 1969, it administers the legal deposit regulations, publishes the national bibliography, Canadiana, and maintains union catalogues from which libraries and researchers can find out where in Canada specific works are held. It assigns International Standard Book Numbers (ISBN) for English-language publications and International Standard Serial Numbers (ISSN) for all Canadian serials. It provides the SDI service for the humanities and social sciences and makes on-line searches available for a minimal fee to libraries and individuals. It has taken a leading part in promoting national bibliographic networks and is developing a federal government libraries network.

In Canada librarians are trained at the universities. Seven postgraduate schools offer master's degrees in library science and two, at the universities of Toronto and Western Ontario, also offer doctoral programs. In addition post-secondary courses for the training of library technicians are available in community colleges in many parts of the country.

Laurier House, the former Ottawa residence of prime ministers Sir Wilfrid Laurier and William Lyon Mackenzie King, is administered by the Public Archives.

Archives

The mandate of the Public Archives of Canada is to acquire, preserve and make available to the public all documents that reflect the various aspects of Canadian life and the development of the country.

At one time, manuscripts were virtually the only objects of interest to researchers. Today, equal importance is given to documents of every kind as authentic sources of information. In addition to its own library, the Public Archives now includes separate divisions for manuscripts, maps and plans, pictures, prints and drawings, photographs, films and sound recordings, and machine-readable archives.

The department has equally important responsibilities in the management of government records. The Records Management Branch aids federal government departments and agencies in establishing and administering effective programs for the management and disposal of records. Microfilms and computer records have important roles in both records and archives, the Central Microfilm Unit of the Departmental Administration Branch provides microfilming services to government departments at cost.

Laurier House, the former Ottawa residence of prime ministers Sir Wilfrid Laurier and William Lyon Mackenzie King, is administered by the Public Archives. Collections of pictures, china and silver enhance the dignified charm of the house, and are viewed every year by more than 25,000 visitors from every part of the country and from abroad.

The Public Archives has also initiated a comprehensive exhibitions program to make the many collections and services of the department better known. To this end, the Archives Branch will present a series of exhibitions and publications on the history of Canada. The first exhibition, scheduled to open in July 1981, will feature historical documents prior to 1700.

Governments and Cultural Policy

Private and Public Responsibilities

All Canadians live their cultures, but very few of them discuss the subject very much. When they do, they usually regard culture primarily as a personal affair. While certain kinds of government support are welcome, any attempt by any government to determine the substance of cultural life would be inconsistent with Canadian values.

Nevertheless, members of the public demand certain kinds of cultural services from their governments. There seems to be increasing public interest in cultural expressions that illuminate the reality of Canada and Canadians. The problems are complicated by the cultural diversity of the population, the decentralization of public authority and the openness of Canada to cultural currents from Europe, the United States and other parts of the world. The resources available from the market and from private patronage, while important, are inadequate to the task; it is recognized that public authorities must also play a part.

Thus cultural policies in Canada are characterized by a search for acceptable ways in which governments may support cultural development and the production and enjoyment of the arts, without imposing official values, control or censorship.

Governments as Proprietors

By historical accident or considered decision, governments own a great deal of property of cultural importance to Canadians. Holdings range from national monuments like the Parliament Buildings to the most representative collections of Canadian painting or the records of obscure 19th century parish priests. From this role as proprietor have emerged important institutions like the provincial and federal archives, historic sites and monuments services, and important art galleries and museums operated at all three levels of government. In short, governments are the predominant collectors and exhibitors in the country.

The responsibilities of proprietorship have been recognized in a number of ways. Collections have been steadily expanded and diversified. Facilities are being improved and interpretation services strengthened so that public holdings may be more readily available and meaningful to the public.

In building construction, governments at all three levels have been prepared to give some weight to aesthetic as well as functional considerations. This extends beyond architectural design to include the use of works of art both in exterior landscaping and in furnishing. Recently there has been a new interest in renovating heritage buildings either for their historic purposes, as was the Kingston City Hall, or for new uses such as government office space.

As proprietors, governments have also been prepared to construct and operate physical facilities for exhibition and performance. Over the past 15 years, there has been quite remarkable progress in building theatres and concert halls. Virtually all the major urban areas, and many smaller centres as well, are now reasonably adequately equipped.

The National Arts Centre in Ottawa.

It is striking that investment in cultural goods and facilities for the enjoyment of the public is not limited to any single level of government. One finds libraries, concert halls, art collections and heritage buildings owned and made available by municipalities and by provincial and federal authorities. Numerous co-operative arrangements have developed between governments to strengthen the services offered and to assist with financing, especially of capital costs. Federal grants to provincial governments and municipalities have been important, especially in building facilities for exhibition and the performing arts; provincial grants to municipalities are essential for the construction and operation of public libraries, cultural centres and many programs offered at the local level. In some provinces, very substantial lottery revenues are allocated to municipal capital expenditure on cultural and recreational facilities.

Underwriting Creativity

Apart from purchasing some of their work for collections or other public purposes, governments took it for granted until the middle of this century that creative people would make it on their own. No substantial expenditures were regularly devoted to the support of people rather than the purchase of product.

The report of the Massey-Lévesque Commission in 1949 was the turning point at which it became apparent that a flourishing cultural life in Canada simply could not be sustained by market revenues, private benevolence and artists living in poverty. Since that time governments have recognized, albeit hesitantly, that it is appropriate for some public funds to underwrite painters, dancers, musicians and other artists, and the institutions within which some of them work. Even now, very few professional artists approach income levels regarded as normal in other professions, but the current level of creative expression in Canada is in some measure a reflection of government support.

Several techniques are used to channel public funds to artists in a rational way, without constraining or attempting to control the direction of their work. A number of arts councils have been established separate from the normal government

The Museum of Anthropology at the University of British Columbia in Vancouver.

structure. The Canada Council, which is the chosen instrument of the federal government, is a statutory foundation, or public trust, that is expected and required to make its own decisions without direction from any authority apart from its legislation. Several provincial governments use this pattern, with modifications to meet regional requirements.

The arts councils in turn are guided by the judgments of the creative community itself and typically rely on recognized practising professionals in a given discipline to advise on the best distribution of the available funds. There are seldom enough funds to meet the need and very hard choices must be made, so the system is designed to identify excellence as objectively as possible.

Governments as Educators

In a broad sense, all education policy is cultural policy. The schools are the most important cultural institutions of Canadian society. Education is a provincial responsibility administered largely at the municipal level; the subject is accordingly diverse, complex and locally oriented, and the paragraphs that follow can suggest only a few general characteristics.

School programs in Canada have always recognized the importance of the arts as an element in general education. Schools have been teaching literature for as long as there have been schools, and in many jurisdictions the current tendency is to increase the stress on contemporary works, particularly Canadian writing. Music is also well established in almost all jurisdictions and many schools offer programs in the visual arts.

Recently there appears to have been increasing concern, reflected both in policy and in student interest, with theatre arts, television and films. Television has appeared both as a teaching aid and as a subject of study and there have been many

"Hark the little angels sing" at a Christmas performance of the Bragg Creek, Alta. kindergarten class.

interesting and rewarding innovations in the use of video technology by students as an additional medium of cultural expression.

In co-operation with school boards, and often with the financial support of other levels of government, many performing arts companies mount presentations to school audiences and associate student companies with their principal endeavours. In addition, many professional companies and community groups offer theatre for young audiences out of school.

Governments as Regulators

Following public opinion, governments have generally avoided any conscious interference with the arts and the cultural life of the community, treating artists and cultural organizations like ordinary private or corporate citizens. Nevertheless, significant regulatory policies have been established in a few defined areas. Space permits only two or three examples.

Governments provide the legal context for artistic production (through legislation respecting copyright and other property rights, for example) and tax policy is designed to favour the arts and other cultural activities by providing tax exemptions for private donations to arts organizations. Sometimes they have also been prepared to intervene to compensate for the economic disadvantage Canadian producers suffer beside foreign competition that can achieve very low unit costs through access to large international markets.

Many provincial and municipal governments have recently shown active interest in legislation designed to protect privately owned heritage buildings and neighbourhoods from demolition or intensive modification. Here again, regulatory policies are often coupled with incentives to encourage the restoration and re-animation of the cultural legacy received from earlier generations.

Building a model at a primary school in Chicoutimi, Que.

Governments as Producers

Apart from a few special cases like the National Arts Centre Orchestra, governments have preferred not to assume managerial responsibility, even indirectly, for artistic performance or the production of cultural works; the work or creation of the artist or company, although often intended for the public, is in the private sector. Where government presence exists it is intended to be unobtrusive, supportive and neutral.

One striking exception to the foregoing is radio and television broadcasting, where the limitations of the technology, the economics of the industry and the character and scale of the country have dictated a mixed public and private system. However, even in the public sector governments have chosen to operate through statutory corporations in order to preserve official detachment from program content, and both public and private sectors are regulated by a separate commission that has no operational responsibilities.

As cultural institutions, the broadcasting enterprises are second in importance only to the schools; indeed some people would rank them first. One could scarcely over-estimate the cultural significance of the radio and television networks of the government-owned CBC, which now serve almost all of Canada in both English and French. At the same time, an important recent development in public sector broadcasting has been the establishment of some provincial educational television services; these are normally operated through statutory corporations and comple-ment the CBC and private services with programming designed for school use, for pre-school children and for adult learners.

In conclusion, the cultural policies of Canadian governments are probably a rough reflection of the cultural characteristics, aspirations and priorities of the Canadian population. Since the population is diverse, dispersed and pluralistic, the policies are equally diverse and sometimes perhaps even contradictory. Like the country itself, cultural policy is a mosaic rather than a melting-pot.

Education

Constitutional Responsibilities

When the four original provinces of Canada were united in 1867, it was a condition of union that responsibility for education be vested in provincial legislatures rather than the federal government. Canada's constitution, the British North America (BNA) Act, was therefore worded to give the provinces exclusive jurisdiction over education and to protect existing educational systems. As other provinces joined Canada, the provisions of the BNA Act respecting education (Section 93) were reaffirmed.

Officially, the BNA Act does not recognize a federal presence in education. However, the federal government has assumed direct responsibility for the education of those outside provincial jurisdiction — native peoples, armed forces personnel and their dependents in Canada and abroad, and inmates of federal penal institutions. As education in Canada has expanded, indirect federal participation in the form of financial assistance has become extensive — support for the construction of vocational and technical schools, contributions to the funding of higher education and assistance to the provinces to promote bilingualism in education.

Provincial Administration

Because each province and territory is responsible for the organization and administration of education within its jurisdiction, no uniform system exists in

The rapture of learning.

Canada. Provincial autonomy has resulted in the establishment of distinctive systems reflecting historical and cultural traditions and socio-economic conditions. Each provincial system is in some ways unique — for example, in local organization, grade structures, funding, curriculum or testing.

Each province has an education department headed by a minister responsible to the legislature. The department is administered by a deputy minister, a public servant and usually also a professional educator, who advises the minister and gives a measure of permanency to the department's policy. Some provinces have separate government departments for post-secondary education and related manpower concerns. Regulation of universities and colleges varies from province to province.

Local Administration

While provincial legislatures and education departments provide the legal framework within which public schools operate, considerable responsibility for the actual operation of schools is delegated to local boards of education composed of elected and/or appointed trustees whose duties are specified in provincial legislation and departmental regulations. Responsibilities of boards vary from province to province, but in general they include school construction, pupil transportation, hiring of teachers and determination of tax rates for local support. In all provinces, school board budgets are reviewed by departments of education.

The structure of local organization for education has changed over the years. Although two provinces have long histories of large school districts (Alberta since 1937 and British Columbia since 1945), the others have traditionally organized in smaller ones; in recent years all have gradually regrouped into larger units. In

Story time at school in Winterton, Nfld.

Lunch time at school in Repulse Bay, NWT.

Saskatchewan, larger school units exist for rural areas but there are still many city and town boards. The same applies in Nova Scotia, where there are geographically large units for rural schools, while most urban municipalities have their own school boards; however, in recent years three amalgamated or regional boards have been established to serve both rural and urban schools in their areas.

School Organization

Provincial variations in the organization of elementary-secondary education are such that no common pattern exists.

Newfoundland has an 11-grade system with an optional kindergarten year. Schools are generally organized on the basis of grades I-VI in elementary schools and grades VII-XI in secondary, but there are local variations. A Grade XI graduate requires four years at university to obtain a pass bachelor's degree. The secondary school curriculum of the province is currently under revision; an additional year (Grade XII) is being introduced for students who enter Grade X in September 1981.

Prince Edward Island, New Brunswick and British Columbia have 12-grade systems, after which four years of university are required for a bachelor's degree. Neither Prince Edward Island nor New Brunswick provides for kindergarten programs in the public schools, but in British Columbia such a program is almost universal. School organization in the two Maritime provinces is generally grades I-VI in elementary schools and grades VII-XII in secondary, in some cases with grades VII-IX as junior secondary; in British Columbia it is usually grades I-VII in elementary schools and grades VIII-XII in secondary, with some grades VIII-X junior secondary schools.

Nova Scotia, Manitoba, Saskatchewan and Alberta all have 12-grade systems with three university years needed for a pass bachelor's degree. In Nova Scotia

Children benefit from physical fitness programs at an elementary school in Calgary, Alta.

Table 1. Elementary and secondary school enrolment, 1979-80[1]

Province or territory	Public[2]	Private	Federal[3]	Total
Canada	4,931,050	193,305	34,055	5,162,290[4]
Newfoundland	150,505	280	—	150,785
Prince Edward Island	27,295	—	50	27,345
Nova Scotia	189,795	1,420	785	192,000
New Brunswick	156,385	395	840	157,620
Quebec	1,164,015[5]	82,300[5]	3,130	1,249,445
Ontario	1,859,910	67,900	7,280	1,935,090
Manitoba	208,920	8,040	8,480	225,440
Saskatchewan	208,120	2,200	6,760	217,080
Alberta	436,330	5,940	4,030	446,300
British Columbia	511,825	24,830	2,700	539,355
Yukon	5,120	—	—	5,120
Northwest Territories	12,830	—	—	12,830

[1] Preliminary data.
[2] Includes provincial schools for blind and deaf and Department of National Defence schools in Canada.
[3] Schools for native peoples operated by the Department of Indian Affairs and Northern Development.
[4] Includes 3,880 students in Department of National Defence schools in Europe.
[5] Estimate.
— Nil or zero.

Creative projects at an elementary school in Prince Edward Island.

kindergarten (known in the province as primary) is universal; it is optional but nearly universal in Manitoba and Saskatchewan, and Alberta has only recently provided it. School organization in all these provinces is generally grades I-VI in elementary schools and grades VII-XII in secondary, with some grades VII-IX junior secondary schools.

Ontario has a 13-grade system for university entrance programs and three years of university study is needed after that for a pass bachelor's degree. It is also possible in Ontario to graduate from high school after Grade XII, but this does not lead directly to university studies. School organization is generally grades I-VIII in elementary schools and grades IX-XIII in secondary. Roman Catholic separate schools, which by law cannot go beyond Grade X, usually operate in conjunction with private schools offering grades XI to XIII.

Quebec has an 11-year system to the end of secondary school, followed by a "collegiate" program of two or three years in a collège d'enseignement général et professionnel (CEGEP). Students who plan to go to university must complete the two-year CEGEP program, after which a three-year university program is necessary to obtain a pass bachelor's degree.

Schools in the Northwest Territories are organized along the same lines as in the Prairie provinces; the Yukon follows the British Columbia pattern.

Elementary-Secondary Education

Elementary education is general and basic, but in the junior high school years there is some opportunity for students to select courses to suit their individual needs. At the secondary level students usually have a choice of several programs and it is possible to tailor a course of studies by selecting from available programs.

At one time secondary schools were predominantly academic, designed to prepare students for continuing their studies at university; vocational schools were separate institutions, designed primarily for those who would not proceed to post-secondary education. Today, while some technical and commercial high schools still exist, most secondary schools are composite schools providing integrated programs for all types of students.

Independent Schools

In all provinces except Newfoundland and Prince Edward Island a number of independent or private elementary-secondary schools operate outside the public school system, and may be either church-affiliated or non-sectarian. Private kindergartens and nursery schools also exist for children of pre-elementary age. In most provinces private schools receive some form of public support.

Separate Schools

Five provinces make some legal provision for establishment of schools with religious affiliation within the publicly supported school system.

Newfoundland has traditionally based public school organization on church affiliation. However, in the mid-1960s the major Protestant denominations (Anglican, United Church and Salvation Army) amalgamated their schools and school boards. Roman Catholic schools, serving the largest single religious group in the province, still exist throughout Newfoundland and are organized into 12 school districts. Two other denominations (Pentecostal Assemblies and Seventh Day Adventist) also operate schools, with one board for each.

Table 2. Full-time enrolment in post-secondary education, 1979-80[1]

	Community colleges and related institutions		Degree-granting institutions and affiliated colleges		Total
	Technical programs	University transfer programs	Undergraduate	Graduate	
Canada	168,420	73,175	329,020	40,905	611,520
Newfoundland	2,020	—	6,240	355	8,615
Prince Edward Island . . .	780	—	1,330	—	2,110
Nova Scotia	2,480	165	16,105	1,605	20,355
New Brunswick	1,790	—	10,440	460	12,690
Quebec	63,400[2]	63,700[2]	74,490	12,220	213,810
Ontario	67,000[2]	—	137,745	17,190	221,935
Manitoba	3,055	—	14,505	1,555	19,115
Saskatchewan	2,400[2]	—	13,440	760	16,600
Alberta	15,265	2,315	27,475	3,140	48,195
British Columbia.	10,230	6,995	27,250	3,620	48,095

[1] Preliminary data.
[2] Estimate.
— Nil or zero.

Laval University in Quebec City.

Quebec has a dual education system — one for Roman Catholic students, the other for non-Catholics — although in recent years the distinction between the two systems on the basis of religion has given way to some extent to a distinction based on language of instruction. Both school systems in the province receive equitable public support.

Legislation in Ontario, Saskatchewan and Alberta permits establishment of separate school districts. In all three provinces, Roman Catholic separate school districts operate a large number of schools, while a few Protestant separate school districts also exist. In Saskatchewan and Alberta, Roman Catholic separate schools span the whole range of elementary-secondary education; in Ontario, however, they receive tax support only for education up to Grade X.

Post-Secondary Education

The 1960s and 1970s have seen extraordinary growth in programs and facilities for continuing education after high school. In past years universities provided almost the only form of post-secondary education. Now every province has public community colleges and institutions of technology.

Degree-Granting Institutions

There are several types of degree-granting institutions in Canada.

Universities usually have degree programs in arts and science at least. Larger institutions offer degrees up to the doctorate level in a variety of fields and disciplines. There were 47 universities in Canada in 1979-80.

University of Lethbridge, Alta.

Liberal arts colleges are smaller institutions with degree programs in arts only. They usually offer some science courses but do not have degree programs in this area. There were two liberal arts colleges in 1979-80.

Theological colleges grant degrees only in religion and theology. There were 12 independent degree-granting theological colleges in 1979-80. In addition, seven colleges were affiliated with universities while granting their own degrees in theology and another seven were affiliated with universities but did not have (or held in abeyance) degree-granting powers.

Other specialized colleges offer degree programs in a single field such as engineering, art or education. There were four such colleges in 1979-80.

The Department of National Defence finances and operates three tuition-free institutions: Royal Military College in Kingston, Ont., Royal Roads in Victoria, BC, and Collège militaire royal in Saint-Jean, Que., which is affiliated with the Université de Sherbrooke.

Admission to university is usually after high school graduation with specific courses and standing. Most universities, however, provide for the admission of "mature students" who do not possess all the usual admission requirements.

Depending on the province, a pass bachelor's degree in arts or science takes three or four years of study. Professional degrees in law, medicine, dentistry, engineering and similar fields normally require the completion of part or all of the requirements for bachelor's degrees. Most universities offer both pass and honours bachelor's degrees; one more year of study is usually necessary for the latter, but in some cases the requirement is for additional courses in the field of specialization.

Admission to a master's degree program is usually contingent on completion of an honours bachelor's degree or equivalent. Most master's programs entail an additional year or two of study plus a thesis. Entrants to doctoral programs must have a master's degree in the same field.

University tuition fees vary among and within provinces. Ontario and Alberta have differential fees for non-Canadian students.

Post-Secondary Non-University Institutions

As an alternative to university education, all provinces have established public non-university institutions — regional colleges in British Columbia, institutes of technology and other public colleges in Alberta, institutes of applied arts and science in Saskatchewan, colleges of applied arts and technology (CAATs) and colleges of agricultural technology (CATs) in Ontario, and collèges d'enseignement général et professionnel (CEGEPs) in Quebec. Other post-secondary colleges for specialized fields such as fisheries, marine technologies and para-medical technologies also exist. Most provinces now provide all nurses' training programs in community colleges rather than in the hospital schools of nursing which were common in the past.

Criteria for admission to public community colleges tend to be more flexible than those of universities. Secondary school graduation is usually required, but "mature student" status allows otherwise ineligible applicants to enrol. Upgrading programs are also provided by some institutions for applicants whose high school standing does not meet regular admission requirements.

In 1979-80, 182 institutions in Canada offered post-secondary non-university instruction — 31 in the Atlantic provinces, 73 in Quebec, 30 in Ontario, 28 in the Prairie provinces and 20 in British Columbia.

Teacher Education

Teacher training was for many years offered at teachers' colleges that operated outside the university system of the province. All of these institutions except the Nova Scotia Teachers' College have either become education faculties of universities or been constituted as institutions offering programs leading to degrees in education. The Nova Scotia Teachers' College works closely with the province's universities so that graduates may continue their studies toward a degree.

Technical and Trades Training

Technical and trades training varies from province to province and often within a province. In addition to the vocational and technical programs available in secondary schools, students may continue this type of education in other institutions, such as public and private trade and business schools, trade divisions of community colleges and related institutions. Trades training is also available through training-in-industry and apprenticeship programs.

Adult Education

In recent years educational programs for adults have assumed increasing prominence in Canada. School boards, community colleges and universities offer extensive adult education in part-time programs either for personal enrichment or leading to a degree. Other programs are provided by professional associations, community organizations, churches, public libraries, departments of government, business and industry. Correspondence courses are also available.

Statistical Highlights

In 1979-80 education was the primary activity of 6,100,000 Canadians, or about 26 per cent of the total population. There were 5,800,000 full-time students being taught by 320,000 full-time teachers in 15,500 educational institutions. Expenditures on education for 1979-80 reached $20 billion, or 8.4 per cent of Canada's gross national product (GNP).

Lower birth rates in recent years and lower levels of immigration have produced an enrolment decline in elementary-secondary schools that is expected to persist in the 1980s. Post-secondary institutions will soon feel the effects of this trend.

Elementary-secondary enrolment in 1979-80 was 5,160,000, a decline of 2 per cent from 1978-79 and of 12 per cent from the all-time high of 5,900,000 recorded in 1970-71. Small annual reductions in elementary enrolment are expected for the rest of the decade — a drop of 22 per cent from the 1968 high of 3,844,000 to a projected low in

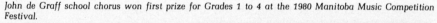

John de Graff school chorus won first prize for Grades 1 to 4 at the 1980 Manitoba Music Competition Festival.

Care of the teeth is memorably explained to an elementary student in Vancouver, BC.

1981 of 3,000,000. After that, enrolment should stabilize for several years and then rise until the mid-1990s. Secondary enrolment patterns resemble those of the elementary level, but they are delayed seven or eight years.

Full-time post-secondary enrolment in 1979-80 was 611,500, a 0.7 per cent decrease from 1978-79. University enrolment made up 60 per cent of the total, but the rate of increase over the past decade was lower than that of the non-university sector, where full-time enrolment increased by 63 per cent, from 142,700 in 1969-70 to 241,600 in 1979-80. At the same time, full-time university enrolment went from 294,100 to 369,900, an increase of 26 per cent.

More than 290,000 students graduated from secondary schools in 1978, a 1 per cent increase over the previous year. About 60 per cent of high school graduates normally enter a post-secondary institution.

In 1978 universities conferred 89,300 bachelor's and first professional degrees, 12,600 master's degrees and 1,800 earned doctorates. Post-secondary non-university institutions awarded 62,400 diplomas.

Expenditures for education from kindergarten through graduate studies reached $20 billion in 1979-80 and preliminary estimates place the 1980-81 figure at around $22.5 billion. Elementary-secondary education consumed about $13.4 billion of the 1979-80 total, universities $4 billion, non-university institutions $1.6 billion and vocational training $1.2 billion.

Education spending per capita of population soared from $208 in 1966 to $852 in 1979; the increase per capita of labour force was from $555 to $1,800. Nevertheless, other indicators point to a decline in education spending as enrolment declines. In 1970, when full-time enrolment was at record levels, expenditures on education were equivalent to 8.8 per cent of GNP and absorbed 22 per cent of government spending, more than any other major area. By 1979 education's share had decreased to 8.4 per cent of GNP and social welfare had become the largest consumer of government resources.

Table 3. Expenditures on education, by level and source of funds, Canada, 1971-72 and 1979-80
(million dollars)

Level of education	Federal[1]	Provincial[1]	Municipal	Fees and other	Total
1971-72					
Elementary-secondary					
Public[2]	203.1	3,201.2	1,694.8	141.4	5,240.5
Private	0.1	27.2	13.8	107.7	148.8
Sub-total	203.2	3,228.4	1,708.6	249.1	5,389.3
Post-secondary					
Non-university	51.3	427.0	3.8	47.9	530.0
University	244.9	1,204.2	1.1	414.3	1,864.5
Sub-total	296.2	1,631.2	4.9	462.2	2,394.5
Vocational training	424.7	107.1	0.1	34.0	565.9
Total.......................	924.1	4,966.7	1,713.6	745.3	8,349.7
Percentage distribution.........	11.1	59.5	20.5	8.9	100.0
1979-80[3]					
Elementary-secondary					
Public[2]	302.0	8,603.2	3,868.2	228.7	13,002.1
Private	2.4	144.9	13.3	277.4	438.0
Sub-total	304.4	8,748.1	3,881.5	506.1	13,440.1
Post-secondary					
Non-university	64.1	1,328.6	25.4	146.5	1,564.6
University	421.0	2,854.9	1.1	651.8	3,928.8
Sub-total	485.1	4,183.5	26.5	798.3	5,493.4
Vocational training	864.6	286.4	0.1	72.8	1,223.9
Total.......................	1,654.1	13,218.0	3,908.1	1,377.2	20,157.4
Percentage distribution.........	8.2	65.6	19.4	6.8	100.0

[1] Federal transfers to provincial governments ($988.3 million in 1971-72 and $2,925.2 million in 1979-80) are included in the provincial contributions.
[2] Includes federal schools.
[3] Preliminary figures.

Hydro technicians using high-frequency measurements check the condition of transformer windings in service at the Pickering nuclear generating station.

Science and Technology

In common with the United States, France and the United Kingdom, Canada has experienced a marked levelling off in the financial support of science and technology in recent years. Growth rates in annual expenditures on research and development declined from about 18 per cent in the mid-1960s to half that value in the mid-1970s.

Canada's gross expenditures on research and development (GERD) in 1978 approximated $2.4 billion. Expressed as a proportion of the gross national product (GNP), Canada's GERD was 0.92 per cent, less than that of any other major country belonging to the Organization for Economic Co-operation and Development (OECD). Increased research and development (R&D) in Canada continues to be a national priority and the target of a GERD/GNP ratio of 1.5 per cent has been reaffirmed. Considerable increases in scientific expenditures and expansion of scientific manpower will be required to meet this goal, and industry will be the main performer in this expansion.

Nearly 26,000 scientists and engineers were employed in research and development in the government, business and university sectors in 1978, with an approximately equal distribution of manpower among the three sectors.

Science Policy

"A nation needs a comprehensive and consistent policy for the support and advancement of science, because there are more opportunities to advance science and technology than there are resources available to exploit them all. Government authorities who are subjected to continuing requests for support from industry, universities, scientific institutions, individual scientists, graduate students and international scientific organizations, as well as from consumers of science within various departments and agencies of government itself, need guidance on how to allocate their funds and their trained manpower. The purpose of a national policy for science is to provide such guidance." (OECD, 1963.)

The Ministry of State for Science and Technology

The Ministry of State for Science and Technology, created in 1971, encourages the development and use of science and technology in support of national goals through the formulation and development of appropriate policies. Canada needs policies for science to ensure that scientific tools will be available. Grants in aid of research through the Natural Sciences and Engineering Research Council, the Medical Research Council and the Social Sciences and Humanities Research Council are an expression of a policy for science that is aimed at generating and maintaining national research capability.

Policies are also needed for the use of science to help Canada achieve non-scientific aims using scientific tools. The maintenance of research laboratories by science-based government departments (such as Energy, Mines and Resources, National Health and Welfare, Agriculture and Environment) and the contracting-out policy are expressions of this aspect of science policy.

The integration of science into public policy formulation is a relatively new development and is the third element of science policy. In order to bring science into policy the Government of Canada is recruiting both natural and social scientists into the federal public service at the policy-making level and using consultative mechanisms to capture the advice of the natural scientific community.

The Science Council of Canada

The Science Council of Canada is a science policy research institute established to advise the federal government and the Canadian public on problems and opportunities in Canadian science and technology. The published results of research in key areas of long-range national science and technology policy are directed throughout Canada to government, industry, academic policy makers and in-creasingly to the public through the mass media. The Council consists of 30 eminent individuals — mostly industrialists or academics — appointed by order-in-council who meet four times yearly to plan and evaluate the Council's research program, which is carried out by a staff located in Ottawa. Publications by the Science Council to date comprise 31 policy reports, including recent Council positions on industrial strategy, national energy policy and the health of university research. Background studies now number 45, including recent papers on Canadian involvement in both international science and world food aid; and on the

Electron beam welding at the National Research Council, a process which uses a focused beam of high energy electrons to fuse metals together.

requirements of Canada's manufacturing sector. Current research is focused on Canada's transportation systems; the telecommunications revolution; the interface between science and the legal process; industrial policies; Canada's scientific and technological contribution to world food; energy; and science education. A catalogue is available from the publications office of the Council, located at 100 Metcalfe Street, Ottawa K1P 5M1.

Science and Technology in Government

Total federal expenditures in the natural and human sciences were expected to be $1.9 billion in 1979-80, an increase of 4 per cent over the preceding year. Nearly one-quarter of the government's expenditures were relevant to the human sciences and the other three-quarters to the natural sciences. Major spenders were the Department of Environment and the National Research Council (NRC) each with 11 per cent of the total government science budget, and Statistics Canada with 7 per cent. Priority areas for expansion of scientific activities were energy and communications.

About 36 per cent of government expenditures were spent extramurally, with $281 million going to industry and $259 million to universities. These expenditures represent increases of 10.5 per cent and 5.7 per cent respectively over expenditures in the 1977-78 period.

Science and Technology in Canadian Industry

While there has been a slight increase in Canadian industry's share of total research and development (R&D) expenditures (from 32.4 per cent in 1971 to 33.9 per cent in 1979) and in its share of R&D performed in Canada (from 41.4 per cent in 1971 to 42.9 per cent in 1979), this country still ranks lower than the other major

The National Research Council's greenhouses, on the campus of the University of Saskatchewan, produce plants required for cell culture work.

industrial nations in overall R&D effort. In most major industrial countries the business sector accounts for 40 to 50 per cent of R&D monies and performs 50 to 65 per cent of all R&D; the proportion of scientists and engineers employed in industries is also much higher than in Canada.

It is agreed by the federal and provincial governments that, if Canadian industry is to make its proper contribution to economic growth and to exploit the opportunities in the many new fields opened by science, its capacity to innovate through research and development must be expanded and reinforced. In recognition of this necessity, they have committed themselves to a much closer collaboration on scientific and technological policies, with particular emphasis on the fostering of industrial R&D capability to respond to regional and national objectives.

The following were among the measures introduced by the federal government to move toward the target of a GERD/GNP ratio of 1.5 per cent: a commitment to use federal procurement to stimulate industrial R&D; 50 per cent tax write-off for increased R&D expenditures over a three-year period; the establishment of up to five industrial research and innovation centres at universities; federal assistance in the development of regional centres of excellence based on the natural and human resources of each area; expansion of the National Research Council's Program of Industry/Laboratory Projects (PILP), which is designed to facilitate technology transfer from NRC laboratories to industry and to extend this program to other departments; expansion of the NRC Technical Information Service; and increased funding of university research into areas of national concern.

University Research

Total federal support of scientific activities in Canadian universities was expected to reach $295 million in the fiscal year ended March 31, 1980. Of this total, science-related activities amounted to $28 million and the support of direct costs of research and development in Canadian universities to $231 million, an increase of 6.7 per cent over 1978-79. A total of $203 million went to research and development in the natural sciences and $28 million to the human sciences. Federal support to universities for related scientific activities was $14 million each for natural sciences and for human sciences.

The three granting councils responsible for the support of university research — Natural Sciences and Engineering Research Council, Medical Research Council, and the Social Sciences and Humanities Research Council — distributed 80 per cent of the federal grants for university research. The balance, $53 million, was distributed by other federal departments and agencies. In response to the government's intention to increase funding of university research, the three granting councils have prepared five-year plans and the government is seeking substantial increases for their budgets in the main estimates for 1980-81 submitted to Parliament — an increase of $42 million or 35 per cent for the Natural Sciences and Engineering Research Council, $10 million or 14 per cent for the Medical Research Council and $6 million or 16 per cent increase for the Social Sciences and Humanities Research Council.

The National Research Council

The National Research Council (NRC) is a national research agency established by Parliament in 1916, to undertake, assist or promote scientific and engineering research to further Canada's economic and social development. The Council operates 11 laboratory divisions and the Canada Institute for Scientific and Technical Information whose main objective is to facilitate the use of scientific and technical information by the government and people of Canada.

A focal point for much of the laboratory research is in Ottawa but numerous other scientific and technical facilities are maintained across the country. These include wind tunnels, nuclear accelerators, ship model tanks, optical and radio telescopes, and the nation's only rocket launching range. Particular projects are undertaken at the request of, or in co-operation with, industries, utilities, federal government departments, provincial or municipal governments.

Approximately one-quarter of NRC's research effort is devoted to basic and exploratory research in order to acquire new knowledge and expertise and to discover new applications of science of potential economic and social benefit. Research on long-term problems of national concern is directed toward the solution of problems in such areas as energy, food, transportation, and building and construction, while research to provide technological support of social objectives includes such areas as health, law, public safety, environment and quality of Canadian life.

In direct support of industrial innovation and development, research is undertaken in promising areas of new technology; effective methods of technology transfer to industry are developed; and technical and financial assistance is given to industry to carry out specific research and development projects to the point of industrial innovation.

In addition, several divisions share the dual responsibilities of maintaining and working to improve a wide range of the nation's standards.

Black Angus cattle in Western Canada.

Scientific Activities

Agricultural Research

Over 50 per cent of agricultural research in Canada is conducted by Agriculture Canada, which employs approximately 900 scientists at about 50 establishments located from coast to coast. Agriculture faculties at universities comprise the second major research group. Private industry and provincial departments have been minor contributors in the past, but are becoming more significant. At all establishments there are probably 2,000 scientists involved, although many in industry and some professors devote only a portion of their time to agricultural research.

The broad traditional areas of crop production and protection, animal production and soils still receive the bulk of the research effort, but in recent years there has been increasing emphasis on food processing. In addition, agricultural scientists are now becoming involved in research directed at protection of the environment, an activity frequently conducted in collaboration with other agencies at the provincial, federal and international levels.

In crops research, plant breeding is a major activity that annually contributes new varieties offering such traits as higher yield, better quality, increased resistance to disease and insects, and earlier maturity. Two spring wheat varieties, Vernon and Dundas, were released in 1978-79 for commercial production in Eastern Canada and Benito, a hard red spring bread wheat with rust resistance superior to Neepawa, was licensed. Licensing was also recommended for a pastry wheat, a bread wheat and a durum wheat. All three have significantly improved quality and yield characteristics. Bedford, a new feed barley, was also licensed and is particularly well adapted to the eastern prairies where it has shown an 8 per cent yield advantage over Klondike.

Rapeseed is the major oilseed crop. In 1978-79, several outstanding lines of *Brassica campestris* were identified. They are superior to current varieties with respect to disease resistance and seed quality characteristics. The oriental mustard, Domo, was licensed and a reselected brown mustard, Blaze, was released.

New lines of soybeans are being developed with improved physiological characteristics and better resistance to one or more diseases. Disease is a major concern in breeding programs. An effective greenhouse screening test for disease has been developed to replace the cumbersome field-rating test.

In forage crops, breeding and evaluation of grasses and legumes for suitability to Canadian environments and higher yield continued at 12 establishments. Elbe, a hardy drought-resistant northern wheatgrass, and the winter hardy Nova were both developed at Lethbridge; Salva, an early improved timothy, was developed at Ottawa; and Cree, a new trefoil, was developed at Saskatoon.

The other major activity in crops research is the development of better means of protection against insects, diseases and weeds. Chemical pesticides are one of the major means of plant protection, but scientists have reduced the number of sprays required by timing them so that they are applied when they are most effective. Biological methods of control have also been developed; such methods include use of insects to control other insects and weeds and of pheromones and sterile male techniques to disrupt insect reproduction. The integration of chemical and biological controls reduces both costs and the risks of environmental pollution. In addition, engineers have developed spray equipment to reduce drift and achieve more effective application.

Storing hay on an Alberta ranch.

Tobacco harvesting in Ontario.

Research in 1978-79 to improve processing technology for the food industry involved cereal, dairy, meat, fruit and vegetable products. The drying process for pasta was improved; new starter cultures, rennet replacers and curing processes were applied to cheesemaking; and at Summerland, BC, a process to extract protein from celery leaves was found to be feasible.

At Winnipeg, the Grain Research Laboratory of the Canadian Grain Commission monitors and assesses the quality of cereal grains and oilseeds grown and marketed in Canada and carries out research on grain quality.

In animal production, breeding projects are under way with sheep, swine, poultry and cattle, conducted mainly by Agriculture Canada. The department has one of the largest research projects on dairy cattle breeding in the world, a project designed to test the feasibility of exploiting hybrid vigour in dairy cattle. At the present time the dairy cattle industry relies heavily on a single breed, the Holstein.

Three British breeds, Hereford, Angus and Shorthorn, have long been the basis of Canada's beef production. In the last decade, ranchers have imported various other European breeds for crossbreeding purposes. Agriculture Canada has a large breeding project to test and assess the value of these imported breeds when crossed with the traditional British ones.

Man-made patterns weaving across the vast productive land of Saskatchewan. ➜

Spraying the potato crop in Prince Edward Island.

Research on reproductive physiology is also being used to improve livestock productivity; an Agriculture Canada program is having excellent success in developing potential areas for major breakthroughs in animal reproduction.

Within Agriculture Canada, research on animal diseases is conducted by the Animal Pathology Division of the Food Production and Inspection Branch, with support from scientists at Canada's three veterinary colleges. The research is aimed at improving present techniques or developing new ones for the accurate and rapid diagnosis of animal diseases, both foreign and indigenous, and for determining the safety and quality of meat and meat products. For example, the following studies are under way: more specific tests for the diagnosis of brucellosis and paratuberculosis in cattle, and bluetongue in cattle and sheep; the determination of heavy metals in beef, pork and poultry tissues; and methods for reducing salmonella infection in poultry and contamination of poultry carcasses.

Soils research is concerned with basic work on soil reactions, on a soil survey to provide information on the soil resources of Canada and on fertilizer practices for various crops. Land capability studies are becoming important because of urban encroachment on prime agricultural land and the looming world food shortage.

Concern for environmental quality is a new thrust in agricultural research. Scientists are monitoring rivers, streams and lakes for contamination by soil nutrients, animal wastes and pesticide chemicals. Food products are carefully checked for freedom from chemical residues. Analytical methodology to permit this monitoring is continually under development.

Environmental Research

The **Environmental Conservation Service** (ECS) is concerned with the wise and careful use of the country's wildlife, water and lands and with promoting the economic potential of renewable resource management and development. The organization consists of three regionalized directorates (Inland Waters, Canadian Wildlife and Lands) responsible for ECS efforts in each resource area. A fourth directorate, Policy and Program Development, is responsible for service-wide planning and policy development and for several national programs which involve input from more than one of the three resource areas. ECS makes major contributions to research and monitoring of toxic substances, developing coastal zone management plans with the provinces and providing baseline information related to major energy developments and to effects of acid rain on aquatic systems and wildlife.

The Canadian Forestry Service (CFS) conducts programs on the management and conservation of the forestry resource and acts as the lead federal agency in forestry. In addition to headquarters which has emphasis on policy and economics work, the service has two national institutes and six forest research centres responding to regional opportunities as well as national goals. Current research priorities of the CFS include forest regeneration, including tree breeding; national forestry data compilation and analysis; combatting the spruce budworm; studying techniques to obtain energy from the forest; toxic substances research, particularly chemical insecticides; research in long-range transport of air-borne pollutants; and the development of biological control of forest pests. Application of research is stressed, as is the environmental impact of forestry practices. Other CFS work involves

Gizzard shad fish are notorious for clogging the cooling water intakes at some Hydro plants. Fish movements are studied in an effort to solve the problem.

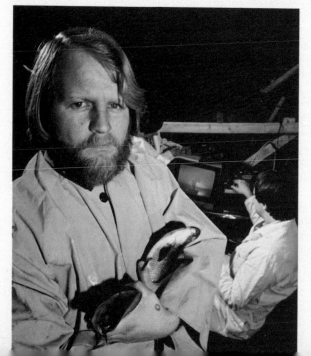

programs with the Department of Employment and Immigration, the Department of Regional Economic Expansion and provincial agencies in the establishment of practices for intensive forest management.

The Canadian Wildlife Service (CWS) conducts programs to manage and protect migratory birds and their habitats in Canada and internationally. Increasing economic development activities which threaten habitat, and growing public interest in wildlife, together provide challenges in carrying out federal responsibilities for migratory birds. CWS surveys and regulates waterfowl hunting in Canada and works to conserve "non-game" bird populations such as seabirds, shorebirds and songbirds. Recent projects include: expanded research efforts on seabirds on the Atlantic and Pacific coasts; studies of shorebirds in James Bay; inventories and research on the great blue heron and double-crested cormorant in Quebec; studies on the feeding ecology and nesting requirements of the common tern on the Great Lakes; and development and management strategies for areas such as Last Mountain Lake in Saskatchewan and the migratory bird sanctuaries in the Northwest Territories. To protect migratory bird habitat, over 40 national wildlife areas have been established across Canada and more are being considered.

CWS also conducts research on wildlife of national interest, other than migratory birds; conserves wildlife habitat; and assists the provinces and territories with their wildlife conservation efforts. Areas of concern are as follows: rare and endangered species; international and interprovincial populations; wildlife on federal lands; and the health of wildlife, with a focus on parasitology, pathology, and the impact of environmental contaminants. Some recent projects are the development of a management plan for the beaver population of the Cap Tourmente national wildlife area in Quebec; studies on furbearers and deer in national parks in Ontario; rehabilitation of wood bison populations in the western provinces; and co-operative research on the caribou in the Yukon with negotiation toward an international agreement for management of caribou.

The Inland Waters Directorate's (IWD) research program is carried out mainly at the National Water Research Institute at Burlington, Ont., and at the National Hydrology Research Institute in the National Capital Region. There are also small research groups in Winnipeg, Calgary and Vancouver.

Water quality research provides a basis for setting water quality objectives and is directed toward measures for the management of Canada's aquatic environment. Specific projects include the pathways by which toxic contaminants move, changes in ecology wrought by human activity and the understanding of the mechanisms leading to these changes, and the role of sediments in regulating water quality.

Water quantity research is based on the needs of water management to solve practical problems that require understanding and quantification of processes in the fields of surface water hydrology, sediment transport, snow and ice hydrology and hydrogeology.

IWD has developed flow prediction models that can be manipulated to receive and test new insights into hydrological processes such as evapotranspiration, snowmelt and glacier melt, soil moisture, and the mechanics of groundwater movement. Research is under way on the hydrology of northern environments and the effects upon it of human activities such as: pipeline and highway construction; the role of glaciers as a natural and variable water storage system; and hydrogeological

Pouch Cove, Nfld.

processes controlling the movement of subsurface contaminants from sources such as landfill, road salts and radioactive wastes.

The Lands Directorate is conducting major research activities in land classification and analysis of the causes and policy implications of land-use change. Land classification research is directed toward establishing better methods of surveying and classifying land according to ecological characteristics, use capabilities and present use. Such techniques are used in major resources investigations to determine land development potential and environmental management requirements. There is emphasis on satellite imagery and high-altitude aerial photography for land resource surveys and land-use monitoring systems. Land-use potential, impact of federal programs on land, use of innovative planning techniques, analysis of change around urban centres and mapping of critical land areas are important aspects under current investigation.

The Lands Directorate is also responsible for the development of a federal policy on land use and represents Environment Canada on the Treasury Board Advisory Committee on Federal Land Management. Planning services of the directorate include advice to provincial and federal agencies regarding native land claims, northern land-use information and land-resources planning. The directorate also advises and assists other countries on land-use policies and studies.

The Atmospheric Environment Service (AES) is concerned primarily with meteorology, the science of the atmosphere. It provides national weather and climatological services for the public and special users. Since 1958 it has been responsible for ice services supporting navigation in Canadian waterways, coastal waters and the Arctic Archipelago. It is also involved in meteorological research, research on effects of pollutants on earth's atmosphere and instrument design.

Research focuses on pollutants such as freons which affect the stratosphere, especially the ozone layer, and lead to potentially harmful effects on human, animal and plant life. Important stratospheric constituents are being measured by AES to establish the current unperturbed stratospheric photochemical balance and to verify photochemical reaction rates needed for input to models of stratospheric behaviour. These models indicate that the effects of pollution are not negligible.

Climatic trends and variability that may seriously affect agricultural production energy and other environmental factors bearing on human welfare are analyzed to determine the basic physical processes in order to make long-range predictions of weather and climate. Particular emphasis is being given to the problem of increasing atmospheric carbon dioxide (CO_2) concentrations and possible effects on climate. Special efforts are being made to help Canadian industries obtain climatic data and consulting services.

A comprehensive system for environmental prediction is being further developed to support many activities going on in the Arctic, especially oil drilling in the Beaufort Sea. New techniques of data assimilation and numerical prediction are applied and more are under development at the Canadian Meteorological Centre. Advanced computer methods for processing satellite data are yielding very high-quality photographs of weather systems for use at Canada's main weather centres.

A major departmental program is under way to establish the causes and impacts of acidic precipitation in Eastern Canada; studies indicate that fossil fuel burning is a major source of the contributing pollutants. The potential impact on Canada's lake and forest ecosystem is being assessed. Negotiations are under way with the US to decrease the acid rain problem.

The Environmental Protection Service (EPS) develops national environmental control guidelines, requirements and regulations in consultation with the provinces and industry. EPS is concerned with air pollution, water pollution, waste management including hazardous waste and resource conservation, contaminants, environmental impact assessment and control, and environmental emergencies. The service carries out the assessment, surveillance, negotiations or enforcement necessary to obtain compliance with federal environmental legislation; co-operatively with provinces, identifies and solves pollution problems; develops and demonstrates pollution control technology; and serves as the focal point for environmental protection matters for federal departments, agencies and the public. Emerging issues of the 1980s such as control of toxic substances, the long-range transport of air pollutants and hazardous waste management are priorities for EPS and the Department of the Environment as a whole.

A forest technician collecting insects from trees for research.

Tulips along the Driveway in Ottawa.

The Air Pollution Control Directorate has undertaken the EPS mandate in air pollution control. One of the most pressing concerns facing Canada today is the transport of pollutants over long distances and the resulting problem of acidic precipitation. The latter, commonly known as acid rain, has deleterious effects on lakes and rivers, forests, farmland and buildings. A federal-provincial committee has been formed to identify, develop and evaluate alternative control strategies.

The directorate's activities in the field of technology development and transfer include: the management of cost-shared programs with Canadian industry for the development and demonstration of new air pollution control technology; the development and certification of analytical techniques required to support regulations and guidelines; the preparation of standard reference material for analytical laboratories across Canada; the provision of a computerized technical information service on air pollution control; and the training and certification of Clean Air Act inspectors, analysts and enforcement officers.

The Environmental Impact Control Directorate is responsible for contaminants control, environmental emergencies and waste management.

The Contaminants Control Branch assesses and evaluates new and existing chemicals to determine whether their use and release into the environment will adversely affect human health and the environment and the development of control instruments pursuant to the Environmental Contaminants Act which is jointly administered with the Department of National Health and Welfare. A technical

A field of flowers on Herschel Island in the western Arctic.

advisory service to the Department of Transport in the development of codes and guidelines for the safe transportation of dangerous goods is also provided.

The Environmental Emergencies Branch is tasked with preventing accidental spills of oils and other hazardous substances, developing contingency plans for dealing with such spills, developing new technology for the control or clean-up of spills and maintaining a national alerting and reporting network to ensure a rapid and effective response to any environmental emergency. This branch is also responsible for co-ordinating federal/provincial/industrial responses to environmental emergencies, where appropriate, through the national environmental emergency team.

The Waste Management Branch is responsible for solid and hazardous wastes management and resource conservation. This includes a comprehensive national program in co-operation with the provinces, industry and the public for the "cradle to grave" management of hazardous wastes.

The Water Pollution Control Directorate operates a national program aimed at cleaning up existing water pollution problems and preventing pollution from new developments to ensure a level of water quality suitable for the protection of fish and suitable for other desirable uses. Programs in the area of technology development are undertaken to design new or improved wastewater treatment processes to solve pollution abatement problems or reduce costs of pollution control; to develop new Canadian technology and equipment for pollution control; and to adapt proven foreign technological developments to solve Canadian water pollution problems.

In view of the ongoing review of the federal role in environmental protection, the future thrust of the national water pollution control program will be modified and will focus more directly on the control of specific toxic substances, the development of site specific control requirements to meet a variety of federal responsibilities including international and interprovincial concerns, and improved collaboration and co-ordination among agencies and industries in technology development.

Energy, Mines and Resources

The Department of Energy, Mines and Resources is the principal component of the federal government responsible for policy formulation and research in the fields of energy and mineral resources. Associated with these activities are surveys and mapping, remote sensing of Canadian lands and waters from aircraft and satellites and efforts to safeguard the environment and the health and safety of Canadians in mining and related work.

This work is carried out in three sectors: the Energy Policy Sector, the Mineral Policy Sector and the Science and Technology Sector. The first two sectors are concerned mainly with studies, analyses and policy recommendations in their respective fields; the third sector, with some of its branches established many decades ago, is concerned primarily with scientific and technical research and with surveys and mapping.

Since the international oil crisis of 1973-74 with its sudden fourfold rise in oil prices and increased uncertainty about future oil supplies, energy policy programs of the Department of Energy, Mines and Resources have been directed toward a national objective of security of energy supply. It has been the department's responsibility to develop and recommend policies to achieve this objective by increasing the domestic availability of energy; accelerating substitution of oil by the more abundant energy sources; and implementing conservation programs. Specific measures have been adopted in support of the policy of uniform price for oil throughout Canada, with the price level being set in relation to Canadian conditions and circumstances.

Announcement was made of a number of policy initiatives in April 1980 at the start of a new Parliamentary session and the department commenced preparation for their implementation. These measures include: establishment of a new blended price for oil to progressively incorporate the costs of the Oil Import Compensation Program while maintaining a single national price for consumers and protecting the right of the producing provinces and corporations to a fair return for their resources and their investment; formation of a Petroleum Price Auditing Agency to investigate and report on oil company costs, profits, capital expenditures and levels of Canadian ownership; promotion of new conservation programs in the transportation, residential and industrial markets; encouragement of consumers to switch from oil to natural gas or electricity and initiation of plans to supply natural gas to eastern Quebec and the Maritime provinces; enlargement of the role of Petro-Canada as an instrument of public policy, with its role to include oil purchase negotiations and agreements with foreign suppliers; preparation of a new Canada Oil and Gas Act to provide new preferential rights for Petro-Canada and other Canadian companies on federal lands, and to establish more demanding regulations for exploration and development of promising frontier areas; creation of an Alternative Energy Corporation to stimulate the development of new and renewable energy sources to replace oil; and adoption of the special goal of at least 50 per cent Canadian ownership of the petroleum industry by 1990.

Changes in the world industrial structure and in world trade patterns have been evident since the initiation of the oil crisis in 1973. The Mineral Policy Sector, through its policy development and policy co-ordinating roles, and the Economic and Policy Analysis Sub-Sector, through its analytical role, are endeavouring in conjunction with the provincial governments and with industry to find ways of assisting the mineral industry to adjust to this new international environment while improving the working and living conditions in mining communities throughout Canada. In order to contribute to the discovery and development of mineral deposits and to the creation of job opportunities, the Mineral Policy Sector co-manages (with DREE) mineral development agreements with several provinces.

The Science and Technology Sector of the department comprises the following branches: the Geological Survey of Canada, the Canada Centre for Mineral and Energy Technology (CANMET), the Earth Physics Branch, the Canada Centre for Remote Sensing, the Surveys and Mapping Branch, the Explosives Branch, the Polar Continental Shelf Project, the Canada Centre for Geoscience Data and the Office of Energy Research and Development.

The dominant concern of the Geological Survey has been the assessment of energy and mineral resources; scientific studies have been formulated in the light of that concern. Field work is being carried out in most regions, with emphasis on the north and offshore areas. In addition to studies aimed at a better understanding of the history and composition of the earth's crust underlying Canada, geologists have undertaken assessments of Canada's oil and gas potential in which cost considerations are an integral part.

Significant advances in the application of geophysical and geochemical techniques in the search for metallic ores culminated in the publication of an 800-page report which is being used in many countries. Studies have been made of the Labrador coast to identify levels of susceptibility in the event of an oil spill and of other terrain to determine the ability of the land to withstand construction of pipelines and other transportation facilities especially in the North. The Geological Survey also continued its study of uranium and other metalliferous deposits to provide a better nationwide basis for the search for mineral wealth.

The laboratory and pilot-plant research of CANMET is carried out in the Ottawa area and in Elliot Lake, Calgary and Edmonton. In recent years the main goal of the branch has been to assure adequate supplies and effective use of Canada's energy and mineral resources. Coal, oil sands and heavy oils have received special attention. Progress has been made in studies of coal-in-oil combustion, fluidized-bed combustion and conversion of coal to oil and gas. In order to aid the Canadian mining industry in achieving cost savings and greater safety in open-pit mining CANMET has published a comprehensive manual on pit slopes. The health and safety of miners have been enhanced through CANMET research to detect and eliminate noxious dust and gases and to improve ground control in underground mines.

Ecological considerations have prompted studies on means of removing acidity and heavy metals from tailings of sulphide ore mines, radium from tailings of Elliot Lake uranium mines and cyanide from gold-mill tailings. The goal of reducing gasoline consumption by making automobiles lighter and to extend automobile life is the reason for a CANMET program of testing aluminum and lighter, high-strength alloys for use in car bodies.

The department's earth physicists carry out research into the seismic, geothermal, geomagnetic, gravity and geodynamic characteristics of the Canadian land mass. New techniques in earthquake detection have been tested off the West Coast of

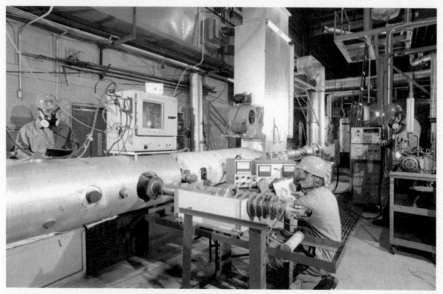

Technicians at Energy, Mines and Resources testing equipment used in combustion-generated air pollution studies.

Canada, and studies are being carried out in British Columbia and Alberta to determine the geothermal energy potential in those areas. Other earth-physics studies concern permafrost distribution and thickness in the Arctic, continental drift, the structure of the ocean floor off Canada, the geophysical development of the Arctic basin and gravity measurements.

The Canada Centre for Remote Sensing is responsible for developing and demonstrating systems, methods and instruments for acquiring, analyzing and disseminating remote sensing data obtained by aircraft and satellite; contributing to the development of effective resource management and information systems relating to Canada's terrain and oceans. Applications include agriculture, forestry, geology, oceanography, engineering, water resource management and ice reconnaissance. Under the guidance of the federal government's Inter-Agency Committee on Remote Sensing (IACRS), the Centre serves federal and provincial government departments and agencies, regional organizations, industry, universities and the general public. In addition, through the Canadian Advisory Committee on Remote Sensing, the Centre co-ordinates remote sensing activities on a national scale. Another function of the Centre is to foster international co-operation in the peaceful use of space technology.

The Surveys and Mapping Branch compiles, prints and distributes topographical maps, aeronautical charts, specialized maps such as electoral and boundary maps and general maps. It establishes and maintains the basic geodetic control survey networks, manages and regulates the boundary and property surveys of Canada Lands and collaborates with the United States in the maintenance of the international boundary. It produces gazetteers and the National Atlas.

The Polar Continental Shelf Project provides logistic communications and accommodation support to research and surveys in the Northern Arctic. The emphasis has been on testing the probable response of the arctic environment and ecology to industrial activity, such as oil exploration and pipeline construction.

The primary mission of the Office of Energy Research and Development is to provide co-ordination and to stimulate improved management of all federal energy research and development.

Medical and Health Research

Biomedical research in Canada is carried out primarily in laboratories located in the universities and their affiliated hospitals. The major part of the financial support for the direct operating costs of this research is provided by the federal government through grants or contributions to investigators whose salaries are, by and large, paid from university funds. Voluntary agencies such as the National Cancer Institute of Canada, the heart foundations, the Arthritis Society and others that derive their monies from public campaigns are providing an increasingly significant share of the support for research in the health sciences. The share provided by provincial governments has also grown in recent years.

In 1979 over 2,500 investigators received research grants from the various funding agencies. Their work ranged from the development of methods for automated reading of X-ray films, through clinical trials of drugs thought to be useful in the prevention of strokes, to research of the most fundamental kind related to the immunology of transplantation. The two federal bodies with primary responsibility in the field of health research are the Medical Research Council, whose main function is the support of university-based research in the health sciences, and the National Health Research and Development Program of the Department of National Health and Welfare, which is concerned particularly with studies relating to the biology of populations, the delivery of health care and the alteration of lifestyles in order to prevent disease.

The Department of National Health and Welfare also carries out research in central laboratories of its own. Research in the department's Health Programs

Migrating caribou in the Arctic.

Scientists' camp at Cunningham Inlet, Somerset Island, NWT.

Branch has seen the development of a preparation for the slow release into the body of the anti-tuberculosis drug isoniazid, permitting larger doses to be given to Inuit, among whom the risk of tuberculosis is greater. There has been substantial progress in field trials of rubella vaccines and increased activity in the study of mental and physical rehabilitation problems.

Northern Research

Canada has long recognized the contribution research makes to the socio-economic development of the North. Moreover, the Canadian North has some unique characteristics that are of particular interest to the scientific community.

Because of this, the Department of Indian and Northern Affairs has designed certain long-term measures to encourage and support northern research. The training of graduate students is assisted by special grants administered by the department. In addition, under its Northern Science Resource Centres Program the department operates the Western Arctic Science Resource Centre at Inuvik and the Eastern Arctic Science Resource Centre at Igloolik to accommodate scientists from government, universities and industry. Plans are being made for science resource centres at Whitehorse, Yukon and at Yellowknife, NWT.

These measures do not, however, meet the need for research to support development programs or to obtain specific information required to support the regulatory and administrative responsibilities of the department. For these purposes substantial short-term programs of applied problem-oriented research have been organized, such as the environmental-social program, the northern pipelines program, the Beaufort Sea project, oil-spill studies, waste disposal studies and regional socio-economic studies.

Recently, the minister initiated various steps in the development of a new framework for science and research in the Yukon and the Northwest Territories; purposing to make science and research more responsive to the northern needs and interests.

Communications

A Telecommunications Revolution

Canada is connected from ocean to ocean, from north to south and even from its geological surface to the stars by a vast telecommunications grid consisting of underground, underwater and surface cables, open lines, microwave towers and a family of celestial satellites. Together, they link Canadians to virtually every telephone, not only within our own borders but throughout the developed world, and provide access to a host of radio, TV and computer facilities.

By the end of the 1970s, these systems had reduced our planet to an electronic global village. Now that the technology is for the most part in place, they entice us with such possibilities as living room television screens that could turn our homes into conference rooms, offices, research libraries, medical clinics or shopping centres.

Such hardware is already well beyond the theoretical stage. In 1978 the federal Department of Communications demonstrated its two-way television system, Telidon. Telidon users can interact directly from their homes or offices with computer-based information sources accessible through adapted television sets, which serve as display screens for text and graphics.

Telidon's advanced graphic capabilities render possible the electronic transmission of a wide variety of illustrations.

Telidon, which is compatible with telephone, cable, broadcast and satellite transmission is now undergoing field trials by Bell Canada (using Telidon technology with Vista, its videotex system); the Manitoba Telephone Company; Alberta Government Telephones; the New Brunswick Telephone Company; the Ontario Educational Communications Authority; and Télécâble-Vidéotron, a Montreal cable firm. During 1980-81, there were 1,500 terminals in use for Telidon field trials in 21 cities, towns and suburbs across Canada.

Breakthroughs on three major technological frontiers during the 1970s contributed to the imminent communications revolution: micro-computers, fibre optics and telecommunications satellites. Within the forseeable future they may bring us as many as 200 television channels on every set; electronic mail delivery; video-telephones; and a wide variety of home services, including print-outs in our living room of tabloid newspapers, dress patterns, recipes and other information materials.

The new generation of small inexpensive computers that proliferated during the past decade enabled voice, visual and data communication formerly transmitted in analogue form to be sent in the much cheaper, faster and more accurate digital form. (Messages transmitted in analogue form are restructured as electronic "pictures" analogous to the original messages. Messages in digital form are not analogous to the original; they are transmitted in a numerical code.)

Fibre optics, a new communications technology, will allow telecommunications carriers to dramatically increase their capacity to carry information and to operate at a significantly lower cost. Fibre-optics transmission uses light pulses sent down hair-thin strands of glass fibre as a replacement for conventional electrical communications signals. By using high frequency light (laser), 1,000 times more information can be carried on glass fibres than on regular telephone copper wires.

Fibre-optics transmission technology is already being field-tested. In February 1979, the federal Department of Communications and the Canadian Telecommunications Carriers Association (CTCA) signed an agreement to conduct a joint $6.1 million field trial over the following five years in the small Manitoba town of Elie.

The first Canadian test in actual field conditions began in October 1977 when Bell Canada and its subsidiary, Bell Northern Research, installed an underground 1.42 km fibre-optics line between two switching centres in Montreal. In December 1978, Bell Canada inaugurated a second field trial in Yorkville, Toronto — the first with fibre optics used for residence telephones. Between 1980 and 1982, Bell Canada expects that the technological development and systems economics of fibre optics will justify its widespread use in transmission systems within metropolitan areas.

As part of a plan to link some Saskatchewan communities with a fibre-optics broadband network by 1984, Northern Telecom (Canada) Limited has been awarded a contract by Saskatchewan Telecommunications for fibre-optics cable and other equipment. To carry out the project, Northern Telecom is building an $11 million fibre-optics manufacturing plant in Saskatoon.

Communications satellite technology is the third area in which progress during the 1970s will affect the telecommunications environment of the 1980s. Satellites are our link to the rest of the world. Functioning much like gigantic microwave towers suspended in orbit over the earth, they are used today for long-distance voice, video and data communication. In addition, satellite transmission costs from Montreal to Toronto are the same as from Montreal to Vancouver. Anik B pilot projects are exploring new applications. These applications include telemedicine, education and community interaction.

Canada has been a leader in satellite technology since 1962 when Alouette I was launched, with several Canadian satellites launched and others on the drawing board. Anik I, the first domestic commercial communications satellite in the world, launched in 1972; and Aniks II and III, back-up satellites launched in 1973 and 1975 respectively, each have a seven-year lifespan. A new series, Aniks B, C and D, will have completely replaced, with greatly expanded ranges, the last of the A series by the mid-1980s. The first of these, Telesat Canada's Anik B, was launched in 1978.

In addition, a powerful new satellite, Hermes, was launched in 1976. It was a forerunner of the direct broadcast satellites and the result of a co-operative program between the Department of Communications and the National Aeronautics and Space Administration (NASA). Hermes was designed and built in Canada and launched by the United States, which provided additional testing and components. Communications experiments began in 1976, with both nations sharing the use of satellite time equally. Hermes' original design lifespan of two years was almost doubled, and the satellite performed successfully until November 24, 1979.

The Science Council of Canada recently summarized the significance of satellites such as Hermes: "It seems likely that long distance communication will be conducted

Canadian providers of information for Telidon, the Canadian-developed videotex and teletext system, have found the system superior for generating, processing and storing of graphics and text.

by high powered satellites using relatively inexpensive low powered ground stations. Low powered parabolic dish receivers designed to sell for under $200 are already being introduced in Japan." Canada is a leader in direct broadcast technology. Using Anik B, small Canadian-designed dishes measuring little more than a metre in diameter are already at about 45 homes and communities in remote locations, pulling in signals from Canadian TV stations. In the near future, community antennas or receivers on home rooftops may be able to pick up satellite signals directly.

The cornucopia of telecommunications marvels that will entice us during this decade may well have hidden within it some surprises. Already Canada's telecommunications carriers, broadcasters and cable-TV operators are beginning to question their future roles. In a 1979 report, the Consultative Committee on the Implications of Telecommunications for Canadian Sovereignty warned, "It is no longer possible, as it was 10 or 15 years ago, to distinguish between the technologies of telegraphy, telephony, radiocommunication and computers. All are used, to a greater or lesser extent, in almost every mode of telecommunication, either in combination or in competition, thus undermining the structure of communications that has developed over the last 130 years."

Federal Regulations and Services

The federal Department of Communications, established in 1969, is responsible for ensuring that all Canadians have the best possible access, at a reasonable cost, to a broad range of communications services. The responsibility includes careful introduction, development and monitoring of the new information technologies, particularly in regard to their impact on Canada's economy, social and cultural values and the quality of Canadian life. The department has four sectors: policy, space, research, and spectrum management and government telecommunications.

The Policy Sector

The policy sector focuses on the far-reaching implications of the coming information revolution. Recently examined issues include communications rights of access; the implications of computerized information systems for personal privacy; the impact of the new technologies on Canadian industry and on the workplace; the effect of new technologies on federal and provincial jurisdictions over telecommunications; the structure and future roles of telecommunications carriers, cable companies, broadcasters and other components of the telecommunications system; and the introduction of pay-television in Canada. The policy sector also plays a major role in co-ordinating planning for communications in the North, including the best way of ensuring efficient communications for oil exploration on the northern continental shelf — especially by satellite. In addition, Canada's relations with the rest of the world in matters relating to telecommunications are handled within this sector.

The Space Sector

The space sector operates Canadian scientific satellites (ISIS); carries out satellite programs such as the successful Hermes and the Anik B communications satellite program; performs research and development; sponsors technology transfer to industry; provides technical support to the international marketing activities of the Canadian space industry; and operates facilities for use by Canadian industry for the integration, testing and reliability assessment of space components, subsystems and complete spacecraft. The sector is carrying out studies on satellite systems to provide mobile radio and television and radio broadcasting services.

The sector is also contributing to a co-operative program involving Canada, France and the United States to develop and evaluate a satellite-aided search and rescue system (SARSAT). Following a December 1978 agreement with the European Space Agency (ESA), Canada has been participating in the Agency's general studies program, as well as in the definition phase of ESA's Large Satellite (L-SAT) program.

The Research Sector

The Department of Communications' research sector carries out research over a broad spectrum of the communications field, both in-house and through a system of university contracts. The sector aids in the development of new communications systems and provides scientific advice to the department. Its principal research facility is the communications research centre, located near Ottawa. In 1977-78 the research sector demonstrated the first fully bi-directional fibre-optics link — a significant advance in lowering costs. The research sector is also the birthplace of Telidon, the two-way television system widely acknowledged to be superior to any other such system in the world. During the past few years the research sector has conducted research projects in transmission and delivery systems, optical communications, space, rural and remote communications, northern communications and new home and business services.

Spectrum Management and Government Telecommunications

The Telecommunications Regulatory Service plans and implements the regulation of the radio frequency spectrum; issues radio station licences (other than for broadcasting stations); sets and conducts examinations for radio operators and regulates the use of radio frequencies; and develops standards to control interference with radio and television reception, as well as technical specifications. The service also tests and approves telecommunications equipment for use in Canada and issues technical and operating certificates for broadcasting stations. The department has five regional offices and 43 district offices across Canada through which it provides many of these services.

The Government Telecommunications Agency is responsible for the overall co-ordination and planning of telecommunications services used by the federal government and its agencies.

The Canadian Radio-television and Telecommunications Commission (CRTC), under the terms of the Broadcasting Act, regulates the Canadian broadcasting system — radio, television and cable television. The Commission issues broadcasting licences and holds public hearings to consider applications relating to broadcasting undertakings, policy and regulatory matters. At these hearings, members of the public may comment or intervene on specific applications or issues. The CRTC also has regulatory powers over Canadian federally regulated telecommunications carriers,

Radio broadcasting at Inuvik, NWT.

including Teleglobe Canada, Bell Canada, the British Columbia Telephone Company, Canadian National Telecommunications and Canadian Pacific Telecommunications.

International Services

Teleglobe Canada, a federal Crown corporation, provides Canadians with a complete range of external communications services: telephone, telegraph, telex, radio and television, leased circuits and computer communications. The corporation operates a worldwide network of telecommunications facilities including trans-oceanic submarine cables and communications satellite circuits. Teleglobe co-ordinates Canada's external telecommunications services with those of other countries.

Statistics on Communications in the 1970s

Telecommunications Carriers

Canada's telecommunications carriers operate a vast telecommunications network. With $17 billion invested in plant and equipment in 1978, the industry is expanding at a rate of more than $2 billion a year. Investment in 1979 was estimated to be about $2.2 billion a year.

A significant increase in direct dialing facilities should enable 80 per cent of Canadian subscribers to dial overseas direct by 1984. By then, close to 90 per cent of outgoing international telephone calls will be customer-dialed. During 1979, Canadians spent 114.2 million minutes on international phone calls which was an increase of 29.2 per cent over 1978.

The federal Northern Communications Assistance Program initiated in 1977 is well on the way to achieving its aim of providing every community in the Northwest

Territories with basic local and long distance service by 1982. Since 1977, 10 communities have been provided with such services. Bell Canada serves the eastern half of the Northwest Territories up to the Arctic Circle, as well as Northern Quebec. In February 1980, Bell put an all electronic digital switching system into service in Broughton Island, a small village near the Arctic Circle. In the western Arctic, 96.2 per cent of the subscribers of Northwest Tel (a subsidiary of Canadian National) can dial long-distance directly. By the end of 1979, Northwest Tel provided 63 telephone exchanges in the Yukon and Northwest Territories west of longitude 102 degrees, and in northern British Columbia, including one digital exchange and 37,736 telephones.

General Statistics

Telephones. The number of telephones in service rose from 14.5 million in 1977 to 15.2 million in 1978, with 64 telephones for every 100 Canadians. Of these phones, more than 10.6 million were residential and about 4.5 million for business. On a per capita basis, Alberta had the most telephones (72.7 for every 100 people), followed by Ontario with 68.5 and British Columbia with 66.3. Canadians averaged 1,020 calls per person in 1978. Telephone company revenues more than doubled between 1973 and 1978, growing from approximately $2.2 billion to $4.6 billion. Their net telephone plant grew from $6.5 billion to $11.7 billion. The number of full-time employees grew from 75,407 to 92,873 during this period.

Telecommunications. Annual operating revenues from the non-telephone telecommunications activities of carriers CN, CP, Teleglobe, Telesat and others rose from $191 million in 1973 to $348 million in 1978. The annual telegram volume declined from almost 3.5 million messages in 1973 to 2.35 million in 1978. Offsetting this trend, the number of cablegrams, including wireless and transatlantic telex messages, grew from 7.4 million in 1973 to 11.2 million in 1978. During 1979-80, more than 5 million telex and Teletypewriter Exchange Service (TWX) messages were switched to overseas points by Teleglobe Canada's facilities. Telex, the first North American dial-and-type printer service, was introduced to Canada by CNCP Telecommunications in 1956. By 1979, it interconnected with some 42,000 telex units in Canada and about 500,000 units around the world. Owned and operated by the TransCanada Telephone system, TWX has some 5,000 subscribers capable of connecting with 119,000 TWX and telex users in the U.S.

Radiocommunications. Licensing of radio stations, other than those that are part of a broadcasting undertaking, and all technical matters dealing with radio, including television, are regulated under the Radio Act. The Radio Act also provides for the technical certification of radio stations that are part of a broadcasting undertaking, but such broadcasting stations (AM radio, TV and FM) and cable TV systems are licensed by the Candian Radio-television and Telecommunications Commission (CRTC) under the Broadcasting Act.

The Canada Shipping Act and the Aeronautics Act authorize the Minister of Transport to make radio regulations concerned with the safety of ships and aircraft.

At the end of March 1980, 1,300,572 radio station licences were in effect, an 8 per cent decline from the previous year. The decrease stemmed mainly from a reduction in General Radio Service (GRS) or citizen's band (CB) radio licences (820,952 in 1980, down from an all-time high of 951,849 in 1979) and elimination of some classes of certificate of registration for US travellers bringing radio equipment into Canada. Mobile stations

The British Columbia Telephone Company traces to origins in 1891 and today serves 97 per cent of the province's population and area.

excluding aircraft showed considerable growth with 334,617 stations in March 1980, up from 300,467 in 1979. Most new mobile stations are located in Montreal, Toronto, Vancouver and in petroleum-producing areas such as Edmonton, Calgary and Grande Prairie. Radio licences are issued for stations operated by federal, provincial and municipal agencies, stations on ships and aircraft registered in Canada, stations in land vehicles operated for public and private use, and GRS stations.

Broadcasting. Canadians are heavy users of radio and television. An estimated 98 per cent of Canadians had a radio in their homes in May 1979, while 86 per cent had an FM radio set. Almost 98 per cent have at least one television set in their homes; 76.6 per cent have colour TV; and 35.5 per cent have more than one TV set in their homes. As of March 1980, Canadians listened to 737 licensed AM radio stations, 470 FM radio stations, 1,100 television stations (including rebroadcasters), 562 cable television systems, and 31 radio and television networks of various types.

The CBC operates coast-to-coast AM radio networks in both French and English, as well as FM radio networks in both languages that approach national distribution. There are no full-time AM or FM national networks operated by private commercial interests, although 55 private stations are affiliated with the English or French networks of the CBC. Many part-time regional networks of privately owned stations operate to present such specific program services as play-by-play accounts of major sporting events.

Networking in television is more pervasive. The CBC operates two nationwide television networks, one in English and one in French. There are two major commercially operated networks: the CTV network provides an English-language program service from coast to coast, and the Réseau de télévision TVA offers French-language programming across Quebec. The privately owned Global Communications

A Grade 1 student in a Vancouver school listening to story for class project.

Ltd. station serves southern Ontario. The provincial governments of Ontario, Quebec and Alberta operate their own educational TV networks.

About 73 per cent of Canadians had access in 1977 to at least one US television channel. About 62 per cent could pick up three US networks, and the US public broadcasting service could be picked up by 57 per cent. English-language programming was accessible to about 62 per cent of the population from four US TV channels while only 46 per cent could receive four Canadian channels. In Quebec, 49 per cent of the population could pick up at least one US channel. Despite CRTC regulation of cable TV and Canadian content regulations, accessibility of US TV channels has meant that Canadians watch a great many US programs. About 70 per cent of all the programming viewed by Canadian audiences on English-language stations was of foreign origin in 1978. For entertainment and sports programming, the figure was 86.5 per cent.

Cable television has expanded dramatically since 1968. Cable was available to 29.9 per cent of Canadian homes in 1968 and only 13.2 per cent of Canadian households actually subscribed to the service. By 1979 an estimated 78 per cent of Canadian homes were passed by cable and 52.5 per cent of Canadian households received the service. In January 1980, an estimated 54 per cent of Canadians were hooked into a cable TV system, making Canada one of the most heavily cabled countries in the world.

Radio Canada International (RCI), the CBC's overseas shortwave service with headquarters in Montreal, broadcasts daily in 11 languages and distributes recorded Canadian programs free to broadcasters throughout the world. RCI attempts to give factual coverage of Canadian and international news and reflects the variety of Canadian opinion on matters of domestic and international concern. In 1973-74, 42,000 discs or tapes were shipped to stations around the world; in 1979-80, the figure was 112,158. The CBC estimates that the RCI shortwave service reaches several million listeners a week in the USSR, the United States, Africa, Europe and Latin America.

The Canadian Broadcasting Corporation

The CBC is a publicly owned corporation established by the Broadcasting Act to provide the national broadcasting service in Canada. Created in November 1936, it reports to Parliament through the Secretary of State, while responsibility for its policies and programs lies with its own directors and officers. It is financed mainly by public funds voted annually by Parliament; these are supplemented by revenues from commercial advertising — mostly on television, since CBC radio is almost completely non-commercial.

The CBC's head office is in Ottawa. The operational centre for English services is in Toronto, and there are several regional production centres across the country. The operations of the French services are centred in Montreal, with local stations at other points in Quebec and in most other provinces.

The corporation's facilities extend from Atlantic to Pacific and into the Arctic Circle, and include both French and English networks in television and in AM and FM stereo radio. A special northern radio service broadcasts in English, French, several Indian languages and Inuktitut, the language of the Inuit; northern television is also beginning to introduce some programming in Inuktitut.

In both radio and television, CBC networks are made up of some stations owned and operated by the corporation, which carry the full national service, and some privately owned affiliated stations, which carry an agreed amount of CBC programming. In many

Terre Humaine, *A CBC drama series depicting the joys, passions and conflicts of everyday life.*

small or isolated locations there are relay or rebroadcast transmitters that carry the national service but have no staff or studios to produce local programs. CBC transmission methods include leased channels on the Canadian space satellite Anik.

Radio Canada International, the CBC's overseas shortwave service, broadcasts daily in 11 languages and distributes recorded programs free of charge for use by broadcasters throughout the world. In other international activities, the CBC sells programs to other countries, is a frequent winner of international program awards and belongs to several international broadcasting organizations. CBC maintains offices in London, Paris, New York and Washington, and news bureaus in the Far East, Moscow and Brussels.

CBC schedules are varied, reflecting the principles set out in the Broadcasting Act that "the national broadcasting service should be a balanced service of information, enlightenment and entertainment for people of different ages, interests and tastes, covering the whole range of programming in fair proportion". Program content is largely Canadian — about 70 per cent in television and usually more in radio — with a selection of programs from other countries.

CBC gives continuing support to Canadian artists and performers through the broadcast of Canadian music, drama and poetry, the commissioning of special works, the sponsorship of talent competitions and the presentation of Canadian films. Selected program material is made available for educational use after broadcast in the form of books, recordings, audiotapes and films.

Scene from A Gift to Last, *a family drama series on CBC's English television network.*

Observers follow the movement of mail by closed-circuit television and computer printouts from the control centre of the handling terminal.

The Postal Service

At the end of the 1978-79 fiscal year, 8,230 postal facilities were in operation across the country and mail delivery by letter carrier totalled 6,210,500 points of call. There were 13,875 full-time and 570 partial letter-carrier routes; 282 post offices provided letter-carrier service. Improvements continue to be made in the frequency and quality of service to isolated and remote communities where mail transportation is normally provided by air.

The coding and mechanization program began in 1972 with the goal of achieving more efficient handling of mail. Automated electronic equipment is capable of sorting first class mail at speeds of from 20,000 to 30,000 pieces an hour by use of the postal code. By the end of 1979 all but two of the proposed 29 mechanized postal plants had been completed.

Other new machinery that has been introduced is capable of sorting flats, or oversize mail, at speeds of up to 6,000 pieces an hour. Since first class parcels and small packets are already being machine-sorted, this means that virtually all classes and kinds of mail can now be sorted mechanically.

The Post Office operates 3,765 motor vehicles for the movement of mail within city boundaries. Mail between centres is moved by a wide variety of contractors using air, rail, highway and waterways as modes of transportation.

The National Postal Museum added a number of unique philatelic and historical postal items to its collection during the past year. In 1979, the museum was visited by approximately 26,500 people. Philatelic items at the museum's pioneer post office have increased in popularity as indicated in the increased volume of sales. The museum's research library is being used extensively by philatelists, historians and writers. The new location of the museum is in downtown Ottawa in larger quarters with considerably more space, providing facilities for meetings and lectures.

Leisure

Industrialization and technological progress in Canada have led to shorter work weeks, longer paid vacations, earlier retirement and hence has provided more time for leisure and recreation.

Definitions of leisure are numerous and reflect a variety of views. Leisure can be simply defined as those groups of activities undertaken in "non-work" time; it has also been described as that group of activities in which a person may indulge of his own free will — to rest, to amuse himself, to add to his knowledge or skills, to enhance his personal, physical and mental health through sports and cultural activities, or to carry out unpaid community work. However, many definitions of leisure exclude activities such as sleeping, eating, commuting to and from work, household duties and personal care. Formal programs of continuing education may be regarded as personal improvement or maintenance just as much as sleeping or eating and therefore may also be excluded from leisure activity. On the other hand, it can be argued that the allocation of all non-work time is at the discretion of the individual and therefore any part of it is potentially time available for leisure. Nevertheless, most people would agree there is a basic minimum time required for sleeping, eating and personal care that cannot in any sense be regarded as being available for leisure activities.

Despite the fact that there is no precise agreement on what constitutes leisure, there is agreement on a core of activities that offer recreation or give pleasure to the participants. Examples would be playing tennis or listening to records. There are

Muttart conservatory in Edmonton. In 1980, Alberta celebrated its 75th anniversary as a province.

Preparing food at camp during a rafting trip in British Columbia.

activities that may be regarded as undesired household tasks in some circumstances, yet pleasurable recreational activities in others, such as mowing the lawn, cooking, dressmaking or house painting. Thus, recreation and leisure may be regarded as qualitative terms that are valued differently according to personal tastes and inclinations. These may vary not only between persons but in different circumstances for the same person.

There is a reciprocal relationship between work and leisure. Longer working hours mean less time for leisure. Additional work time normally provides additional income, while additional leisure time typically leads to increased expenditures. The distribution of time between work and leisure is theoretically a matter of choice, but in practice most employed persons have only limited freedom in determining how long they work. This is because working hours and holidays in Canada are normally fixed, either by employers or as a result of collective bargaining, according to current legislation and accepted norms. As a result Canadian workers are typically committed to working a fixed number of hours a day and days a week.

The normal work week in Canada is from 35 to 40 hours spread over five working days. Most employees receive at least 10 paid holidays annually and a two-week annual vacation, which is usually extended to three, four or more weeks after several years of service with the same employer. Allowing for weekends, paid holidays and annual vacations, most employed persons in Canada have at least 124 days free from work each year. The net amount of non-work time available to Canadians depends also on the proportion of the population in the labour force and whether or not they are employed or seeking employment. Those outside the labour force are by definition non-working and therefore have more free time at their disposal. Typical of these are persons who have retired early or are elderly.

Events and Attractions

Every year, in all parts of Canada, annual events and attractions draw large numbers of vacationers and travellers seeking diversion, excitement and relaxation. Events such as the Quebec Winter Carnival and the Calgary Stampede are organized to promote or celebrate historical, social or cultural occasions. On the other hand, attractions can be either natural or man-made physical features of a permanent nature that provide facilities for displaying distinctive architectural or geographic qualities or for recreational or cultural activities. In this category are museums, parks, mountains and city nightlife; specific examples would be a natural phenomenon like Niagara Falls or a man-made attraction such as Lower Fort Garry in Selkirk, Man.

Outstanding events take place in each province and territory. One of the oldest sporting events in North America is Newfoundland's annual regatta, held in St. John's. Prince Edward Island's capital city, Charlottetown, features Country Days and Old Home Week, with musical entertainment, agricultural and handicraft displays, harness racing and parades. Nova Scotia events include Highland Games in the centres of Cape Breton, while in New Brunswick there are a variety of festivities related to the province's fishing resources, such as the Shediac Lobster Festival and the Campbellton Salmon Festival.

Craft Village near Fredericton, NB.

Tobogganing in Quebec City.

In Quebec attractions include Man and his World, Montreal's permanent cultural and ethnic exhibition, and the Sherbrooke Festival des Cantons, which features "Québécois" shows, horse-pulling, soirées and gourmet cuisine. Drama festivals in Stratford and Niagara-on-the-Lake are examples of happenings in Ontario.

Western Canada's events reflect its cultural diversity and pioneering heritage. Examples include the National Ukrainian Festival in Dauphin, Man., and an Oktoberfest in Vancouver, BC. Both Saskatchewan and Alberta had special events throughout 1980 to celebrate their 75th year as provinces.

Special events are held each summer in the North. In Yellowknife, NWT, a Midnight Golf Tournament is held each year late in June. In Dawson City, Yukon, the discovery of gold in 1896 is celebrated on Discovery Day in August by raft races on the Klondike River and by dances, sports and entertainment relating to the period.

Art students painting in Quebec.

Fishing in the Yukon.

Recreation

The types of leisure activities undertaken vary widely according to the age, sex, income and occupation of the individual. Popular sports or physical recreational activities include swimming, ice skating, tennis, golf and ice hockey. In recent years cross-country skiing has become increasingly popular with adults and families in many parts of Canada.

According to a survey of selected leisure activities, conducted in February 1978, most popular activities included watching television, listening to radio, reading newspapers, listening to records or tapes and reading magazines. Visits to bookstores, movies, sports events and public libraries were also popular.

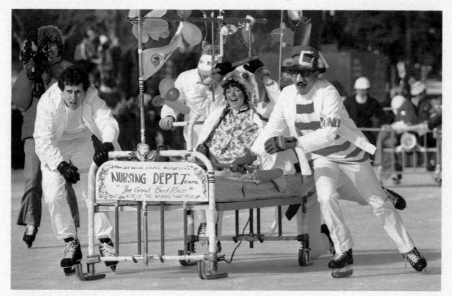

Winterlude in Ottawa.

Government Programs

All levels of government play an active role in enriching the leisure time of Canadians and several federal agencies have major programs related to leisure. Among these is the Fitness and Amateur Sport Branch of the Secretary of State, which is mainly responsible for recreation and physical fitness programs and which carries out a number of programs aimed at encouraging citizens of all ages to take part in physical fitness activities; it provides financial and consultative assistance to recreational agencies such as the YMCA, boys' and girls' clubs, Scouts, Guides and youth hostels, and it also assists Canada's native people in increasing their participation in sports and recreation. The Canadian Government Office of Tourism assists in advertising our special events and attractions nationwide and outside Canada. National Museums of Canada promotes interest in and awareness of Canadian heritage and regional variety through the National Museums, the Associate Museums and the Museums Assistance programs. The responsibilities of Fisheries and Oceans Canada and Environment Canada include recreational programs such as sport fishing, the conservation of migratory game birds, the provision of interpretive centres on wildlife and the construction and maintenance of wharf facilities for small recreational craft.

For the area in and around Ottawa–Hull, the National Capital Commission plays an important role in conserving and developing space for outdoor recreation. The facilities it provides include Gatineau Park, an area of 357 km² (square kilometres) similar to a national or provincial park, a system of scenic driveways and bicycle paths and a greenbelt of land forming a semi-circle of recreational land to the south of Ottawa; it also maintains the longest outdoor skating rink in the world on the Rideau Canal during the winter and rents out garden plots in the greenbelt during the summer.

Banff National Park in Alberta.

Parks Canada

National Parks

Canada's national parks system began with a 26 km² reservation of land around the mineral hot springs in what is now Banff National Park. From this nucleus the system has grown to include 28 national parks that preserve more than 129 500 km² of Canada's natural areas.

Canada's national parks reflect the amazing diversity of the land. The program now extends from Terra Nova National Park, on the rugged eastern coast of Newfoundland, to Pacific Rim National Park, where breakers pound magnificent Long Beach on the west coast of Vancouver Island, and from Point Pelee, Canada's most southerly mainland point, to Auyuittuq National Park on Baffin Island.

There is at least one national park in each province and territory. The mountain parks of British Columbia and Alberta, among the oldest in the system, are noted for their craggy peaks, alpine lakes and meadows, glaciers and hot springs.

At Waterton Lakes National Park, which together with Glacier National Park of the US forms an international park, the mountains rise dramatically from the prairie without the usual transitional foothills. Aspen and spruce forests contrast with the surrounding flat farmland in Elk Island National Park, Alta. Prince Albert National Park, Sask., displays three vegetation zones — boreal forest, aspen parkland and prairie — and within the park's boundaries are hundreds of lakes, streams, ponds and bogs. In Riding Mountain National Park, situated on the summit of the Manitoba escarpment, northern and eastern forests and western grasslands form a diverse landscape that shelters a broad variety of plant and animal life.

There are four national parks in Ontario — Georgian Bay Islands, Point Pelee, St. Lawrence Islands and Pukaskwa. La Mauricie in the Laurentian Mountains and Forillon on the historic Gaspé peninsula are located in Quebec.

Seven national parks in the Atlantic provinces conserve areas of acadian and boreal forest, harsh sea coast and sandy beaches, and the lake-dotted interior of Nova Scotia.

There are now four parks located partially or completely above the 60th parallel of latitude. Wood Buffalo National Park straddles the Alberta–Northwest Territories border and is home to the largest remaining herd of bison on the continent. Kluane, Yukon, contains Mount Logan, Canada's highest peak, while in Nahanni National Park, NWT, the spectacular Virginia Falls of the South Nahanni River plunge 90 m (metres) to the valley below. On Baffin Island, Auyuittuq, which in Inuit means "the place that does not melt", is Canada's first national park above the Arctic Circle.

The magnificent scenery and numerous recreational possibilities of the national parks attract visitors year-round, whether to camp, sightsee, hike, mountain-climb, swim, fish, ski or snowshoe. Interpretive programs include guided walks, displays, films and brochures that explain the natural history of the park regions.

Ice fields in Kluane National Park in the Yukon.

National Historic Parks and Sites

To preserve Canada's past the National Historic Parks and Sites Branch of Parks Canada commemorates persons, places and events that played important parts in the development of Canada. Since 1917, when Fort Anne in Nova Scotia became the first national historic park, 55 major parks and sites and over 700 plaques and monuments have been established at significant sites. At present, some 30 more sites are under development.

Sites are selected on the basis of their cultural, social, political, economic, military or architectural importance and include major archaeological discoveries. Two finds in Newfoundland are the ancient Indian burial ground at Port au Choix and the Norse settlement at L'Anse aux Meadows believed occupied about 1000 A.D..

Many historic parks and sites recall the early exploration of Canada and struggles for its possession. Cartier-Brébeuf Park in Quebec City marks Jacques Cartier's first wintering spot in the New World and is, in addition, the site of the Jesuit order's first residence in Canada.

The pursuit of furs led to extensive exploration of Canada and construction of many posts and forts to expand and protect the fur trade. Such posts include Port Royal, the earliest French settlement north of Florida, Fort Témiscamingue, a strategic trading post in the upper Ottawa Valley, and Fort Prince of Wales, the most northerly stone fort in North America. Lower Fort Garry, near Winnipeg, has been restored to recreate a 19th century Hudson's Bay Company post; here one can see women baking bread and spinning and weaving fabric at the "Big House", a blacksmith at work in his shop and furs, once the mainstay of Canada's economy, hanging in the loft above the well stocked sales shop — the hub of fort activity.

Restoration of Province House in Charlottetown, PEI.

Prince Albert National Park, Sask. In 1980 Saskatchewan celebrated its 75th year as a province.

Military fortifications that have been protected as national historic sites range from the massive Fortress of Louisbourg on Cape Breton Island, built by the French in the 18th century to protect their dwindling colonial possessions, through a series of French and English posts along the Richelieu and St. Lawrence rivers, to Fort Rodd Hill on Vancouver Island, site of three late 19th century British coastal defences.

The fur-trading posts of Rocky Mountain House in Alberta, Fort St. James in northern British Columbia and Fort Langley in British Columbia, where the province's salmon export industry also began, recall the expansion of trade and settlement in the West. The orderly development of Western Canada was due in large part to the North-West Mounted Police, who are commemorated at Fort Walsh, Sask., first headquarters of the force.

The major route to the Klondike Gold Rush is being marked and protected by the Klondike Gold Rush International Historic Park. In Dawson City, the boom town of 1898, the Palace Grand Theatre, the Robert Service Cabin and the paddlewheeler *S.S. Keno* have been restored, while other historic buildings are in the process of restoration or stabilization.

Province House in Charlottetown, PEI, is a national historic site and at the same time continues to serve as the legislative chambers of the province. The childhood homes of two of Canada's prime ministers, Sir Wilfrid Laurier and William Lyon Mackenzie King, have also been protected. Bellevue House National Historic Park in Kingston, a superb example of the "Tuscan Villa" style of architecture, was once occupied by Sir John A. Macdonald.

Agreements for Recreation and Conservation

Agreements for Recreation and Conservation (ARC) was introduced by Parks Canada in 1972 to satisfy increasing demands for heritage conservation and the provision of outdoor recreational opportunities. ARC is based on the concept of federal and provincial co-operation in the planning, development, operation and management of areas containing important heritage resources.

ARC is comprised of three program activities: heritage canals, co-operative heritage areas, and the proposed system of heritage rivers.

Heritage Canals. The canals of Canada were initially constructed as defence or commercial trading routes to serve a new country. At Confederation, canals came under the jurisdiction of the federal government because of their importance to the nation's transportation system.

Certain of these canals, with roles as commercial routes diminished, are now the responsibility of Parks Canada. The canals are operated and maintained as significant examples of early engineering technology in Canada. They also serve as examples of land and its water courses adapted by man to suit his needs for transportation and communication. In addition, the canals provide outstanding opportunities for recreational use and public enjoyment of significant heritage features which are being preserved, protected and presented for present and future generations.

Co-operative Heritage Areas. An area that contains natural or cultural resources which are of Canadian significance because of their quality or quantity is a heritage area. When the resources are owned, operated and maintained collectively by separate agencies under the Agreement for Recreation and Conservation, it is a co-operative heritage area. The co-operative approach produces opportunities for comprehensive programs in the field of heritage protection, heritage presentation and recreational activities that would not be possible for individual agencies through unilateral action. Acting in conjunction with provincial governments and others, resources and expertise can be combined to develop programs that are broader in scope and more effective as a complete presentation of an area.

Co-operative heritage areas may be of several types. In some cases there may be a variety of distinctive natural and cultural resources concentrated in an area which, in combination, are of Canadian significance. In other cases there may be an example of one particular type of heritage resource which is considered to be of national significance, (e.g. historic land and water routes or rural cultural landscapes) and whose preservation requires co-operative action. At present "co-operative heritage areas" is an umbrella term for areas where joint action is required to protect and present significant resources.

Heritage Rivers. There is a proposal to establish a system of heritage rivers across Canada. Our country has an abundance of free flowing rivers which are an important part of the natural and the cultural heritage. Some of the best examples of this heritage should be protected. The ARC branch is now in the process of consulting with the provinces and the territories to establish a mechanism whereby Parks Canada can undertake a joint program to initiate and establish such a system. The nature of the system which has been under discussion is a co-operative one in which nomination and management of designated waterways would remain entirely with the level of government which is constitutionally responsible for the resource (e.g. the provinces on provincial waterways; the federal government in national parks; and the federal government in co-operation with the Yukon and Northwest territorial governments on territorial waterways).

Provincial Parks

Most provinces have set aside vast areas of land for the conservation of the natural environment and the enjoyment of residents and visitors. The areas of provincial parks total about 298 600 km², which when added to the area of the national parks brings the total federal and provincial parkland available to more than 1.6 ha (hectares) for each resident of Canada.

Some of the oldest parks in Canada were created by the provinces. In 1895 the Quebec government's concern for the conservation of the caribou led to the establishment of Laurentide Park, one boundary of which is only 48 km north of Quebec City. In Ontario the first park was Algonquin, created in 1897, which covers an area of 7 540 km² and extends to within 240 km of the city limits of both Toronto and Ottawa; this park, like many of the others in Ontario and the other provinces, features camping, canoeing and sport fishing.

In addition, provincial governments administer a variety of recreational programs, manage natural resources, hunting and fishing and provide recreational facilities, both directly and through municipal programs.

Dinosaur Provincial Park, a World Heritage Site in Alberta.

Tourism

Tourism affects the lives of all Canadians. It has an impact on our lifestyle and provides a change of pace from contemporary social pressures. It also contributes to national unity by increasing understanding among people of the different regions which form the country.

Tourism is a major earner of foreign exchange for Canada. At the same time tourism is a significant generator of domestic spending. It has a considerable impact on consumption, investment and employment and is a source of substantial tax revenue for governments; it also spreads its benefits widely across Canada, playing a prominent role in helping to alleviate regional socio-economic disparities.

According to the World Tourism Organization, with monetary figures in US dollars, global tourism in 1979 involved 270.2 million international arrivals (up 4.2 per cent from 1978) and these travellers spent an estimated $75 billion in their countries of destination (up 15.4 per cent from 1978). In the world context, Canada ranked ninth in 1978 in terms of international travel receipts and sixth in terms of international travel spending by its residents. Tourism was a business worth $12.3 billion to Canada as a whole in 1979, an amount equivalent to about 5 per cent of the gross national product. The spending of Canadians travelling within Canada amounted to nearly $9.4 billion. The balance of $2.9 billion was earned from spending in Canada by visitors from other countries — our sixth largest source of foreign exchange after autos and auto parts, lumber, newsprint, wood pulp and natural gas.

Peggy's Cove, NS.

Ontario Place in Toronto, Ont.

In 1979, visitors from the United States numbered 31.2 million, down 1.3 per cent from 1978. Non-resident travellers from countries other than the US numbered 2 million, an increase of 20.1 per cent over 1978. Of this number 1,315,595 came from Europe and arrivals from the United Kingdom, the largest source of tourists after the US, totalled 516,438. Visitors from other major tourist-producing countries included 234,954 from the Federal Republic of Germany, 158,582 from Japan, 127,568 from France, 100,979 from the Netherlands, 51,348 from Australia and 61,400 from Italy.

The value of tourism spending in Canada should not, however, be measured solely in terms of the $12.3 billion direct travel expenditure. Subsequent rounds of spending spread throughout the economy and create additional business.

For example, when a traveller rents a hotel room he contributes in the first instance to the gross margin of the hotel owner. Part of this margin will be paid out to employees in the form of wages. These wages will subsequently be spent to the benefit of the owner of a corner store, for example. The money will then pass to the wholesaler who supplied the goods purchased and then to the manufacturer, who in turn probably purchases his raw materials from another Canadian firm, and so on. Counting this "multiplier" effect, the $12 billion generated in 1979 could have amounted to approximately $20.5 billion or 7.9 per cent of the GNP.

Receipts and payments on travel between Canada and other countries, 1974-79
(million dollars)

Country	1974	1975	1976	1977	1978	1979
United States						
Receipts........................	1,328	1,337	1,346	1,525	1,650	1,881
Payments......................	1,196	1,587	1,956	2,280	728	1,006
Balance	+132	−250	−610	−755	2,378	2,887
Other countries						
Receipts........................	366	478	584	500	2,553	2,457
Payments......................	782	955	1,165	1,386	1,531	1,498
Balance	−416	−477	−581	−886	4,084	3,955
All countries						
Receipts........................	1,694	1,815	1,930	2,025	−903	−576
Payments......................	1,978	2,542	3,121	3,666	−803	−492
Balance	−284	−727	−1,191	−1,641	−1,706	−1,068

Tourism also generated the equivalent of one million jobs across Canada in 1979 — or about 8.7 per cent of the labour force. It involved governments at every level and almost 100,000 individual private enterprises of diverse kinds, such as transportation companies, accommodation operators, restaurateurs, tour wholesalers and operators, travel agents, operators of activities and events, and trade associations.

Beach on Kalamalka Lake at Vernon, BC.

Story Book Park in London, Ont.

Another important feature of travel consumption in Canada is the low import content of the products consumed. As travel is predominantly service-oriented, travel spending is on goods and services with a relatively high domestic labour content. Furthermore, the goods purchased by tourists are usually home-produced — food and drink by Canadian farmers and processors and souvenirs by Canadian craftsmen, for example.

The growth of tourism in Canada is no accident. Canada possesses many basic tourism assets. It has an enviable location at the crossroads of the northern hemisphere and adjacent to the world's most affluent travel market. It is endowed with an abundance of open space, for which world demand is sure to intensify. Its northern territories constitute one of the world's few remaining tourist frontiers. It possesses immense supplies of a most precious recreational resource — water — and of a most promising one — snow. The variety, quantity and quality of Canada's wildlife compare favourably with those of any country. Canada's scenic, cultural and ethnic diversity add to its travel appeal, as do its heritage buildings and the developing attractions of its major cities.

Above all, Canada enjoys a worldwide reputation for friendliness and hospitality. But the growth of tourism also reflects the efforts of 10 provincial tourism departments and two territorial tourism departments, the services and promotion effected by the thousands of businesses catering to Canadian tourism and the work of the Canadian Government Office of Tourism.

The Economy

Canada's Economic Performance, 1979-80

Overall, real gross national product (GNP) increased 2.9 per cent during 1979, according to preliminary estimates, continuing the pattern of relatively moderate growth which has characterized the Canadian economy since 1977. Leaving out government final spending on goods and services (including government investment) real GNP grew almost 4 per cent. However, even the performance of the private sector was mixed with strength evident in business fixed capital spending, moderate growth in consumer demand, and a decline in residential construction activity. The international trade sector, which was a major source of growth in 1977 and 1978, was a negative force in 1979 as the real balance of trade in goods and services deteriorated.

Among the components of final demand particular strength was evident in business fixed capital formation. Business investment spending on plant and equipment began to strengthen in mid-1978, following three years of virtually no growth, in response to increased corporate profits and higher capacity utilization rates in many industries. This strength continued into 1979 when business final capital formation grew over 10 per cent in real terms, with similar advances occurring in both spending on machinery and equipment and non-residential construction.

Housing activity continued to wind down in 1979, however. Dwelling starts totalled 198,000 units during the year, down from 234,000 units in 1978, 244,000 units in 1977 and 277,000 units in 1976. The fall in the real value of business spending on residential construction in 1979 was smaller, at 7.4 per cent, than was the decline in housing starts due mainly to a continued marked shift in the composition of housing starts toward single family units and away from multiples.

Consumer spending on goods and services increased 2.3 per cent in 1979, its lowest annual rate of growth since 1970. The principal reason for the sluggish performance of consumer spending was the slow growth in real personal disposable income, which increased only 2.6 per cent in 1979 compared to an average rate of increase of over 5.5 per cent per year during the 1970s as a whole. Modest growth in real personal disposable income in 1979 may be traced to the effects of inflation. Remuneration failed to keep pace with inflation for the second year in a row, as average weekly earnings in the industrial sector declined 0.5 per cent in 1979.

Regina, Sask.

Sudbury, Ont.

International trade, which had been a source of relative strength in the Canadian economy in 1977 and 1978, was a negative force in 1979, at least regarding its impact on overall economic activity. The rapid growth in the volume of exports evident over the previous two years eased in 1979 as real merchandise exports increased only 2.6 per cent. The slowdown in export growth was most clearly evident in the area of motor vehicles and parts, exports of which declined by almost 14 per cent in response to a weakening US auto market and the impact of gasoline shortages in the United States in the second quarter. In contrast to the slowdown in export growth, merchandise imports accelerated in 1979, increasing by 9.2 per cent in real terms compared to 4.5 per cent in 1978. To a large extent this reflected increased spending by Canadian business on machinery and equipment, much of which is not produced in Canada.

Despite a widening in Canada's deficit on international trade in goods and services measured in constant dollars, the deficit on the current account of the balance of international payments actually narrowed somewhat to a level of $3.3 billion. The merchandise trade balance measured in current dollars benefited from an improvement in the terms of trade, as export prices increased more rapidly than did import prices, and posted an unexpectedly large surplus of $4 billion for the year as a whole. The deficit on non-merchandise transactions continued to deteriorate as in previous years, although at a somewhat slower pace. A principal reason for the reduced growth in the services deficit in 1979 was the stabilization of Canada's deficit on international travel, which in turn can be traced to the impact of the decline in the international value of the Canadian dollar together with slow real income growth among Canadian consumers.

Government spending on final goods and services (including government investment spending) declined by almost 1 per cent in real terms in 1979. The weakness in spending was evident at all levels of government and reflects the commitments to restraint made in recent years. It continues the pattern of rather steady decreases in the growth in government spending which have characterized the Canadian economy over the past five years. The overall deficit of the government sector on a national accounts basis declined in 1979 from $8.9 billion to $5.8 billion. However, the government sector budget position was expected to deteriorate markedly during 1980, particularly at the federal level.

A sharp increase in stockbuilding characterized the economy throughout 1979. The increase in inventory accumulation began in the fourth quarter of 1978 and continued throughout the following year. For the year 1979 as a whole, inventory accumulation exceeded $2 billion 1971 dollars (compared to $500 million in 1978), and accounted for in excess of one-half of the increase in real gross national expenditures. This in turn resulted in an inventory/sales ratio that was considerably in excess of its long-term trend by year end, and strongly suggested that an inventory correction would take place in 1980.

Inflation remained high throughout 1979, and in fact accelerated according to several measures. The consumer price index (CPI) increased by 9.1 per cent for the year 1979 as a whole, up marginally from an 8.9 per cent advance in 1978. By the end of 1979, however, consumer prices were running 9.5 per cent of their levels a year earlier. The broader implicit price index for gross national expenditures increased by almost 10 per cent in 1979 compared to only 6.4 per cent in 1978. A significant proportion of that increase was accounted for by higher export prices — which increased by 19 per cent in 1979 compared to an increase of 8 per cent in 1978 — but there were also broadly based accelerations in the deflators for the domestic demand components.

Given the high rates of inflation, the growth of labour earnings in Canada over 1978-79 was moderate. Average weekly earnings in the industrial composite fell in six of the eight quarters ending with the fourth quarter of 1979, and also declined on an annual basis during both years. The only other extended period of decline in real average weekly earnings in Canada during the past 20 years was in 1973-74. In 1973 real earnings fell during three consecutive quarters, while in 1974 earnings barely kept pace with inflation. This period was followed by a sharp acceleration in wage settlements and in nominal earnings as labour attempted to recover lost ground: in 1975 real earnings grew 3 per cent followed by a further 4.3 per cent gain in 1976.

While there was some evidence, in early 1980, of an acceleration in nominal earnings it was unlikely that the experience of the mid-1970s would be repeated. A sharp rebound in real earnings appeared unlikely, and expectations were that real earnings would remain essentially flat in 1980. This, in turn, suggested that

Quebec City, Que.

consumer spending would continue to be constrained by the slow growth in the household income.

By late 1979 all signs pointed to an imminent cyclical downturn in the economy. The US economy was poised to enter a period of recession which implied an additional decline in the markets for Canadian exports. Canadian automobile exports were expected to decline substantially again during 1980. Housing starts in the United States, the major determinant of the demand for Canadian lumber exports, were expected to fall by over 600,000 units. As a result of these two factors, Canadian exports were expected to decline by over 2 per cent in real terms in 1980.

Moreover, high US inflation was expected to result in continuing upward pressure on Canadian price levels, which in turn would severely limit the growth of real disposable income and, hence, consumer spending in Canada. Canada is very susceptible to foreign inflation, as approximately 40 per cent of Canadian prices are determined outside the country (primarily in the United States), given a constant exchange rate. Consumer prices in Canada were expected to rise by almost 10 per cent in 1980, with a higher rate of inflation possible depending on the timing and extent of an acceleration in the adjustment to higher oil prices.

Finally, in order to prevent a further depreciation in the Canadian dollar, policy makers allowed interest rates in Canada to rise in response to the sharp increase in rates in the United States beginning in the fall of 1979. By the end of 1979 real interest rates (after adjusting for inflation) were high in Canada and this situation was expected to persist throughout 1980, despite the decline in nominal interest

Tank trucks loading nitrogen fertilizer in southern Alberta.

rates which took place during the spring. The high real interest rates were expected to have a dampening effect on real economic growth, and particularly to affect interest sensitive sectors of the economy. The hardest hit areas were expected to be purchases of new homes and purchases of large consumer durable items such as cars. Businesses would also be affected as the cost of holding excessive inventories had increased significantly.

Overall, these negative factors were expected to result in a year of no real economic growth in the Canadian economy in 1980. The growth of consumer spending was predicted to be even lower than in 1979, while residential construction activity would decline further. Government spending was also expected to decline in real terms. Business capital spending on plant and equipment was foreseen to continue to be a source of relative strength in an otherwise weak economy, but it would not match the growth rate in 1979. Finally, no net inventory accumulation was expected in 1980, as stock/sales ratios were brought back into line following the inventory build up during 1979.

The weak outlook for overall economic activity in 1980 implied that the rapid growth in employment, which took place in 1978 and 1979, would wind down. Employment growth was expected to slow to 2 per cent from 4 per cent in 1979, while the unemployment rate would rise throughout 1980 to average about 7.8 per cent for the year compared to 7.5 per cent in 1979. By the end of 1980, the unemployment rate was expected to exceed 8 per cent once again.

For 1981 there are few obvious sources of strength evident in the economy, and hence a strong cyclical recovery seems unlikely. Much will depend on the performance of the US economy as the most likely prospect for recovery would be export-led growth. Apart from that possibility the most probable engine of growth in the Canadian economy is energy investment. However, there may well be a protracted period of weakness before the Canadian economy returns to a strong growth path.

CHARLES A. BARRETT

Natural Wealth

Agriculture

Farm Income, Expenses and Investment

Although farming takes place in every province, 79 per cent of Canada's farmland is in the Prairies and in 1979, 55 per cent of all farm income was earned in the Prairie provinces. In 1979, total net farm income was approximately $4,105 million, or on a regional basis, $124 million in British Columbia, $2,250 million in the Prairie provinces, $1,044 million in Ontario, $562 million in Quebec and $124 million in the Maritime provinces.

Cash receipts from the sale of crops reached $5.9 billion in 1979 and represented about 42 per cent of total farm cash receipts. Wheat continues to be the crop with the most economic value in Canada as cash returns from wheat and Wheat Board payments reached an estimated $2.4 billion in 1979.

Seventy-nine per cent of Canada's farmland is in the Prairies.

Harvesting cucumbers in Ontario.

On the expense side, depreciation charges continued to be the largest single farm expense, closely followed by feed and interest expenses with fertilizer, petroleum products, machinery repairs and parts, and wages to hired farm labour representing the other more significant farm expenses.

While the number of farms is slowly decreasing, increasing average farm size and mechanization have raised capital investment in farming from $24 billion in 1971 to more than $84 billion in 1979. The average total capital value per farm in 1979 was $256,316 of which $190,222 was invested in land and buildings, $38,951 in machinery and equipment and $27,143 in livestock and poultry.

Field Crops

The major grains and oilseeds occupied approximately 22 348 300 ha (hectares) in 1979 or approximately 50 per cent of the total improved farmland in Canada.

Of the major field crops, wheat is dominant in terms of the area it occupies and in terms of the volume and value of grain and product exports. Spring wheat contributes significantly to the economy of Western Canada and in 1979 was grown on approximately 10 199 000 ha of the Prairie provinces. Ontario generally produces most of the winter wheat, but in 1978 Ontario production was surpassed by that of Alberta. The production of feed grains, particularly oats and barley in the Prairie provinces and corn in Ontario, is essential to the Canadian livestock industry. The importance of oats in Western Canada, however, has declined over the years with the 1 335 000 ha sown to oats in the Prairie provinces in 1979 at a record low. Field crop production tends to be more diversified outside the Prairie provinces with increased emphasis on dairy and livestock production resulting in a larger

Table 1. Area and production of the major Canadian field crops, 1978 and 1979

Item	Area		Production	
	1978	1979	1978	1979
	'000 hectares	'000 hectares	'000 tonnes	'000 tonnes
Winter wheat	298.0	311.0	809.4	909.2
Spring wheat.............	8 809.0	9 056.9	17 483.7	15 037.7
Durum wheat	1 477.0	1 133.0	2 852.2	1 798.9
All wheat................	10 584.0	10 500.9	21 145.3	17 745.8
Oats for grain	1 828.9	1 541.1	3 620.5	2 977.9
Barley for grain...........	4 258.6	3 724.3	10 387.4	8 460.1
All rye	318.1	330.0	605.4	524.7
Flaxseed.................	526.0	927.0	571.5	835.7
Rapeseed	2 825.0	3 439.0	3 497.1	3 560.7
Corn for grain	783.0	891.0	4 032.5	4 963.3
Soybeans	285.0	283.0	515.6	671.7
Mustard seed.............	98.0	62.0	103.3	53.3
Sunflower seed...........	91.5	164.0	120.2	220.9
Tame hay................	5 607.0	5 514.0	26 911.7	26 461.2
Fodder corn..............	496.0	486.0	14 135.9	14 467.6

proportion of land devoted to forage crops, pasture and feed grains. In Ontario, grain corn is an important crop for livestock feed as well as for industrial uses; in 1979 production amounted to 4 298 100 t (tonnes), over 85 per cent of the Canadian total. Quebec produced 457 100 t of grain corn and 3 528 700 t of fodder corn in 1979.

The oilseeds — rapeseed, flaxseed, soybeans and sunflower seed — have become a major component in Canadian field crop production. Rapeseed in particular has become an important agricultural export. Domestically, the oilseed crops are processed to produce vegetable oils for human consumption or industrial use and high protein meal for livestock feed. Production of rapeseed, flaxseed and sunflower seed is concentrated in the Prairie provinces, while soybean production is located in Ontario. In 1979, the area seeded to these crops increased dramatically over 1978 in response to higher prices and good market prospects. Rapeseed is Canada's third most extensively sown annual crop and the 1979 area of 3 439 000 ha was a record high. In 1979 there were 927 000 ha planted to flaxseed, 283 000 ha to soybeans and 164 000 ha to sunflower seed.

Tobacco is a field crop with a relatively high cash value. Most of Canada's tobacco production is concentrated in southern Ontario, although some occurs in Quebec and the Maritime provinces.

Horticultural Crops

Fruit and vegetable production comprises a major part of Canadian agriculture. There are over 30 fruit and vegetable crops grown commercially in Canada which together account for an annual farm value in excess of $460 million. The apple

Fruit and vegetable production comprises a major part of Canadian agriculture.

continues to be the most important fruit grown in Canada. Two popular varieties are the McIntosh and the Delicious, representing 42 per cent and 25 per cent respectively of the total production. Apple orchards are located throughout Eastern Canada and British Columbia. The production of peaches, cherries and grapes is limited to the Niagara region of southern Ontario and the Okanagan Valley in British Columbia. In recent years the cultivation of berry crops — strawberries, blueberries and raspberries — has gradually increased. Commercial plantings of berry fruits are found in the Maritimes, Quebec, Ontario and British Columbia.

In 1978, the farm value of potatoes at $178 million accounted for 63 per cent of all farm income derived from the sale of vegetables, making the potato the most important vegetable grown in Canada. The Maritime provinces are recognized as the major growing region in the country. The production of potatoes in 1978 amounted to 2 495 000 t.

The Canadian mushroom industry is expanding. Domestic production in 1978 was 20.6 million kg (kilograms) and with recent changes in tariff rates and increased investment, production is expected to continue to increase for the next few years.

The food processing industry in Canada requires considerable quantities of fruits and vegetables mainly for canning and freezing. Peas, corn, beans and tomatoes are the main vegetables processed while apples, grapes and berry crops are the main fruits. Many of the processed commodities are grown under contract to processors; however, the proportion of items grown under this system is decreasing.

In 1978 there were 1,575 greenhouses across Canada producing floricultural products and vegetables. Despite increasing input costs and continued high levels of imported products, greenhouse sales reached a record $181.4 million. Roses, chrysanthemums and carnations continued to be the cut flowers most demanded by Canadians. Sales by the 539 Canadian nurseries reached a record high of $150.9 million in 1978. Nurserymen in Ontario, consistently the largest producing province, operated 56.1 per cent of the country's 22 572 ha of land used for nursery purposes.

Approximately 70 per cent of the world's maple syrup is produced in the four Canadian provinces of Quebec, Ontario, Nova Scotia and New Brunswick. Quebec, especially the Eastern Townships and the Beauce region, has the best maple forests in the world as the climate is advantageous for tree development. In recent years plastic tubing and vacuum pumps have replaced the traditional bucket system of sap collection on about 25 per cent of all the tappings made in Canada. Although the

There are over 1,500 greenhouses across Canada.

Commercial daffodil growing at Bradner, BC.

new system requires a large initial equipment investment it is more efficient, more hygienic and requires less costly manpower than the bucket system and increases yields without affecting tree growth. The maple sap collected is used to make a variety of products including syrup, sugar, taffy and butter. Canada exports large volumes of these products, especially to the United States.

Canada, with 30 585 t of honey in 1978, ranks among the world's top 10 honey-producing nations. Honey is produced commercially in all provinces except Newfoundland although the bulk of the crop comes from the three Prairie provinces. The number of beekeepers continues to increase to meet consumers' demands for over 0.9 kg of honey per person annually.

Livestock

On January 1, 1980, total cattle and calves on farms in Canada, (excluding Newfoundland which had 6,300 cattle and calves at July 1, 1979) were estimated at 12,403,000, up 1 per cent from 12,328,000 on January 1, 1979. This was the first sign of an increase in the cattle population since it peaked in 1975. Inspected slaughter of cattle in 1979 dropped to 2,954,317 head, down 14 per cent from 1978, while calf slaughter was 324,890 in 1979, down 34 per cent. The average warm weight per

Spring cattle drive in the Porcupine Hills of southern Alberta.

Table 2. Estimated meat production and disappearance, 1978 and 1979

Animal	Year	Animals slaughtered[1] No.	Production t	Imports[2] t	Exports[2] t	Domestic disappearance t
Beef.	1978	3,987,900	1 022 795	97 565	44 609	1 075 092
	1979	3,431,500	917 243	83 193	52 035	948 017
Veal	1978	736,100	37 338	4 747	399	41 474
	1979	518,000	28 763	4 104	527	32 880
Pork	1978	10,026,600	619 600	54 345	56 592	615 382
	1979	12,216,000	749 904	33 535	79 673	703 850
Mutton & Lamb. .	1978	221,100	4 284	16 572	62	19 848
	1979	211,700	4 188	21 293	270	25 003
Offal.	1978	. . .	61 830	5 299	39 659	28 471
	1979	. . .	61 126	6 261	47 335	19 932

[1] Includes federally inspected, other commercial, and farm slaughter.
[2] Sources: External Trade Division, Statistics Canada.
. . . Not applicable.

carcass of cattle slaughtered was 273.5 kg in 1979, up from 262.3 kg in 1978. The weighted average price per 100 kg of A1 and A2 steers weighing 453.6 kg and over at Toronto was $176.88 in 1979 compared to $136.84 in 1978. Cattle exports to United States for slaughter in 1979 were 199,286 head, down 28 per cent from 275,733 head in 1978. The same trend occurred in imports from United States which were 19,142 head in 1979, a significant decrease from the 1978 figure of 47,541.

On January 1, 1980, there were 9,096,000 pigs in Canada (excluding Newfoundland which had 16,200 pigs at July 1, 1979) an increase of 14 per cent from January 1, 1979. This increase is a continuation of the upward part of the cycle which commenced in the latter half of 1975. Federally inspected slaughter of pigs in 1979 was 11,030,840 head, up 23 per cent from the 1978 slaughter of 8,934,470. Average warm weight per carcass in 1979 was 77.1 kg virtually the same as 1978, which was 77.2 kg. The increased slaughter caused the average weighted price at Toronto for Index 100 pigs to drop from $153.88 per 100 kg in 1978 to $141.43 in 1979. Imports of pork in 1979 were 33 535 000 kg down 38 per cent from 1978, while exports were 79 673 000 kg up 41 per cent from 1978.

Sheep numbers showed a substantial increase from an estimated 430,000 head on January 1, 1979 to a January 1, 1980 estimate of 480,800, an increase of 12 per cent.

Farm near Wainwright, Alta.

The 1979 estimate was the first increase in sheep numbers since 1957. Newfoundland which was not included at January 1, 1980 had 10,700 sheep and lambs at July 1, 1979. Federally inspected slaughter of sheep and lambs in 1979 was 92,825, down 5 per cent from 1978. This caused the price at Toronto for lambs weighing 36.3 kg and over to increase to $191.84 per 100 kg in 1979, compared to $174.45 in 1978. Imports of sheep and lambs in 1979 were 17,667 head, down 39 per cent from 1978, and imports of mutton and lamb were 21 293 000 kg in 1979, up 28 per cent from the previous year.

Table 3. Inventory of selected classes of livestock on farms in Canada, Jan. 1, 1974-80[1]
(thousands)

Year	Total cattle	Milk cows and heifers[2]	Beef cows and heifers[2]	Total pigs	Total sheep
1974 .., ...	13,481.0	2,546.4	5,333.9	6,972.0	529.4
1975	14,278.0	2,560.6	5,691.5	6,030.5	497.1
1976	14,048.0	2,541.4	5,576.7	5,692.1	458.3
1977	13,709.5	2,455.1	5,467.0	6,154.5	410.1
1978	12,869.5	2,410.3	5,019.3	6,652.8	388.9
1979	12,328.0	2,334.4	4,827.7	8,009.0	430.0
1980	12,403.0	2,350.2	4,849.6	9,096.0	480.8

[1] Excluding Newfoundland.
[2] One year of age and older.

Table 4. Milk and cream sold off farms, by region, 1978 and 1979
(kilolitres)

Region	Year	Farm sales of milk and cream			
		Fluid purposes	Sold for industrial purposes		Total farm sales
			Delivered as milk	Delivered[1] as cream	
Maritimes	1978	184 884	135 501	27 537	347 922
	1979	191 956	147 219	27 186	366 361
Quebec and Ontario.....	1978	1 563 345	3 449 468	104 706	5 117 519
	1979	1 589 909	3 421 709	93 731	5 105 349
Prairies................	1978	431 674	385 438	167 901	985 013
	1979	458 111	381 718	140 868	980 697
British Columbia	1978	281 305	130 768	1 420	413 493
	1979	294 836	141 180	1 318	437 334
Total, Canada	1978	2 461 208	4 101 175	301 564	6 863 947
	1979	2 534 812	4 091 826	263 103	6 889 741

[1] Farm separated cream expressed as milk equivalent.

Dairying

During 1979, 6 889 741 kL (kilolitres) of milk were sold off farms, with Ontario and Quebec accounting for 74 per cent of the total. Thirty-seven per cent of this milk was used for fluid purposes with the remaining 63 per cent used for manufacturing purposes. Farm value of milk sold off farms in 1979, including supplementary payments, was $1,978,340,000, 11 per cent greater than in 1978. The number of farms reporting dairy cows in the 1976 Census was 96,900, compared with 145,300 in 1971. Of these farms 91,300 had incomes of over $1,200 in 1976, compared with 129,800 farms in 1971.

Poultry and Eggs

A high degree of specialization and concentration has been developing recently in the production of poultry and eggs, particularly in the egg, broiler chicken and turkey industries. The producers of eggs, turkeys and broiler chickens operate within the constraints of supply-management programs directed by provincial producer marketing boards. The activities of egg producers and turkey producers at the provincial level are co-ordinated by national agencies (the Canadian Egg Marketing Agency and the Canadian Turkey Marketing Agency, respectively), which operate under federal government charters.

Turkey farm at Beiseker, Alta.

Harvesting celery, tomatoes and onions.

In recent years consumers have substituted poultry and pork for beef.

Furs

Fur statistics have been collected and published annually since 1920. The value of wildlife pelts in 1978-79 was $81,747,855 or 65 per cent of total pelts; the value of fur farm pelts increased from $25,544,687 to $43,539,362 for the 1978-79 season.

Per Capita Food Consumption

Total apparent Canadian consumption of fruits remained stable in 1978 at 102.1 kg per person. The largest increase occurred in juice disappearance which increased by 2.1 kg from 1977 mainly due to large imports of citrus juices. Tomatoes, citrus fruits and apples continued to be Canadians' favourite fruits.

An increase of several kilograms per person was experienced in apparent vegetable consumption in 1978. The major contributors to the increase were carrots, cabbage and green and wax beans due to increased domestic production of these crops. A good harvest of white potatoes as well as high opening inventories boosted potato disappearance 3.6 kg to 74.9 kg in 1978 despite increases in the quantities moving to processors.

Consumers substituted poultry and pork for beef in 1978 as Canada moved on the down side of the beef cycle and less cattle were slaughtered. Beef disappearance at 45.6 kg was at its lowest level since 1974. The continued expansion of the hog industry helped to maintain pork supplies.

The increase of 2.4 L in fluid partly skimmed milk disappearance in 1978 was offset slightly by a decrease in the apparent consumption of whole milk. Disappearance of fluid skim milk and chocolate drink increased marginally. Fluid partly skimmed milk exhibited the largest apparent consumption.

Cheese disappearance increased again in 1978. The increase was attributed to increased demand for process and specialty cheeses. Apparent consumption of cheddar cheese continued to decline to 1.3 kg, the lowest level since 1966.

Disappearance of coffee increased in 1978 after low levels due to the poor Brazilian crop and high prices in 1977. Tea disappearance decreased slightly as consumers substituted coffee for tea. Apparent consumption of cocoa also declined slightly due mainly to low opening inventories.

Shipping in Vancouver, BC. Canada's forests are among our greatest renewable resources. One in 10 jobs in Canada depends on this resource.

Forestry

Canada's forests are among our greatest renewable resources. Stretching across the continent in an unbroken belt 500 to 2 100 km wide, they provide raw material for the great lumber, pulp and paper, plywood and other wood-using industries so vital to the country's economy. One in 10 jobs in Canada depends on this resource, which also accounted for over $10,448 million in the 1979 balance of trade for wood, wood products and paper. In addition, the forests of Canada control water run off and prevent erosion, shelter and sustain wildlife and offer unmatched opportunities for human recreation and enjoyment.

Forest land — that available for producing usable timber — covers more than 1 635 000 km² (square kilometres). The total volume of wood on these lands is estimated at 17 230 million m³ (cubic metres), of which four-fifths is coniferous and one-fifth deciduous.

Seventy-five per cent of Canada's productive forest area is known as the boreal forest; it stretches in a broad belt from the Atlantic Coast westward and then northwest to Alaska. The forests of this region are predominantly coniferous, with spruce, balsam fir and pine the most common species. Many deciduous trees are also found in the boreal forest; poplar and white birch are the most widespread.

The Great Lakes–St. Lawrence and Acadian regions are south of the boreal region. Here the forests are mixed and many species are represented. Principal conifers are eastern white and red pine, eastern hemlock, spruce, eastern white cedar and fir; the main deciduous trees are yellow birch, maple, oak and basswood.

Entirely different in character is the coastal region of British Columbia. Here the forests are coniferous and, because of a mild, humid climate and heavy rainfall, very large trees are common — 60 m (metres) tall and more than 2 m in diameter. This region contains less than 2 per cent of the country's forest area, but supplies almost one-quarter of the wood cut. Species are western red cedar, hemlock, spruce, fir and Douglas fir.

The coniferous forests of the mountainous regions of Alberta and the British Columbia interior are mixed; distribution and characteristics of species depend on local climate, which ranges from dry to very humid. Production in this area has expanded rapidly in recent years, with the establishment of many new pulp mills.

The only true deciduous forests in Canada occupy a relatively small area in the southernmost part of Ontario, which is predominantly an agricultural district.

A tractor-loader piling wood chips for processing at the pulp and paper plant in The Pas, Man.

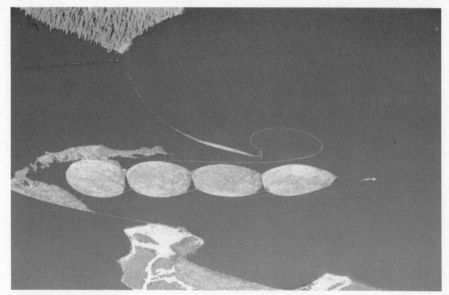
Logs in transit in Quebec.

Ownership and Administration of Forests

Ninety per cent of Canada's productive forest land is publicly owned. Under the British North America Act, the various provincial governments were given the exclusive right to enact laws regarding management and sale of public lands within their boundaries, including the timber and wood on those lands. In the northern territories, which contain only about 5 per cent of the country's productive forest land, the forests are administered by the federal government.

For many years the policy of both federal and provincial governments has been to retain in public ownership lands not required for agricultural purposes. In some of the older settled areas of Canada, however, a high proportion of land is privately owned, especially in the three Maritime provinces, where nearly 64 per cent of the productive forest area is owned by individuals and companies. Thus, the administration and protection of most of Canada's productive forest area is vested in the various provincial governments, which make the forests available to private industry through long-term leasing and other arrangements.

Forest Industries

The forest industries group includes logging, the primary wood and paper manufacturing industries, which use roundwood as their chief raw material, and the secondary wood and paper industries, which use lumber, wood pulp and basic paper as raw materials to be converted into numerous wood and paper products. This group of industries accounted for approximately 18.1 per cent of all Canadian exports in 1978, up from 17.8 per cent in 1977 mainly because of large increases in the quantity and value of wood and paper products exported to the United States.

Table 5. Principal statistics of the pulp and paper industry, 1975-78

Item		1975	1976	1977	1978
Establishments	No.	147	147	145	144
Employees	No.	84,046	86,995	84,533	85,601
Salaries and wages	$'000	1,091,675	1,415,843	1,541,355	1,696,769
Value of shipments of goods of own manufacture	$'000	5,122,093	5,992,723	6,636,533	7,648,960
Value added — manufacturing activity	$'000	2,569,650	2,845,278	3,056,481	3,503,545
Pulp shipped	'000 t	5 649	6 768	7 066	8 021
	$'000	1,982,617	2,254,714	2,270,938	2,461,919
Paper and paperboard shipped	'000 t	9 891	11 341	11 880	13 167
	$'000	2,861,471	3,383,315	3,964,571	4,729,638
Newsprint exported	'000 t	6 348	6 997	7 266	7 868
	$'000	1,741,990	1,997,371	2,381,265	2,886,214

Logging. Production consisting of sawlogs, veneer logs, pulpwood, poles and other roundwood products increased from 145 262 000 m³ in 1977 to 156 745 000 m³ in 1978. Sawlog production increased from 103 707 000 m³ in 1977 to 112 386 000 m³ in 1978, during this same period there was an increase in pulpwood production east of the Rockies from 36 732 000 m³ to 38 832 000 m³. British Columbia showed a substantial increase in overall production, up from 69 971 000 m³ in 1977 to 75 164 000 m³ in 1978.

Mechanized harvesting equipment in Canada's forests.

Reforestation in Canada. The total area burned in forest fires in Canada during August 1980 was 240 686 hectares.

The value of exports of roundwood decreased about 9 per cent, from $71 million in 1977 to $67 million in 1978. Exports of sawlogs, logs and bolts were down by 28 per cent in quantity and 18 per cent in value in 1978.

The value of shipments by the logging industry in 1978 was $4,046 million, up from $3,498 million in the previous year as a result of both increased unit values and increased quantities shipped.

In 1978, 45,944 people were employed in logging, an increase of about 10 per cent from 1977; wages in 1978 were $808 million, compared to $693 million in 1977.

Sawmills and Planing Mills. This industry is particularly dependent upon the general economic condition of the country and the state of foreign markets, particularly the market in the US. Because of substantial strength in residential construction in Canada and particularly in the US, the lumber market grew steadily throughout 1977 and 1978. Lumber production in Canada increased 7.8 per cent from 41 633 thousand m³ in 1977 to 44 887 thousand m³ in 1978. Exports of Canadian lumber rose 9.1 per cent from 29 059 thousand m³ in 1977 to 31 713 thousand m³ in 1978. The long-term trend toward increased size of individual sawmills and more complete automation is continuing, particularly in the interior of British Columbia, where the sawmill industry is becoming more and more integrated with the pulp and paper industry.

Pulp and Paper. The manufacture of pulp and paper is the second leading industry in Canada in terms of value of shipments, however, it still ranks first in employment, in salaries and wages paid and in value added by manufacture. The manufacturing value added by this one industry in 1978 accounted for 1.5 per cent of Canada's total GNP and it contributed 10.9 per cent to the total value of domestic exports in 1978 (11.4 per cent in 1977). Canada is the second largest producer of wood pulp in the world (20 152 457 t in 1978), after the US (46 000 000 t), and the

Loading pulp in Quebec.

largest exporter. It is by far the largest producer of newsprint (8 739 405 t in 1978, which is close to 33 per cent of the world total).

Although the pulp and paper industry is engaged primarily in the manufacture of wood pulps and basic papers and paperboard, it also produces converted papers and paperboards and even chemicals, alcohol and other byproducts. Approximately 60 per cent of the wood pulp manufactured in 1978 was converted in Canada to other products, particularly newsprint. Ninety per cent of the rest was exported.

Quebec had the largest share of Canada's pulp and paper industry and accounted for 33 per cent of the total value of production in 1978. It was followed by British Columbia, with 27 per cent, and Ontario, with 20 per cent.

Paper-converting Industries. These include asphalt roofing manufacturers, paper box and bag manufacturers and other paper converters. In 1978 this group had 555 establishments (502 in 1977), employed 41,182 persons (39,930 in 1977) and paid $585,000,000 in salaries and wages ($538,000,000 in 1977); the value of factory shipments set a new record of $2,548,325,000 ($2,301,149,000 in 1977). In contrast to the basic pulp and paper industry the paper-converting industries are dependent primarily on the domestic market.

Other Wood Industries. This group includes the shingle mills, veneer and plywood mills and particleboard plants that, like the sawmills and pulp and paper mills, are primary wood industries. It also includes the secondary wood industries that further manufacture lumber, plywood and particleboard into flooring, doors, sashes, laminated structures, prefabricated buildings, boxes, barrels, caskets and woodenware. In 1978 the veneer and plywood industry, the single most important of this group, accounted for $844,457,000 in shipments of goods of own manufacture, an increase of 30.6 per cent over the 1977 shipments of $646,779,000.

Split and salted cod drying in the sun and wind at Dildo, Nfld.

Squid are left to dry on lines on Fogo Island, Nfld. Dried squid are exported to Japan.

Fisheries

Canada's fish harvest in 1979 continued the upward trend of recent years, reinforcing the promise of a resurgence of the nation's oldest primary industry.

Total landings in Canada in 1979 amounted to 1 402 414 t, compared to 1 375 000 t in 1978. Landed value of the catch totalled $858 million, up $167 million from the previous year.

Cape Breton Island, NS.

The value of Canadian exports of fishery products continued to rise, with the 1979 total valued at $1.32 billion, up by $189 million over 1978. Following the trend of previous years, some 49 per cent of Canadian exports went to the US and 25 per cent to European countries.

Tuna fishing near Prince Edward Island.

The Arctic Harvester *fishing boat, owned and operated by the Sechelt Indian band, having completed an eight-day fishing trip, returned to British Columbia with 235 tonnes of fish in its hold.*

Canada continued to play a major role at the United Nations (UN) Law of the Sea negotiations, seeking support of changes in international sea law. On January 1, 1977, the government officially extended Canadian fishing jurisdiction to 200 miles off both east and west coasts. Landings on the Atlantic Coast in 1979 totalled 1 171 100 t, up 18 000 t from the previous year. The 1979 landed value of the Atlantic catch was $476.5 million up $60 million over 1978 values. A significant increase in the value of herring catches was a contributing factor in the substantial increase in landed values on the Pacific Coast. The 1979 total of 171 300 t, up 72 000 t from the previous year, meant a $94.5 million increase in landed value for Pacific Coast fishermen, for a total of $346.6 million. The market value of all Canadian fisheries products in 1979 was an estimated $1,642 million, an increase of approximately $85 million over 1978.

The number of commercial fishermen in Canada was approximately 73,500, of which some 67 per cent were located on the Atlantic Coast and 23 per cent on the Pacific Coast; the remainder were engaged in the inland fisheries. The size of the fishing fleet operating in the sea fisheries was approximately 38,000 vessels.

Minerals and Energy

Minerals

The value of production of Canadian minerals increased to $26,098 million in 1979, from $20,261 million in 1978 and $18,473 million in 1977. Metallic minerals accounted for 31 per cent of the value of Canadian mineral production in 1979. In order of importance, the principal metallic minerals produced in Canada were iron ore, copper, zinc, nickel, uranium, gold, silver and lead. Headed by crude oil and natural gas, mineral fuels accounted for 56 per cent of the total value of production. Non-metallic minerals and structural materials accounted for 14 per cent. The main structural materials were cement, sand and gravel, and stone; the non-metallic minerals group was dominated by potash, followed by asbestos. The leading mineral commodity in 1979 was crude oil, with a production value of $7,611 million, up from $5,811 million in 1978 and $423 million in 1960.

Nickel production in Canada in 1979 amounted to 131 579 t valued at $826 million, an increase from 128 310 t valued at $635 million in 1978. Most of Canada's nickel was mined in the Sudbury, Ont. region by INCO Limited and Falconbridge Nickel Mines Limited.

Copper production in 1979 amounted to 643 754 t, valued at $1,515 million; the figures for 1978 were 659 380 t and $1,084 million. The major producing provinces were British Columbia (286 509 t), Ontario (184 888 t) and Quebec (80 663 t).

A gas processing plant at Carstairs, Alta. Natural gas must be conditioned before it can be sent to market.

The Wapiti gas plant in the Deep Basin in western Alberta went officially onstream in November 1979.

Iron ore production in 1979 amounted to 60 185 000 t worth $1,889 million; in 1978 it was 42 930 803 t worth $1,222 million. Zinc production was 1 148 498 t, valued at $1,107 million in 1979; in 1978, 1 066 902 t worth $818 million were produced.

Asbestos production in 1979 was 1 501 000 t, valued at about $641 million. Eighty-nine per cent of the asbestos produced in Canada came from the province of Quebec; the rest came from British Columbia and Newfoundland. Canada produces over 25 per cent of the world's total supply of asbestos and is the world's second leading producer.

Cement was the most important structural material produced in Canada, with about two-thirds of the production coming from Ontario and Quebec.

Among the minerals of previously lesser importance whose production has increased significantly in the past few years are potash, molybdenum and coal.

Table 6. Mineral production, by class, 1967-79
(million dollars)

Year	Metals	Non-metals	Fossil fuels	Structural materials	Total
1967	2,285	406	1,234	455	4,380
1968	2,493	447	1,343	440	4,722
1969	2,378	450	1,465	443	4,736
1970	3,073	481	1,718	450	5,722
1971	2,940	501	2,014	507	5,963
1972	2,956	513	2,368	571	6,408
1973	3,850	615	3,227	678	8,370
1974	4,821	896	5,202	835	11,753
1975	4,795	939	6,653	959	13,347
1976[r]	5,315	1,162	8,109	1,107	15,693
1977[r]	5,988	1,362	9,873	1,249	18,473
1978	5,698	1,478	11,578	1,508	20,261
1979	8,000	1,833	14,529	1,737	26,098

[r] Revised figures.
Figures may not add to totals owing to rounding.

Table 7. Mineral production, by province, 1977-79

Province or territory	1977[r]		1978		1979[1]	
	Value $'000	%	Value $'000	%	Value $'000	%
Newfoundland	867,146	4.7	675,028	3.3	1,100,152	4.2
Prince Edward Island. . .	1,863	- -	2,068	- -	2,200	- -
Nova Scotia	159,426	0.9	210,659	1.0	208,718	0.8
New Brunswick	289,393	1.6	339,610	1.7	529,926	2.0
Quebec.	1,674,927	9.1	1,796,050	8.9	2,247,850	8.6
Ontario.	2,980,082	16.1	2,697,852	13.3	3,271,369	12.5
Manitoba	563,733	3.1	459,636	2.3	585,438	2.2
Saskatchewan.	1,207,562	6.5	1,581,850	7.8	1,814,743	7.0
Alberta.	8,576,327	46.4	10,087,206	49.8	12,884,740	49.4
British Columbia	1,686,511	9.1	1,882,652	9.3	2,741,467	10.5
Yukon.	209,898	1.1	218,804	1.1	299,564	1.2
Northwest Territories . .	255,659	1.4	309,639	1.5	412,100	1.6
Total.	18,472,528	100.0	20,261,053	100.0	26,098,267	100.0

[r] Revised figures.
[1] Preliminary estimates.
- - Figures too small to be expressed.
Figures may not add to totals owing to rounding.

The value of Canadian potash production increased from less than $1 million in 1960 to $695 million in 1979, as a number of mines were opened in Saskatchewan between 1962 and 1970. About 95 per cent of the world's potash is used as fertilizer.

A natural gas treatment plant at Taylor Flats, BC.

Canada is second only to the US among the producers of molybdenum. The value of production increased from $1 million in 1960 to $330 million in 1979, with over 90 per cent of the Canadian production coming from British Columbia.

Elemental sulphur production increased from 5 752 000 t in 1978 to 6 718 000 t in 1979 and its value increased to $145 million from $101 million. Natural gas is the major source of elemental sulphur in Canada, so its production is in direct proportion to natural gas production regardless of the price of sulphur. Nearly all sulphur is transformed into sulphuric acid, of which one-half is used in the manufacture of fertilizers.

Although gold production decreased to 49 175 kg in 1979 from 53 967 kg in the previous year, its value increased to $543 million from $382 million in 1978 because of increases in world prices.

Petroleum and Natural Gas

Awareness of the energy sector as a key determinant of economic well-being has obviously increased with the constantly rising prices of energy products. Of the industrialized countries, Canada is fortunately endowed with significant reserves of most forms of energy, although the proven reserves of hydrocarbon energy now represent relatively few years of oil and gas production.

In 1979 the petroleum industry extracted about $13,671 million worth of hydrocarbon products, an increase of 26.6 per cent over 1978. The increase in value is primarily the result of price increases as the volume of crude production increased 17.0 per cent to 89 320 000 m³ (cubic metres) while natural gas production increased 6.2 per cent to 94 116 000 000 m³. Natural gas liquids production increased 18.2 per cent to 19 290 000 m³.

Table 8. Mineral production, by kind, 1977-79

Mineral	Unit	1977r	1978	1979[1]
		'000	'000	'000
Metallics				
Antimony	kg	..	..	..
Bismuth	kg	165	145	112
Cadmium	kg	1 185	1 151	1 256
Calcium	kg	491	575	477
Cobalt	kg	1 485	1 234	1 381
Columbium (Cb₂O₅)	kg	2 509	2 473	2 406
Copper	kg	759 423	659 380	643 754
Gold	kg	54	54	49
Indium	kg	1	4	..
Iron ore	t	53 621	42 931	60 185
Iron, remelt	t	..	..	..
Lead	kg	280 955	319 809	315 751
Magnesium	kg	7 633	8 309	9 172
Molybdenum	kg	16 568	13 943	11 187
Nickel	kg	232 512	128 310	131 579
Platinum group	kg	14	11	6
Selenium	kg	161	122	107
Silver	kg	1 314	1 267	1 184
Tantalum (Ta₂O₅)	kg	..	..	..
Tellurium	kg	35	31	33
Tin	kg	328	360	362
Tungsten (WO₃)	kg	2 284	2 886	..
Uranium (U₃O₈)	kg	6 824	8 211	6 956
Zinc	kg	1 070 515	1 066 902	1 148 498
Non-metallics				
Asbestos	t	1 517	1 422	1 501
Barite	t	..	..	..
Fluorspar	t	..	—	—
Gemstones	kg	..	..	..
Gypsum	t	7 234	8 074	8 105
Magnesitic dolomite and brucite	t	..	..	..
Nepheline syenite	t	575	599	617
Nitrogen	m³	..	..	..
Peat	t	386	435	409
Potash (K₂O)	t	5 764	6 344	7 046
Pyrite, pyrrhotite	t	24	9	31
Quartz	t	2 317	2 165	2 246
Salt	t	6 039	6 452	6 672
Soapstone, talc, pyrophyllite	t	72	62	88
Sodium sulphate	t	395	377	452
Sulphur in smelter gas	t	736	676	605
Sulphur, elemental	t	5 207	5 752	6 718
Titanium dioxide, etc.	t	..	..	..
Mineral fuels				
Coal	t	28 520	30 477	33 019
Natural gas	m³	91 517 960	88 610 000	94 116 000
Natural gas by-products	m³	16 703	16 313	19 290
Petroleum, crude	m³	76 579	76 348	89 320

Table 8. Mineral production, by kind, 1977-79 (concluded)

Mineral	Unit	1977[r]	1978	1979[1]
		'000	'000	'000
Structural materials				
Clay products (bricks, tile, etc.).		..	..	..
Cement	t	9 640	10 558	11 835
Lime.	t	1 900	2 034	2 092
Sand and gravel	t	262 905	272 092	275 127
Stone	t	120 163	122 144	114 989

[r] Revised figures.
[1] Preliminary estimates.
.. Not available.

Oil refineries at Oakville, Ont.

Gold miners waiting to go underground at Yellowknife, NWT.

Domestic sales of refined petroleum products were 102 460 000 m³ in 1979 including 38 285 000 m³ of motor gasoline, 30 715 000 m³ of middle distillates, 15 932 000 m³ of heavy fuel oils and 17 528 000 m³ of other products.

To develop new reserves as production depletes present supplies, $3,917 million of capital expenditures were undertaken in 1978. Seventy-two per cent of this expenditure was in Alberta, a reflection of industry's increasing activity in frontier areas. Alberta accounted for 90 per cent of the value of crude oil, natural gas and natural gas byproducts produced. In addition to conventional reserves Canada possesses significant volumes of bituminous tar sands. According to one estimate the ultimate recoverable reserves of synthetic crude oil from all Alberta's bituminous deposits amounts to 40 000 000 000 m³ of which 4 200 000 000 m³ is considered recoverable by methods similar to those now in use at the two plants operating near Fort McMurray. Other techniques will be needed to recover the remainder of the resource.

The Gulftide drilling rig was used in the discovery of a new gas field off the east coast of Sable Island, NS. On a jack-up rig, the legs of the structure actually set on the ocean floor and the platform is raised above the surface of the water.

Table 9. Production of coal, by province, 1977-79

Province	Type of coal	1977	1978	1979
			Tonnes '000	
Nova Scotia	Bituminous	2 165	2 650	2 157
New Brunswick	Bituminous	277	315	310
Saskatchewan.	Lignite	5 479	5 058	5 013
Alberta.	Sub-bituminous	7 725	8 278	9 575
	Bituminous	4 289	5 115	5 349
	Total Alberta	12 014	13 393	14 924
British Columbia	Bituminous	8 585	9 061	10 616
Total.		28 520	30 477	33 019

Open-pit coal mining in south eastern British Columbia. After the coal is mined, these areas are re-seeded with grass and trees are planted. Coal is exported to Japan.

Coal

Production of coal in Canada increased from 30 476 846 t in 1978 to 33 018 960 t in 1979. The preliminary value of coal production in 1979 increased to $858 million from $780 million in 1978. Japanese steel producers, Canada's main export customers, accounted for approximately 77 per cent of all coal exports.

Electricity

Canada's total generating capacity increased from a modest 133 MW (megawatts) in 1900 to approximately 74 507 MW in 1978.

Although water power traditionally has been the main source of electrical energy in Canada, and still is, thermal sources are becoming more important and this trend is expected to continue. The choice between the development of a hydroelectric power site and the construction of a thermal generating station must take into account a number of complex considerations, the most important of which are economic. The heavy capital costs involved in constructing a hydroelectric project are offset by maintenance and operating costs considerably lower than those for a thermal plant. The long life of a hydro plant and its dependability and flexibility in meeting varying loads are added advantages. Also important is the fact that water is a renewable resource. The thermal station, on the other hand, can be located close to areas where power is needed, with a consequent saving in transmission costs; however, pollution problems at these plants are an undesirable factor.

The marked trend toward the development of thermal stations that became apparent in the 1950s can be explained to some extent by the fact that, in many parts of Canada, most of the hydroelectric sites within economic transmission distance of load centres have been developed and planners have had to turn to other sources of electrical energy. Although recent advances in extra-high voltage transmission techniques have given impetus to the development of hydroelectric sites previously considered too remote, thermal stations will probably be the more important of the two sources in the long run.

Water Power Resources and Developments. Substantial amounts of water power have been developed in all provinces except Prince Edward Island, where there are no large streams. The hydroelectric plant at Churchill Falls in Labrador, with its 5 225 MW capacity, is the largest single generating plant of any type in the world. Quebec, however, is richest in water power resources, with over 37 per cent of the total for Canada, and has the most developed capacity. Even this considerable figure will double as plans for the development of a number of rivers flowing into James Bay become a reality; this development could result ultimately in an additional 10 000 MW.

A hydroelectric dam on Lac St-Jean, Que.

Conventional Thermal Power. Prince Edward Island, Nova Scotia, New Brunswick, Ontario, Saskatchewan, Alberta and the Northwest Territories depend on thermal stations for most of their power requirements. Quebec's wealth of water power has so far limited the application of thermal power in that province to local use and the James Bay project will maintain hydro pre-eminence. Manitoba and British Columbia both have substantial amounts of thermal capacity, but current development is still of hydroelectricity.

Nuclear Thermal Power. Development of commercial electric power generation in thermal plants using the heat generated by nuclear reactors is one of Canada's major contributions to energy resource technology. This development has centred around the CANDU reactor, which uses a natural uranium fuel with a heavy water

Point Tupper heavy water plant on Cape Breton Island, NS.

moderator; heavy water as a moderator provides a high-energy yield and facilitates the handling of spent fuel. The first experimental reactor went into use in 1962 at Rolphton, Ont., with a capacity of 20 MW. Since then, four major nuclear projects have been undertaken. The first full-scale nuclear plant is situated at Douglas Point on Lake Huron; it consists of a single unit, completed in 1967, with a capacity of 220 MW. The second project is a four-unit 2 160 MW capacity plant built at Pickering, east of Toronto; its four units came on line from 1971 to 1973. Both the Douglas Point and the Pickering plants use heavy water as a coolant. The third nuclear plant is a 250 MW unit situated at Gentilly, Que.; it uses boiling light water as a coolant. The fourth plant, the 3 200 MW Bruce Station in Ontario, began generating electricity in 1978.

Power Generation and Utilization. In 1978 Canada's generating facilities produced 335 641 120 MWh (megawatt hours) of electric energy, 70 per cent in hydroelectric stations. Energy exported to the US exceeded by 19 493 292 MWh the energy imported, bringing the total available to Canadian users to 316 147 828 MWh. Average domestic and farm consumption continues to rise year by year. In 1978 it was 10 388 kWh (kilowatt hours), ranging from a low of 5 931 kWh in Prince Edward Island to a high of 13 062 kWh in Quebec. The average annual bill for domestic and farm customers was $292.07.

Hydro workers are transported by helicopter to erect transmission towers in the Revelstoke area of British Columbia.

Employment

The Labour Force

In 1979 the Canadian labour force averaged 11,207,000 persons, or 63.3 per cent of the total population 15 years of age and over (excluding inmates of institutions, full-time members of the Canadian Armed Forces, residents of the Yukon and the Northwest Territories and residents of Indian reserves); it was composed of 10,369,000 employed and 838,000 unemployed persons. Table 1 shows the growth in this labour force during the 1970-79 period. From 1970 to 1979 this growth was generated by increases in both the size of the population aged 15 and over and the

Table 1. Labour force characteristics, annual averages, 1970-79

Year	Population[1] '000	Labour force '000	Employed '000	Unemployed '000	Participation rate %	Unemployment rate %
1970	14,528	8,395	7,919	476	57.8	5.7
1971	14,872	8,639	8,104	535	58.1	6.2
1972	15,186	8,897	8,344	553	58.6	6.2
1973	15,526	9,276	8,761	515	59.7	5.5
1974	15,924	9,639	9,125	514	60.5	5.3
1975	16,323	9,974	9,284	690	61.1	6.9
1976	16,706	10,206	9,479	727	61.1	7.1
1977	17,057	10,498	9,648	850	61.5	8.1
1978	17,381	10,882	9,972	911	62.6	8.4
1979	17,691	11,207	10,369	838	63.3	7.5

[1] Persons 15 years of age and over, excluding inmates of institutions, full-time members of the Canadian Armed Forces, residents of the Yukon and the Northwest Territories and residents of Indian reserves.

participation rate. (The participation rate is the percentage of the working age population in the labour force.) The main source of growth in the overall participation rate continued to be the increase in the rate for women of all ages.

Table 2 shows an employment increase of 397,000 between 1978 and 1979. Between 1978 and 1979 persons aged 15 to 24 years accounted for 139,000 or 35 per cent of total employment growth, in contrast with their 28 per cent share of the growth between 1970 and 1978. The growth from 1978 to 1979 for those aged 25 years and over was 258,000, or 65 per cent.

Table 3 shows the distribution of unemployment by principal age and sex groups for 1970 and 1979 and the shift in the proportions of total unemployment from adult men to adult women and persons aged 15 to 24 years. Specifically, men aged 25 years

Table 2. Employment by age and sex, annual averages, 1973-79
(thousands)

Age and sex	1973	1974	1975	1976	1977	1978	1979
Total employed............	8,761	9,125	9,284	9,479	9,648	9,972	10,369
Men....................	5,678	5,870	5,903	5,965	6,031	6,148	6,347
Women.................	3,083	3,255	3,381	3,515	3,617	3,824	4,022
Employed aged 15-24.......	2,230	2,374	2,376	2,393	2,417	2,493	2,632
Men....................	1,230	1,310	1,299	1,299	1,317	1,352	1,428
Women.................	1,000	1,064	1,077	1,094	1,100	1,141	1,204
Employed aged 25+........	6,531	6,751	6,908	7,086	7,231	7,479	7,737
Men....................	4,448	4,559	4,605	4,666	4,714	4,796	4,919
Women.................	2,083	2,192	2,304	2,421	2,517	2,683	2,818

Table 3. Unemployment by age and sex and by province, annual averages, 1970 and 1979

Age and sex	No. unemployed		Province	Unemployment rate	
	1970 '000	1979 '000		1970 %	1979 %
Total unemployed	476	838	Nfld.	7.3	15.4
Men......................	312	452	PEI	- -	11.3
Women...................	164	386	NS	5.3	10.2
			NB	6.3	11.1
Unemployed aged 15-24........	214	393	Que.	7.0	9.6
Men......................	133	218	Ont.	4.4	6.5
Women...................	81	175	Man.	5.3	5.4
Unemployed aged 25+.........	262	445	Sask.	4.2	4.2
Men......................	178	234	Alta.	5.1	3.9
Women...................	84	211	BC	7.7	7.7

- - Based on too small a sample for publication.

Preparing meals at a lumber camp in northern Quebec.

Table 4. Average weekly earnings for all employees, selected industries and industrial composite[1], annual averages, 1961, 1978 and 1979

Industry and province	Average weekly earnings (dollars)			Percentage increase	
	1961	1978[2]	1979[2]	1961 to 1979[2]	1978 to 1979[2]
Industry					
Forestry..............................	79.02	326.48	360.89	356.7	10.5
Mining, incl. milling..................	95.57	376.40	419.40	338.8	11.4
Manufacturing........................	81.55	285.67	311.19	281.6	8.9
Durables............................	88.22	305.97	331.44	275.7	8.3
Non-durables........................	76.17	266.13	291.33	282.5	9.5
Construction	86.93	389.64	422.28	385.8	8.4
Transportation, communications and other utilities	82.47	313.28	341.45	314.0	9.0
Trade...............................	64.54	201.79	218.75	238.9	8.4
Finance, insurance and real estate.......	72.82	248.43	272.10	273.7	9.5
Service	57.87	180.00	193.30	234.0	7.4
Industrial composite[1]	78.24	265.37	288.25	268.4	8.6
Industrial composite by province					
Newfoundland........................	71.06	248.36	271.64	282.3	9.4
Prince Edward Island..................	54.91	196.72	209.77	282.0	6.6
Nova Scotia	63.72	223.72	245.23	284.9	9.6
New Brunswick.......................	63.62	232.89	256.49	303.2	10.1
Quebec.............................	75.67	262.82	284.37	275.8	8.2
Ontario.............................	81.30	264.04	285.57	251.3	8.2
Manitoba	73.66	239.71	259.00	251.6	8.0
Saskatchewan	74.38	250.44	275.79	271.1	10.1
Alberta	80.29	276.32	306.79	282.1	11.0
British Columbia.....................	84.99	301.26	324.14	281.4	7.6

[1] "Industrial composite" is the sum of all industries except agriculture, fishing and trapping, education and related services, health and welfare services, religious organizations, private households, and public administration and defence. All statistics are based on returns received from employers having 20 or more employees in any month of the year.

[2] Preliminary data.

Table 5. Average hourly earnings and average weekly hours for hourly-rated
wage-earners, annual averages, 1961, 1978 and 1979

Industry and province	Average hourly earnings (AHE)			Average weekly hours (AWH)			Increases in AHE		Changes in AWH	
							1961 to 1979[1]	1978 to 1979[1]	1961 to 1979[1]	1978 to 1979[1]
	1961 $	1978 $	1979[1] $	1961 No.	1978 No.	1979[1] No.	%	%	%	%
Industry										
Mining, incl. milling	2.13	8.75	9.66	41.8	40.5	41.1	353.5	10.4	−1.7	+1.5
Manufacturing	1.83	6.84	7.44	40.6	38.8	38.8	306.6	8.8	−4.4	−
Durables	2.00	7.30	7.90	40.9	39.6	39.5	295.0	8.2	−3.4	−0.3
Non-durables	1.69	6.34	6.93	40.3	37.9	38.1	310.1	9.3	−5.5	+0.5
Construction	2.06	10.28	11.04	40.9	39.0	39.4	435.9	7.4	−3.7	+1.0
Building	2.16	10.35	11.24	38.9	37.3	37.9	420.4	8.6	−2.6	+1.6
Engineering	1.90	10.18	10.68	44.8	42.1	42.6	462.1	4.9	−4.9	+1.2
Manufacturing by province[2]										
Newfoundland	1.69	6.33	6.79	40.5	37.4	37.6	301.8	7.3	−7.7	+0.5
Nova Scotia	1.58	6.03	6.65	40.3	38.1	38.3	320.9	10.3	−5.2	+0.5
New Brunswick	1.55	6.24	6.79	40.9	38.5	38.8	338.1	8.8	−5.4	+0.8
Quebec	1.65	6.22	6.80	41.5	39.1	38.9	312.1	9.3	−6.7	−0.5
Ontario	1.94	6.91	7.48	40.5	39.3	39.4	285.6	8.2	−2.8	+0.3
Manitoba	1.67	6.01	6.53	39.7	37.2	37.3	291.0	8.7	−6.4	+0.3
Saskatchewan	1.98	7.30	8.06	39.0	37.4	37.0	307.1	10.4	−5.4	−1.1
Alberta	1.96	7.46	8.21	39.7	37.8	37.9	318.9	10.1	−4.7	+0.3
British Columbia	2.23	8.95	9.73	37.7	36.4	36.3	336.3	8.7	−3.9	−0.3

[1] Preliminary data.
[2] Data for Prince Edward Island are not available.
— Nil or zero.

and over represented 37 per cent of the unemployed in 1970 but only 28 per cent in
1979, while women in the same age group increased from 18 per cent to 25 per cent
and persons aged 15 to 24 years moved from 45 per cent to 47 per cent. The figures in
Table 3 also show that the range in provincial unemployment rates increased
between 1970 and 1979.

Earnings and Hours of Work

Statistics Canada obtains information on average weekly earnings, average
weekly hours and average hourly earnings from its monthly survey of Employment,
Payrolls and Manhours. The survey covers larger companies that have 20 or more
employees in any month of the year; these companies account for almost 75 per cent
of the total commercial non-agricultural employment in Canada.

Average Weekly Earnings. Average weekly earnings of all employees in all of
the industries surveyed were $288.25 in 1979; this was an 8.6 per cent rise from the
1978 level. The industrial gains ranged from 7.4 per cent in service to 11.4 per cent in
mining (including milling). Among the provinces, gains ranging from 6.6 per cent in
Prince Edward Island to 11.0 per cent in Alberta were recorded.

Average Hourly Earnings.[1] In 1979 average hourly earnings rose 10.4 per cent in mining, 8.8 per cent in manufacturing and 7.4 per cent in construction. By province, average hourly earnings in manufacturing registered gains ranging from 7.3 per cent in Newfoundland to 10.4 per cent in Saskatchewan.

Average Weekly Hours.[1] From 1978 to 1979 average weekly hours increased in all industries except manufacturing which remained unchanged. Average weekly hours in manufacturing increased in all provinces except Quebec, Saskatchewan and British Columbia which decreased.

The Public Service Commission

The Public Service Commission is an independent agency responsible to Parliament and having the exclusive right to make appointments to the public service and from within the public service. The commission also operates staff development and training programs, assists deputy heads with these concerns, and, since 1972, has been charged with investigating cases of alleged discrimination of various kinds in connection with the application and operation of the Public Service Employment Act.

The commission may establish boards to decide on appeals against certain staffing decisions and to rule on allegations of political partisanship.

The commission may delegate any of its powers, other than those relating to appeals and inquiries, to deputy heads, and has done so with regard to the operational and administrative support categories. Authority has also been delegated for the administrative and foreign service, technical, and scientific and professional categories, while at the same time preserving the commission's authority as the public service's central recruiting agency.

The commission is the guardian of the merit principle as it applies to its major task — staffing the public service — ensuring that high standards are maintained in the service, consistent with adequate representation of the two official language groups, a bilingual capability to the extent prescribed by the government, equal employment and career development opportunities irrespective of sex, race, national origin, colour or religion, and encouragement of equal opportunities for the handicapped and for under-represented groups.

The Public Service Commission offers interdepartmental courses in government administration, occupational training and managerial improvement, acts as a consultant to deputy heads, and makes training and development facilities available for specific occupations or for promotion in administration and management.

The commission ensures that employees are qualified to meet relevant linguistic requirements, and where they do not, ensures that those who require it receive training in their second official language. The commission is also responsible for establishing the method used in assessing language knowledge and the degree of language knowledge or proficiency of candidates.

---

[1] Data on average hourly earnings and average weekly hours pertain only to those wage-earners from whom data on hours were available.

Labour Organizations

Membership in labour organizations active in Canada totalled 3,396,721 in 1980. About 68.5 per cent of the members were in unions affiliated with the Canadian Labour Congress (CLC); 5.5 per cent were affiliates of the Confederation of National Trade Unions (CNTU); 1.3 per cent were affiliated with the Centrale des syndicats démocratiques (CSD); 0.8 per cent were affiliates of the Confederation of Canadian Unions (CCU); the remaining 23.8 per cent were members of unaffiliated national and international unions and independent local organizations.

Of the total union members, 46.3 per cent belonged to international unions with headquarters in the United States.

Sixteen unions reported memberships of 50,000 or more in 1980. The five largest unions were the Canadian Union of Public Employees (257,180); the United Steelworkers of America (203,000); the National Union of Provincial Government Employees (195,754); the Public Service Alliance of Canada (155,731); and the International Union, United Automobile, Aerospace and Agricultural Implement Workers of America (130,000).

Average weekly earnings of all employees in all of the industries surveyed (covering companies that have 20 or more employees in any month of the year) were $288.25 in 1979.

Among the provinces, gains in weekly earnings in 1979 ranging from 6.6 per cent in Prince Edward Island to 11.0 per cent in Alberta were recorded.

Unemployment Insurance

The Unemployment Insurance Act was passed in 1940. Since that time the basic structure of the Act has remained unaltered, although various amendments have brought new categories of workers into the plan and contributions and benefit rates have been raised periodically to keep abreast of changing economic conditions.

In 1968, when Parliament approved upward revisions of both contributions and benefit rates and broadened the scope of coverage, the Unemployment Insurance Commission (now the Canada Employment and Immigration Commission) was instructed to carry out a full-scale investigation of the program and recommend appropriate changes in approach and structure. The Unemployment Insurance Act of 1971 was the result of extensive studies. Its basic objectives are (1) to provide assistance in coping with an interruption of earnings resulting from unemployment, including unemployment due to illness, and (2) to co-operate with other agencies engaged in social development. During 1979 benefit payments under the Act amounted to $4,008 million.

In 1972, coverage was extended to include virtually all paid workers in the labour force and members of the armed forces. The main exceptions are salaried and hourly paid persons working less than 20 hours weekly, those on piece-work and commission earning less than 30 per cent of the maximum weekly insurable earnings ($79.50 per week in 1979) and persons 65 years of age and over. Coverage, contributions and benefit entitlement cease at age 65. The number of insured persons was estimated at 10 million in December 1979.

Employers and employees absorb the cost of administering the program as well as the cost of initial regular benefits plus the labour force extended benefits up to a threshold rate of unemployment (based on an eight-year moving average) for that year. They also pay for the entire cost of special benefits (sickness, maternity and retirement). The federal government is responsible for regionally extended benefits, the cost of benefits to self-employed fishermen and also for the excess of initial regular benefits and the labour force extended benefits over the calculated threshold rate. There is no fund, and employer and employee contributions are adjusted yearly. In 1979, the maximum weekly contribution by an employee was $3.58. The employer's rate is 1.4 times the employee's rate.

The duration of benefit under the new program is not determined solely by the length of time a person has worked. A claimant can draw to a maximum of 50 weeks, depending on his or her employment history and the prevailing economic conditions, provided that (1) he or she has had at least 10 weeks of contributions in the last 52 and (2) he or she has been available, capable of and searching for work. Persons with 20 or more weeks of insured earnings (called a "major labour force attachment") are eligible for a wider range of benefits that includes payments when the interruption of earnings is caused by illness or pregnancy and three weeks' retirement benefit for older workers. A claimant is not entitled to be paid benefit until he or she has served a two-week waiting period that begins with a week of unemployment for which benefits would otherwise be payable.

Sickness benefits are available up to a maximum of 15 weeks for persons with a major labour force attachment who have suffered an interruption of earnings due to illness, injury or quarantine (excluding cases covered by Workmen's Compensation). Maternity benefits are available for a maximum of 15 weeks to women who have had a major labour force attachment; they must also have been part of the labour force for at least 10 of the 20 weeks prior to the 30th week before the expected date of confinement.

Retirement benefit is available for three weeks. It is paid in a lump sum to major attachment claimants who are 65 years of age. In the case of those over 65 the application must be made within 32 weeks of the 65th birthday, as employment weeks are no longer earned after that time. The benefit is paid without a waiting period and without regard to earnings or availability.

The benefit rate for all claims is 60 per cent of a person's average insured earnings in the qualifying period, to a maximum in 1979 of $159 a week. The maximum insurable earnings and the maximum benefit are subject to annual adjustment based on an index calculated from earnings of Canadian employees. In 1979 maximum weekly insurable earnings were $265.

Income from employment in excess of 25 per cent of the benefit rate is deducted from the benefits payable. In the case of sickness or maternity, proceeds of wage-loss plans are not deducted from unemployment benefits during the waiting period but are deducted afterwards. All work-related income is deducted both during the waiting period and after the waiting period has been served.

Oil refinery near Edmonton, Alta.

Industry

Industrial Growth and Change

In Canada the long expansionary phase of domestic output that was such a remarkable characteristic of the 1960s faltered in the early 1970s and ended in 1974. From 1974 to 1975 there was virtually no growth in output. In the second half of 1975 a modest recovery started, and it continued into 1976. From mid-1976 on, the recovery lost impetus and was followed by slower growth for the rest of the decade.

The 1961-71 Period

The expansion of the 1960s was evident throughout most of the major divisions of the economy. While real domestic product grew by 75.4 per cent between 1961 and 1971, the resource-based industries (excluding mines), construction, retail trade, local government and federal government failed to equal this rate of growth. The 83.1 per cent growth of mines, quarries and oil wells from 1961 to 1971 reflected strong increases over the decade in iron mines, crude petroleum and natural gas. Gains in the manufacturing industries brought the aggregate growth for manufacturing to 83.3 per cent above 1961, the largest gains being recorded in the transportation equipment industries (particularly motor vehicle manufacturers), chemical industries, metal fabricating industries and machinery industries. A wide range of service industries recorded 1961-71 output growth rates that exceeded the aggregate for real domestic product. Air transport and rail transport, at 253.2 per cent and 82.9 per cent respectively, and education, at 132.5 per cent, were service industries showing the largest rates of growth. Two large aggregations of industries — community business and personal services, and finance, insurance and real estate, which together contribute over one-quarter of domestic output — showed 1961-71 growth rates of 87.6 per cent and 76.9 per cent respectively.

Industrial growth and change from 1961 to 1971 should be viewed as part of a pattern of overall change in the domestic economy. Some of the changes are very long term and enduring; others are short term and temporary.

Probably the most fundamental change, one that Canada has in common with many developed economies, is the transition from a predominantly goods-producing economy to a predominantly services-producing economy. This particular process of change started before there were statistics to measure it. In 1949, for example, 53 per cent of domestic production occurred in the goods-producing industries; in 1971 it was 40 per cent.

Forest products sawmill at Victoria, BC.

Recently expanded oil refinery at Saint John, NB.

Much of the change occurred as the resource-based industries, particularly agriculture, declined in their relative contributions to total domestic output. The relative contribution of resource-based industries — agriculture, forestry, fishing, trapping, mines, quarries and oil wells — approximately halved, from 16.6 per cent of total output in 1949 to 8.1 per cent in 1971. Manufacturing also declined in relative importance in the same period, from 28 per cent to 23 per cent of total domestic output. Within manufacturing, considerable decline was evident in the relative contribution of the non-durable goods-producing industries, whereas durable goods-producing industries showed an increase that in part reflected increases in contributions of motor vehicle parts and accessories manufacturers and electrical products manufacturers.

The relative growth of education and related services industries produced the most dramatic of the shifts in industrial structure. These more than quadrupled their contributions to total domestic output, from 1.6 per cent in 1949 to 6.5 per cent in 1971, which reflected the increase in post-secondary school education.

Another large change was in the health and welfare services industries, which grew from a 2.3 per cent share of total domestic output in 1949 to one of 5.3 per cent in 1971. The large aggregation of industries identified as the finance, insurance and real estate industries increased their share of output from 9.1 per cent in 1949 to 12.0 per cent in 1971 and growth in computer-related services also added to service-industry growth.

The 1971-79 Period

This period was ushered in with a record level of output for agriculture and very high levels of output in the transportation equipment industries, especially in motor vehicle manufacturers. However, agriculture declined substantially in 1972 and failed to rally much in 1973, a year in which most divisions of the economy were achieving high levels of output.

The marked slowdown in activity that began in 1974, while reflecting a slowing of the growth of the services-producing industries, was mainly the result of sharp declines in the goods-producing industries. For the one-year period from the first quarter of 1974 to the first quarter of 1975 services-producing industries slowed from the 1971-74 average growth rate of 5.9 per cent to 2.5 per cent; goods-producing industries reversed from the 1971-74 growth rate of 4.9 per cent to a decline in that one-year period of 5.3 per cent.

There was little clear indication of recovery until the last quarter of 1975; then a strong resurgence in the goods-producing industries fuelled the recovery until May 1976. The change from October 1975 to May 1976 for the goods-producing industries, services-producing industries and total domestic product were 8.7 per cent, 2.6 per cent and 4.9 per cent respectively.

Calgary, Alta. — a rapidly growing city.

The slower rate of growth in output from May 1976 to the end of the year was most clearly due to a decline in non-residential construction, although there were a number of other industries that also declined during this period and thus contributed to the slower growth rate, including pulp and paper, smelting and refining, residential construction, and the transportation equipment industries.

On the other hand, the services-producing industries showed generally strong growth in this period. Retail trade, the industries in the finance, insurance and real estate group and those in the community, business and personal services group, all of which contribute nearly 40 per cent of aggregate domestic output, showed strong growth between May and December 1976.

For the remainder of the decade, from 1976 to 1979, no division of the economy showed any particular strength: the growth in output for the total domestic economy was lower in this period than in the early 1970s. From the closing months of 1979 and into the early months of 1980 the economy showed signs of faltering into recession. Thus the opening of the decade of the 1980s may be clouded by the prospect of even slower economic growth than had been experienced in the later years of the 1970s.

Aircraft jet engines being repaired and overhauled for the Canadian Armed Forces at a plant in Mississauga, Ont.

Field crew install curtain wall for the 32-storey Trizec Tower, Winnipeg's tallest office building.

Capital Expenditures

A sustained rising income in Canada depends upon, among other things, the capacity to produce and sell goods and services. This capacity and its efficiency in turn depend largely on the amount invested in new mines, factories, stores, power generating installations, communications and transportation equipment, hospitals, schools, roads, parks and all other forms of capital expenditure that encourage the production of goods and services in future periods.

Surveys of these capital expenditures are made at regular intervals every year. On each occasion statistics are published for expenditures on housing, non-residential construction, and machinery and equipment by all sectors of the Canadian economy. Approximately 24,000 establishments are surveyed for their investment intentions. In order to approximate full coverage, adjustments are made for non-

Table 1. Summary of capital and repair expenditures, by sectors, 1979[1] and 1980[2]
(million dollars)

Sector		Capital expenditures			Capital and repair expenditures		
		Construction	Machinery and equipment	Sub-total	Construction	Machinery and equipment	Total
Agriculture and fishing	1979	831.1	3,529.9	4,361.0	1,159.2	4,165.1	5,324.3
	1980	967.3	3,938.0	4,905.3	1,347.2	4,683.2	6,030.4
Forestry	1979	140.0	162.7	302.7	190.5	370.5	561.0
	1980	135.1	189.2	324.3	187.1	407.3	594.4
Mining, quarrying and oil wells	1979	4,311.1	961.5	5,272.6	4,734.7	2,057.3	6,792.0
	1980	5,764.8	1,399.7	7,164.5	6,219.0	2,566.9	8,785.9
Construction industry	1979	155.3	815.7	971.0	179.5	1,438.8	1,618.3
	1980	170.1	894.1	1,064.2	193.6	1,577.0	1,770.6
Manufacturing	1979	1,663.6	5,656.8	7,320.4	2,273.0	8,942.1	11,215.1
	1980	1,820.1	7,252.6	9,072.7	2,496.5	10,794.9	13,291.4
Utilities	1979	6,099.8	5,783.5	11,883.3	7,195.0	8,367.2	15,562.2
	1980	6,802.6	6,165.8	12,968.4	8,005.0	8,984.6	16,989.6
Trade	1979	456.0	912.2	1,368.2	582.4	1,102.2	1,684.6
	1980	495.2	988.1	1,483.3	631.8	1,190.1	1,821.9
Finance, insurance and real estate	1979	2,778.7	333.2	3,111.9	2,981.8	407.4	3,389.2
	1980	3,077.7	373.1	3,450.8	3,303.5	456.3	3,759.8
Commercial services	1979	491.4	2,782.3	3,273.7	552.8	3,069.5	3,622.3
	1980	566.4	3,225.8	3,792.2	633.5	3,535.9	4,169.4
Institutions	1979	1,378.2	372.9	1,751.1	1,654.0	472.2	2,126.2
	1980	1,492.1	389.0	1,881.1	1,797.7	494.2	2,291.9
Government departments	1979	5,683.6	659.5	6,343.1	6,715.5	872.8	7,588.3
	1980	5,975.6	725.0	6,700.6	7,061.2	946.1	8,007.3
Housing	1979	11,481.7	—	11,481.7	14,152.6	—	14,152.6
	1980	11,529.5	—	11,529.5	14,540.2	—	14,540.2
Total	1979	35,470.5	21,970.2	57,440.7	42,371.0	31,265.1	73,636.1
	1980	38,796.5	25,540.4	64,336.9	46,416.3	35,636.5	82,052.8

[1] Preliminary estimate.
[2] Forecast.
— Nil or zero.

surveyed and for non-reporting firms. In a few areas, including agriculture, fishing and housing, expenditure estimates are arrived at independently on the basis of current trends and expert opinion in these fields.

Information on capital spending intentions provides a useful indication of market conditions both in the economy at large and in particular industries. Since such expenditures account for a large and relatively variable proportion of gross national expenditures, the size and content of the investment program provides significant information about demands to be placed upon the productive capacities of the economy during the period covered by the survey. In addition, information on the relative size of the capital expenditures program planned, both in total and for individual industries, gives an indication of the views managements hold on prospective market demands in relation to present productive capacity. Non-capitalized repair expenditures on structures and on machinery and equipment are also given, but these are shown separately. By including these outlays, a more complete picture is provided of all demands likely to be made on labour and materials in accomplishing the program.

Table 2. Summary of capital and repair expenditures, by province, 1979[1] and 1980[2]

(million dollars)

Province or territory		Capital expenditures			Capital and repair expenditures		
		Construction	Machinery and equipment[3]	Sub-total	Construction	Machinery and equipment	Total
Atlantic region:							
Newfoundland	1979	689.3	309.9	999.2	806.8	548.7	1,355.5
	1980	702.9	386.0	1,088.9	831.2	638.8	1,470.0
Prince Edward Island.	1979	134.0	55.6	189.6	164.5	81.9	246.4
	1980	144.6	64.9	209.5	178.8	93.8	272.6
Nova Scotia	1979	896.6	471.7	1,368.3	1,122.4	704.0	1,826.4
	1980	991.5	497.7	1,489.2	1,240.2	752.0	1,992.2
New Brunswick	1979	916.4	714.3	1,630.7	1,078.1	924.7	2,002.8
	1980	852.0	620.3	1,472.3	1,030.0	847.9	1,877.9
Total, Atlantic region.	1979	2,636.3	1,551.5	4,187.8	3,171.8	2,259.3	5,431.1
	1980	2,691.0	1,568.9	4,259.9	3,280.2	2,332.5	5,612.7
Quebec..............	1979	7,743.4	4,316.1	12,059.5	9,395.0	6,226.0	15,621.0
	1980	7,967.5	4,824.1	12,791.6	9,797.7	6,899.8	16,697.5
Ontario..............	1979	9,213.0	7,613.9	16,826.9	11,538.5	11,003.0	22,541.5
	1980	9,695.2	9,537.1	19,232.3	12,260.6	13,214.5	25,475.1
Prairie region:							
Manitoba	1979	1,155.2	871.5	2,026.7	1,451.9	1,249.1	2,701.0
	1980	1,178.3	949.4	2,127.7	1,509.9	1,369.5	2,879.4
Saskatchewan.......	1979	1,695.1	1,344.5	3,039.6	2,046.6	1,773.8	3,820.4
	1980	1,959.1	1,543.1	3,502.2	2,339.6	2,029.0	4,368.6
Alberta.............	1979	8,161.4	3,415.3	11,576.7	9,051.5	4,521.3	13,572.8
	1980	9,663.3	3,716.5	13,379.8	10,656.7	4,913.3	15,570.0
Total, Prairie region ..	1979	11,011.7	5,631.3	16,643.0	12,550.0	7,544.2	20,094.2
	1980	12,800.7	6,209.0	19,009.7	14,506.2	8,311.8	22,818.0
British Columbia	1979	4,473.0	2,702.3	7,175.3	5,297.4	4,017.1	9,314.5
	1980	5,263.5	3,178.8	8,442.3	6,165.4	4,591.4	10,756.8
Yukon and							
Northwest Territories	1979	393.1	155.1	548.2	418.3	215.5	633.8
	1980	378.6	222.5	601.1	406.2	286.5	692.7
Total, Canada	1979	35,470.5	21,970.2	57,440.7	42,371.0	31,265.1	73,636.1
	1980	38,796.5	25,540.4	64,336.9	46,416.3	35,636.5	82,052.8

[1] Preliminary estimate.
[2] Forecast.
[3] Capital expenditures on machinery and equipment include an estimate for "capital items charged to operating expenses", in the manufacturing, utilities and trade totals.

Provincial Expenditures

The expenditures shown for each province or territory represent the value of construction and of machinery and equipment acquired for use within the province or territory. Such expenditures represent gross additions to the capital stock of the province or territory and are a reflection of economic activity in that area. However, the actual production of these assets may generate its major employment and income-giving effects in other regions. For example, the spending of millions of dollars on plants and equipment in Western Canada may generate considerable activity in machinery industries in Ontario and Quebec as well as construction activity in the western provinces.

It should be appreciated that there are statistical difficulties in making a precise geographic allocation of past or anticipated investment, since many business firms operating in several provinces neither record nor plan their capital expenditures geographically. As a result, it has been necessary to use approximate breakdowns in many cases. Such is the case for investment in railway rolling stock, ships, aircraft and certain other items.

The recently expanding Clarkson oil refinery in Ontario.

Housing

Canada Mortgage and Housing Corporation (CMHC) is the principal agent of the federal government in its pursuit of housing objectives, and in this role it administers the National Housing Act (NHA). It has two main types of operations, both directed to the attainment of the government's housing policy objectives. First are the direct mortgage lending and mortgage insurance programs of CMHC, in the administration of which CMHC acts primarily as a financial institution. Second are operations of a departmental nature. These include the management of social housing and related programs; the administration of grants, contributions and subsidies; policy advice to government; and activities related to research, demonstration and housing standards, as well as negotiations with provincial housing agencies.

In 1979, CMHC's direct lending and investment commitments declined sharply. This reflected policy and legislative changes completed early in the year which were aimed at increasing reliance on private rather than public funds for mortgage lending under the terms of the National Housing Act. This change in emphasis is being accompanied by a growth in subsidization and an increased assumption of risk by CMHC through NHA mortgage insurance.

CMHC is empowered to make new loan and investment commitments under its annual capital budget approved by government. In 1979, the capital budget for these commitments was dramatically below the levels authorized up to 1977. In that year the approved budget totalled $1,862 million; for 1978 it was reduced to $1,273 million, and then it was cut to $495 million in 1979. The reductions affected most types of lending by CMHC but were particularly marked in social housing, market housing, municipal infrastructure and land assembly.

Direct loans authorized for social housing were down from $488 million in 1978 to $170 million, although, with provision for NHA mortgage insurance, annual subsidies on private loans for non-profit and co-operative projects, and increased rent supplement activity, CMHC's authority to make commitments in terms of the numbers of dwelling units to be subsidized was unchanged from the previous year. The decline in direct lending for social housing did not apply to CMHC's Rural and Native Housing Program which remained unchanged from 1978 to 1979.

Lending authorized for market housing was reduced from $207 million in 1978 to $58 million in 1979 because mortgage lending was terminated under the Assisted Home Ownership Program and the Assisted Rental Program.

Direct lending programs for municipal infrastructure ceased at the end of 1978, except for certain increases to loans approved before that time. Direct lending for this purpose, and the loan forgiveness that accompanied it, were replaced by the Community Services Contribution Program, under which contributions are made by the federal government to defray the costs of a wide range of municipal undertakings. Similarly, direct loans through CMHC for land assembly were not available after 1978. Under joint federal-provincial agreements, investment continued for the development of lands already acquired but was discontinued for land acquisition purposes.

Lending authorized for residential rehabilitation diminished in 1979 but not as severely as the other reductions. As with the action taken on social housing, this

Mining community at Strathcona Sound, Baffin Island, NWT.

reduction did not apply to subsidies, but only to the provision of public funds for loans, with other arrangements being made to encourage private lending for this purpose at least for rental properties. The number of dwelling units authorized to receive subsidies was unchanged from 1978 to 1979.

Despite the marked reduction in the level of commitments authorized for direct lending in CMHC's 1979 capital budget, the actual commitments approved during the year fell significantly below the authorized levels. This decrease was partly due to the introduction of certain program amendments during the second quarter of 1979 which caused delays in the start of new projects. It was also to some extent attributable to changes in economic conditions which reduced housing and mortgage lending activity.

Altogether, direct lending and investments by CMHC amounted to $350 million in 1979 compared to the approved budget of $495 million. Direct loan commitments for social housing were only $134 million, compared to a budgeted total of $170 million; market housing commitments were made for $29 million, half of the amount provided. Only under the Residential Rehabilitation Assistance Program was most of the loan commitment authority used — $125 million out of $151 million.

Housing starts declined in 1979 from the 1978 level of 227,667 units to 197,049 units and housing completions decreased to 226,489 units from 246,533 units the previous year.

Of the 197,049 dwellings started in 1979, 48,703 units benefited from some form of assistance under the NHA including loan insurance. Of this total, 12,209 units were social housing, which included public housing and units being constructed by non-profit and co-operative groups, all for low- and moderate-income people. The remaining 36,494 units started with some form of assistance were directed at the same income groups, but largely financed by the private sector.

Manufacturing

Manufacturing is the largest of Canada's goods-producing industries. Because of its importance to the growth of national productivity, its high demand for capital goods and its contribution to exports, it plays an important role in the economy.

A monthly sample survey of households produced an estimate that an average number of 2,046,000 persons were being paid salaries or wages by the manufacturing industries in 1979, out of a total for all industries of 9,298,000. This household survey yields a somewhat higher estimate of employees in manufacturing than a monthly survey of employees, which showed an average employment of 1,873,900 for 1979. (The difference in figures is believed influenced by the employees of manufacturing companies who were not working in units classified to manufacturing by the employer survey.)

Cutting room at a plant in Winnipeg, Man.

Table 3. Manufacturing industries, selected years, 1920 to 1979

Year	Establishments	Employees	Salaries and wages	Value added by manufacture	Value of shipments of goods of own manufacture[1]
	No.	No.	$'000	$'000	$'000
1920	22,532	598,893	717,494	1,621,273	3,706,545
1929	22,216	666,531	777,291	1,755,387	3,883,446
1933	23,780	468,658	436,248	919,671	1,954,076
1939	24,805	658,114	737,811	1,531,052	3,474,784
1944	28,483	1,222,882	2,029,621	4,015,776	9,073,693
1949	35,792	1,171,207	2,591,891	5,330,566	12,479,593
1953	38,107	1,327,451	3,957,018	7,993,069	17,785,417
1954	38,028	1,267,966	3,896,688	7,902,124	17,554,528
1955	38,182	1,298,461	4,142,410	8,753,450	19,513,934
1956	37,428	1,353,020	4,570,692	9,605,425	21,636,749
1957	33,551	1,340,948	4,778,040	..	21,452,343
1958	32,446	1,272,686	4,758,614	9,454,954	21,434,815
1959	32,075	1,287,809	5,030,128	10,154,277	22,830,827
1960	32,852	1,275,476	5,150,503	10,371,284	23,279,804
1961	33,357	1,352,605	5,701,651	10,434,832	23,438,956
1962	33,414	1,389,516	6,096,174	11,429,644	25,790,087
1963	33,119	1,425,440	6,495,289	12,272,734	28,014,888
1964	33,630	1,491,257	7,080,939	13,535,991	30,856,099
1965	33,310	1,570,299	7,822,925	14,927,764	33,889,425
1966	33,377	1,646,024	8,695,890	16,351,740	37,303,455
1967	33,267	1,652,827	9,254,190	17,005,696	38,955,389
1968	32,643	1,642,352	9,905,504	18,332,204	42,061,555
1969	32,669	1,675,332	10,848,341	20,133,593	45,930,438
1970	31,928	1,637,001	11,363,712	20,047,801	46,380,935
1971	31,908	1,628,404	12,129,897	21,737,514	50,275,917
1972	31,553	1,676,130	13,414,609	24,264,829	56,190,740
1973	31,145	1,751,066	15,220,033	28,716,119	66,674,393
1974	31,535	1,785,977	17,556,982	35,084,752	82,455,109
1975	30,100	1,741,159	19,156,679	36,105,457	88,427,031
1976	29,053	1,743,047	21,799,733	39,921,910	98,280,777
1977	27,715	1,704,415	23,592,410	44,110,091	108,852,431
1978[2]	31,963	1,790,849	26,577,136	51,682,554	129,022,512
1979		1,873,900[3]	30,643,519[3]	60,210,004[4]	151,625,000[5]

[1] Before 1952, data represent gross value of production.
[2] Preliminary figures. Increase in number of establishments due to improved coverage.
[3] Based on monthly surveys of employment and earnings.
[4] Estimate.
[5] Based on monthly survey of shipments of manufacturers.
.. Not available.
Note: Revised SIC and new establishment concept applied to data as of 1957. Employment includes total activity of manufacturing industries as of 1961.

Preliminary data from another monthly survey show that Canadian manufacturers shipped $151.6 billion of their own products in 1979, an increase of 17.5 per cent over 1978. (By comparison, the annual average index of selling prices of manufacturing industries increased 14.4 per cent over the same period and the annual average index of industrial production increased 3.3 per cent.)

A new redesigned electric kettle on test at Barrie, Ont.

An exact measure of exports of manufacturers is not routinely compiled, but if exports of fabricated materials and end products are accepted as roughly equivalent to manufactured products, Canadian manufacturers did some processing on about seven dollars out of every 10 of exports of Canadian products in 1979. Domestic exports of fabricated materials amounted to $24.4 billion, compared with $20.8 billion for end products.

However, the end products — roughly equivalent to highly manufactured goods, though including very small values of non-manufactured goods — have increased in value 29.5 times since 1961, when they amounted to only $706 million, while those of fabricated materials have risen more than eightfold from a 1961 figure of $2,916 million. This is a striking reflection of the growth of those sectors of Canadian manufacturing producing more highly fabricated goods. For various reasons, these values are not strictly comparable with the value of overall shipments of manufactures by Canadian factories, but they give an impression of the approximate intensity of export activity as measured by shipments. The relative importance of production for export would be appreciably higher if it were feasible to use a measure of the Canadian value added that is exported, as the overall manufacturing shipments of Canadian manufacturers necessarily contain double counting of output from manufacturers supplying each other with inputs.

Most manufacturing activity in Canada is highly mechanized and Canadian factories thus constitute a large market for equipment. This is partly because many types of natural resources processing are inherently capital-intensive; that is, they employ a great deal of machinery, equipment and buildings in proportion to employees. Industries producing highly manufactured goods — like machinery and automobiles — are becoming increasingly important. In addition high living standards, reflected in high wages, create an incentive to economy in the use of workers and this often leads to increased mechanization.

In 1980, according to a survey of investment intentions, it was anticipated that the manufacturing industries would be accounting for 28 per cent of all capital expenditures by business and government for new machinery and equipment. These expenditures represent, of course, not only the expansion of productive capacity but presumably some "deepening" of capital (an increase in capital per employee or per unit of product).

Increasing capital intensity of production has probably been a prime cause of the rise in productivity of each employee in the manufacturing industries. Physical output in the manufacturing industries, by man-hour worked, increased at an average rate of 3.9 per cent over the 1961-79 period.

The leading manufacturing industry in Canada in 1979, measured by the value of shipments of its own products, was petroleum refining. With a total value of $12.3 billion, this industry's shipments were approximately $2.1 billion greater than in 1978, prices having increased by 18.3 per cent during the year. There have been substantial price increases in this industry in recent years in attempts to reach world market prices.

The second-ranking industry in 1979 was motor vehicle manufacturers at $11.0 billion, with an increase of $0.9 billion in shipments from the previous year. Prices have increased by 12.2 per cent over 1978 while production has decreased as a result of weak consumer and export demand and the substitution of more fuel-efficient foreign imports. Pulp and paper mills had the third largest value of shipments at $9.4 billion, an increase of approximately $1.8 billion from 1978. The industry's real domestic product rose 2 per cent over 1978, a small increase in comparison with a 19.3 per cent increase in prices over the same period. There has been a continuing strong export demand for Canadian pulp and newsprint despite a slowing down of the US economy.

Eleven industries, in descending order of magnitude, had shipments in the $2 billion to over $6 billion range in 1979: slaughtering and meat processing, $6.6 billion; iron and steel mills, $5.9 billion; sawmills and planing mills, $5.4 billion; motor vehicle parts and accessories, $4.3 billion; miscellaneous machinery and equipment manufacturers, $4.2 billion; dairy products, $3.9 billion; metal stamping and pressing, $3.0 billion; miscellaneous food processors, $2.5 billion; smelting and refining, $2.4 billion; commercial printing, $2.2 billion; and manufacturers of industrial chemicals (organic), $2.0 billion. Twenty-four industries had shipments of between $1 billion and $2 billion. These preliminary estimates for 1979 were based on a monthly survey of shipments, inventories and orders in the manufacturing industries and are subject to revision by the results of the annual census of manufactures.

A quarterly survey on business conditions conducted by Statistics Canada helps overcome some problems involved in projecting changes in the manufacturing sector by asking executives for their qualitative assessments. A recent survey disclosed that in April 1980 respondents representing 77 per cent of manufacturing shipments expected the volume of production in the following three months to be higher than or about the same as in the previous quarter. This was an increase in expectations of 7 percentage points from the survey conducted in January of the same year. Shortages of skilled labour and working capital were major sources of production difficulty for 15 per cent of the respondents.

The largest four enterprises or groupings of commonly controlled companies had 80 manufacturing establishments in 1976 and accounted for 7.9 per cent of all manufacturers' shipments, 7.1 per cent of manufacturing value added and 5.4 per cent of total employees. The largest 16 enterprises accounted for approximately 22 per cent of manufacturing shipments. (While these data are not issued annually, figures on the size of manufacturing establishments are compiled each year.) The average size of a manufacturing establishment in 1978 was $4.0 million worth of shipments of goods of own manufacture — or about 56 persons, measured by the number of persons employed. These averages are, however, greatly affected by the large number of small establishments operated by local or regional entrepreneurs in manufacturing industries throughout Canada. Actually, 50.4 per cent of the total work force in the manufacturing industries was in establishments employing 200 or more persons and there were 139 manufacturing establishments with more than 1,000 persons employed in 1977.

An automatic nut tapping machine.

The proximity of the US, the interest of foreign firms in fabricated materials for use in foreign industry and the generally profitable character of Canadian manufacturing over many years have led to widespread investment in Canadian manufacturing by companies outside Canada. However, a special analysis of the census of manufactures for 1976 showed that Canadian-controlled firms nonetheless accounted for 59 per cent of all employment in the manufacturing industries; the proportion of manufacturing value added was somewhat lower, 52 per cent.

The 1979 profits of incorporated companies classified as manufacturing industries amounted to 8.4 per cent of total revenue, before taxes and certain extraordinary items. Average weekly wages and salaries in Canadian manufacturing in a preliminary March 1980 figure amounted to $335.61.

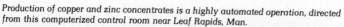

Production of copper and zinc concentrates is a highly automated operation, directed from this computerized control room near Leaf Rapids, Man.

Eaton Centre in Toronto, Ont.

Trade

Domestic Trade

The means by which goods and services are transferred from producers to end users are usually referred to as the channels of distribution. In Canada these encompass three distinct sectors of the domestic economy — retail trade, wholesale trade and community, business and personal services. Businesses generally operate within one or another of these sectors, although some are active in two or all three sectors (manufacturers' sales branches and co-operatives, for example, may be engaged in either wholesaling or retailing activities or both).

The channels of distribution are characterized by continuous change. During the past few years, the volume of business transacted by franchised operations has increased rapidly especially within the food-serving industry. In the retail food and general merchandise sectors, a small number of firms continue to be dominant.

The growth of regional shopping centres has decreased in recent years due to difficulty in securing suitable sites and to the high cost of land acquisition and construction. However, there has been a growing movement in construction of shopping malls in central business districts of many major metropolitan areas as well as the refurbishing of existing shopping centres in downtown areas and in the suburbs. Although independent retailers appear to be holding their share of the retail market, many individual retailers are facing difficulties in competing directly with the larger chain operations. Within the next few years, an increasing number of bankruptcies and closures among marginal retailers may occur.

The commodity mix and services offered by retailers are expanding in a variety of directions and the spread of businesses into new areas and types of operation (for example, home improvement centres and catalogue showroom operations) continues unabated. However, continuing high credit costs may slow the rate of growth in these areas.

Montreal, Que.

The produce department of a Canadian grocery store.

In the midst of such change has come a significant increase in the kinds of business that compete for the consumer dollar and in the types of specialized agencies — some of which did not even exist 10 years ago — that serve the varied needs of modern businesses. Although all sectors of the economy have shared in these developments, it is in the service trades that the greatest impact has been felt. Increases in income and leisure time have contributed to the substantial sales growth in services and goods of a recreational nature and rising expertise in the marketing function has spurred the growing use of data processing services, market research houses, public relations firms, mailing-list agencies and other marketing and management consulting businesses.

Retail Trade

In 1978 sales in retail locations reached an estimated $68,799 million, an increase of 11.6 per cent over 1977. During the period 1973-78 for which comparable data are available, total retail sales rose 79.5 per cent. The largest sales increases during this period occurred in Alberta (121.4 per cent), in the Yukon and the Northwest

Table 1. Summary statistics on retail trade, 1973 and 1978
(million dollars)

	1973			1978		
	Chain stores	Independent stores	All stores	Chain stores	Independent stores	All stores
Kind of business						
Combination stores (groceries and meat)	4,738	2,211	6,949	9,206	3,701	12,907
Grocery, confectionery and sundries stores......	259	1,387	1,646	525	2,761	3,286
All other food stores.......	68	720	787	106	1,070	1,176
Department stores	4,316	—	4,316	7,695	—	7,695
General merchandise stores	969	253	1,222	1,383	365	1,748
General stores............	130	606	736	396	951	1,347
Variety stores	547	164	711	683	219	902
Motor vehicle dealers	98	7,325	7,422	182	13,298	13,480
Used car dealers	—	130	130	—	268	268
Service stations...........	406	2,093	2,499	923	3,656	4,579
Garages	—	479	479	—	957	957
Automotive parts and accessories stores	117	638	754	179	1,190	1,369
Men's clothing stores......	127	431	557	294	546	840
Women's clothing stores ...	278	366	643	675	573	1,248
Family clothing stores.....	223	340	563	430	502	932
Specialty shoe stores	13	27	40	53	39	92
Family shoe stores	197	158	355	378	206	584
Hardware stores	71	381	452	[1]	[1]	706
Household furniture stores.	101	398	499	162	906	1,068
Household appliance stores	38	131	169	[1]	[1]	248
Furniture, TV, radio and appliance stores	130	274	404	92	403	495
Pharmacies, patent medicine and cosmetic stores	197	910	1,107	464	1,653	2,118
Book and stationery stores .	48	102	150	142	183	325
Florists..................	7	130	1·37	11	250	261
Jewellery stores	129	185	313	266	330	596
Sporting goods and accessories stores	14	359	373	89	728	816
Personal accessories stores	106	467	574	253	731	985
All other stores...........	2,332	2,015	4,347	4,073	3,699	7,771
Total, all stores	15,658	22,677	38,335	28,604	39,995	68,799
Province						
Newfoundland	253	464	717	484	811	1,295
Prince Edward Island......	56	119	176	107	229	335
Nova Scotia	492	735	1,227	927	1,313	2,240
New Brunswick	397	580	977	739	1,006	1,745
Quebec..................	3,110	6,587	9,697	5,702	11,472	17,174
Ontario.................	6,610	7,896	14,505	11,892	13,292	25,184
Manitoba	731	968	1,699	1,225	1,502	2,727
Saskatchewan............	492	1,041	1,533	998	1,876	2,874
Alberta..................	1,373	1,697	3,070	3,009	3,789	6,798
British Columbia	2,097	2,549	4,646	3,630	4,605	8,235
Yukon and Northwest Territories ...	48	41	89	90	102	192

— Nil or zero.

Figures may not add to totals owing to rounding.

[1] Confidential.

A gladioli farm in Ontario.

Territories (115.7 per cent) and Prince Edward Island (90.3 per cent), while Ontario and Manitoba experienced the lowest rates of growth (73.6 per cent and 60.5 per cent respectively). Although Ontario and Quebec continued to account for nearly two-thirds of all retail sales in Canada, their share of the retail market has been declining for many years, reaching a low of 61.6 per cent in 1978.

By kinds of business, the most substantial increase in sales for the period 1973-78 was recorded by specialty shoe stores (130.0 per cent), followed by sporting goods stores (118.8 per cent), book and stationery stores (116.7 per cent), household furniture stores (114.0 per cent), used car dealers (106.2 per cent) and garages (99.8 per cent). No specific kind of business lost ground between 1973 and 1978, however, several kinds of business recorded increases that were well below average, for example, furniture, television, radio and appliance stores, variety stores, general merchandise stores and household appliance stores.

The largest shares of the retail market were held during 1978 by motor vehicle dealers (19.6 per cent of total sales) and combination stores selling groceries and meats (18.8 per cent). If the sales of other food stores, used car dealers, service

Coquitlam Centre, one of Western Canada's largest shopping centres.

stations, garages and automotive accessories stores were also included, well over half (55.4 per cent) of every dollar spent by households or personal consumers in 1978 was used to purchase food, cars or automotive services. The inclusion of stores selling mainly clothing and footwear — other "basic necessities" of life — would only increase this total by 11.1 per cent. The only other kind of business with a significant volume of sales was department stores; they captured 11.2 per cent of the retail market, a slight decrease from the 11.3 per cent held in 1973.

Within the framework of retail trade, chain store organizations (those that operate four or more stores in the same kind of business under the same legal ownership) compete with independent retailers for a share of the consumer dollar. The market position of the chains, which has been improving slowly but steadily over the years, showed further gains during the 1973-78 period. In 1973 chain stores accounted for 40.8 per cent of total retail sales; by 1978 this figure had risen to 41.9 per cent. With department stores excluded from both chain and total retail sales, the market share of chain organizations accounted for 33.3 per cent in 1973 and 34.5 per cent in 1978.

Between 1973 and 1978 the share of the market held by chains increased in 16 of the 28 kinds of business with data available (including all other stores), and declined

Split Lake, Man. Loading whitefish on plane to be flown to markets while still fresh.

in 9. Chain store organizations accounted for at least half of the total sales of department stores, in which all firms are classified as chains (100 per cent), general merchandise stores (79.1 per cent), variety stores (75.7 per cent), combination stores selling groceries and meat (71.3 per cent), family shoe stores (64.7 per cent), specialty shoe stores (57.6 per cent), women's clothing stores (54.1 per cent) and all other stores (52.4 per cent).

Independent retailers had an increase of 76.4 per cent in sales for the period from 1973 to 1978. Kinds of business in which independent retailers increased their market share, even if only slightly, included general merchandise stores, variety stores, automotive parts and accessories stores, household furniture stores, furniture, television, radio and appliance stores, florists and other stores.

Direct Selling

Retail stores account for only a part (although the largest part) of the total volume of purchases made by household or personal consumers. Other channels of distribution that completely bypass the traditional retail outlet are direct selling agencies, coin-operated vending machines and campus bookstores, which reported total sales of $2,036.2 million during 1977. Of this total, the direct selling activities of manufacturers, importers, wholesalers, mail-order agencies, book, newspaper and magazine publishers and other specialized agencies accounted for $1,683.0 million, or 4 per cent of sales registered by comparable kinds of business in retail stores. In addition, vending machine operators reported total sales in 1977 of $286.5 million and campus bookstores contributed an additional $92.7 million during the 1977-78 academic year.

The 1977 survey of direct selling in Canada showed that the largest proportion of such "non-store retailing" continues to be made by means of door-to-door canvassing. Sales of commodities such as cosmetics and costume jewellery, dairy products, newspapers and household electrical appliances, made on a door-to-door basis, accounted for 62.1 per cent of total direct selling. Sales of furniture re-upholstering and repairs, furniture, frozen foods and household electrical appliances in the showrooms and other premises of manufacturers provided an additional 15.6 per cent. Mail-order sales of such goods as books, phonograph records, magazines and newspapers represented 16.9 per cent while sales through other channels accounted for the remaining 5.4 per cent of total direct selling.

Table 2. Consumer credit in Canada-balances outstanding, selected holders, selected year ends
(million dollars)

Credit holders/types of credit	1965	1970	1975	1976ʳ	1977ʳ	1978	Percentage change 1977-78
Sales finance and consumer loan companies:							
Instalment financing	1,198	1,136	1,156	1,122	1,073	1,164	+8.5
Cash loans under $1,500	628	525	252	231	204	178	−12.7
Cash loans over $1,500	348	1,190	1,504	1,501	1,462	1,488	+1.8
Chartered banks' personal loans	2,241	4,663	13,175	16,213	18,777	21,689	+15.5
Quebec savings banks' personal loans . .	16	22	58	72	87	104	+19.5
Life insurance companies' policy loans. .	411	759	1,149	1,227	1,277	1,341	+5.0
Credit unions and caisses populaires . . .	813	1,493	3,243	3,884	4,512	5,465	+21.1
Department stores and other retail dealers	1,313	1,551	2,418	2,318	2,411	2,597	+7.7
Other credit-card issuers.	72	186	338	305	330	371	+12.4
Public utility companies	99	155	295	373	444	492	+10.8
Trust and mortgage loan companies	—	—	199	301	385	659	+71.2
Total.	7,140	11,680	23,787	27,547	30,962	35,549	+14.8

— Nil or zero.
ʳ Revised.

Onions from Ontario and potatoes from Prince Edward Island en route to consumers.

Consumer Credit

Consumer credit arises through an advance of cash, merchandise or services to an individual or household for personal (non-commercial) consumption purposes, through authorized use of credit cards, promissory notes or conditional sales agreements, in exchange for a promise to repay the lender at a later date, generally by instalments. Statistics on consumer indebtedness do not include fully-secured loans, home improvement loans and residential mortgages, nor do they include interpersonal loans, bills owed to doctors, dentists, lawyers and other professional practitioners, or credit extended by clubs and personal service establishments.

As can be observed from Table 2 there has been a significant shift since 1965 in the nature of consumer credit and in the relative market share of the various institutions and organizations — financial and merchandising — which serve consumers' needs for credit. In 1965 the need for vendor credit holdings of outstandings tied directly to acquisitions of goods and services amounted to $2,583 million or 36

View of Expo in Montreal, Que.

per cent, of the total balances outstanding of $7,140 million. By 1978 vendor credit balances increased to $4,132 million but this amount now accounts for only 11.6 per cent of the total balances outstanding of $35,549 million. Consumers' preference for cash credit has swollen this category of credit to $31,417 million — the remaining 88.4 per cent of balances outstanding.

The largest share of total consumer credit outstanding at the present time, approximately 61 per cent is held by the chartered banks, whose balances increased 15.5 per cent during 1978 to reach $21,689 million by year end. The balances of cash loans and sales financing held by sales finance and consumer loan companies increased by 3.3 per cent over the year to $2,830 million by year-end 1978.

Wholesale Trade

Wholesalers are primarily engaged in buying merchandise for resale to retailers, to farmers for use in farm production, to industrial, commercial, institutional or professional users or to other wholesalers. Also forming part of wholesale trade are those who act as agents, or brokers, in such transactions and who derive commissions from the purchase and/or sale of goods on behalf of others.

For statistical purposes wholesalers are grouped into two categories, the largest and most important of these being wholesale merchants; the other group comprising agents and brokers. The wholesale merchant category includes import and/or export merchants, manufacturers' sales branches, voluntary group wholesalers, cash-and-carry wholesalers, drop shippers or desk jobbers, mail-order wholesalers, truck distributors and rack jobbers, all of whom buy and/or sell merchandise mainly on their own account.

On a current basis a monthly survey of wholesale merchants provides estimates of sales and stocks for selected kinds of business. Estimated sales during 1978-79 are shown in Table 3.

Sales of wholesale merchants in every kind of business group increased during 1979 reaching $72,574 million, a 17.1 per cent increase over the $61,965 million sold in 1978. The more significant increases occurred during the year in electrical machinery, equipment and supplies where sales rose from $3,200 million in 1978 to $3,805 million or 18.9 per cent in 1979; farm machinery and equipment, from $3,327 million in 1978 to $4,313 million or 29.6 per cent; other machinery and equipment, from $8,770 million to $11,014 million or 25.6 per cent; and metals and metal products, from $1,926 million in 1978 to $2,621 million or 36.1 per cent in 1979.

Service Trades

Intercensal surveys which provide partial coverage of this large and diverse sector show that accommodation receipts reached $3,306.1 million in 1977, of which hotel receipts amounted to $2,692.3 million, a 112.2 per cent increase over 1971. Restaurant, catering and tavern receipts totalled $6,847.4 million in 1978, an increase of 184.9 per cent over 1971. Receipts of motion picture theatres and drive-ins rose to $326.2 million (including taxes) in 1978, an increase of 110.6 per cent over 1971. Other intercensal surveys carried out for the year 1978 in the service trade sector produced the following results: computer service industry, $1,411.6 million; motion picture production, $113.3 million; and motion picture distribution (film exchanges), $197.2 million.

Table 3. Estimated sales of wholesale merchants, 1978 and 1979

Trade group	Sales		Percentage change 1978-79
	1978 $'000,000	1979 $'000,000	
Total, all trades[1]	61,965	72,574	+17.1
Farm products (excluding grain)	513	575	+12.1
Paper and paper products	1,303	1,562	+19.9
Food..	12,899	14,617	+13.3
Tobacco products......................................	1,246	1,374	+10.3
Drugs and toilet preparations	884	990	+12.0
Apparel and dry goods..................................	1,725	1,959	+13.6
Household furniture and house furnishings	1,154	1,278	+10.7
Motor vehicles	2,033	2,162	+6.4
Automotive parts, accessories and supplies	3,282	3,605	+9.9
Electrical machinery, equipment and supplies	3,200	3,805	+18.9
Farm machinery and equipment	3,327	4,313	+29.6
Machinery and equipment (not elsewhere specified)	8,770	11,014	+25.6
Hardware...	1,221	1,373	+12.4
Plumbing and heating equipment, etc...	1,496	1,738	+16.2
Metals and metal products	1,926	2,621	+36.1
Lumber and building materials	7,466	8,370	+12.1
Scrap and waste materials...............................	605	892	+47.4
Wholesalers (not elsewhere specified)[2]...	8,915	10,325	+15.8

[1] Excluding grain and petroleum product dealers.
[2] Also includes general merchandise and coal and coke dealers.

The Consumer Price Index

Based on annual averages the all-items consumer price index (CPI) advanced 9.1 per cent in 1979, virtually unchanged from the 9.0 per cent increase recorded in 1978. The increases in the latest two years reflect a considerable acceleration in the rate of price changes over the increases of 7.5 per cent and 8.0 per cent in 1976 and 1977 respectively. In 1978, the food index climbed sharply by 15.5 per cent after advancing by 8.4 per cent in 1977, while the all-items excluding food index decelerated somewhat from an increase of 7.8 per cent in 1977 to 6.4 per cent in 1978. These relative rates of increase were reversed in 1979 with the all-items excluding food index recording an increase of 7.9 per cent while the increase in the food index decelerated to 13.2 per cent. As a result of this shift in relative rates of increase, the contribution of higher food prices to the overall annual change in the all-items index fell from slightly over two-fifths in 1978 to slightly over one-third in 1979.

Table 4. The consumer price index and its major components for Canada, percentage change between annual average indexes

	1974 1973	1975 1974	1976 1975	1977 1976	1978 1977	1979 1978
All-items..........................	10.9	10.8	7.5	8.0	9.0	9.1
Food............................	16.3	12.9	2.7	8.4	15.5	13.2
All-items excluding food.............	8.9	10.0	9.4	7.8	6.4	7.9
Housing.........................	8.7	10.0	11.1	9.4	7.5	7.0
Clothing.........................	9.6	6.0	5.5	6.8	3.8	9.2
Transportation	10.0	11.7	10.7	7.0	5.8	9.7
Health and personal care............	8.7	11.4	8.7	7.4	7.2	9.0
Recreation, reading and education ...	8.7	10.4	6.0	4.8	3.9	6.9
Tobacco and alcohol	5.5	12.1	7.2	7.1	8.1	7.2

Based on annual averages, the goods component of the CPI rose 10.1 per cent and 10.6 per cent in 1978 and 1979 respectively, while the service component recorded increases of 6.8 per cent and 6.9 per cent respectively.

The consumer price indexes for selected cities measure changes in consumer prices within the specified cities. Beginning in October 1978 city indexes were reconstructed from January 1971 onward in order to render them consistent with the concepts and methods used in the construction of the Canada CPI. As shown in Table 5 increases in all-items ranged from 7.7 per cent in Vancouver to 9.8 per cent in St. John's.

The purchasing power of the 1971 consumer dollar, which stood on average at 67 cents in 1976, declined to 52 cents in 1979.

Table 5. Consumer price indexes and major components for selected cities, percentage change between 1978 and 1979

(based on annual averages)

City	All items	Food	Hous- ing	Cloth- ing	Trans- porta- tion	Health and personal care	Recreation, reading and education	Tobacco and alcohol
St. John's, Nfld........	9.8	16.1	7.6	6.9	7.9	10.4	9.8	6.8
Charlottetown-Summerside, PEI.....	8.6	12.2	7.1	8.8	8.0	7.5	6.8	6.0
Halifax, NS............	8.9	13.3	6.1	9.1	8.6	7.6	7.5	10.2
Saint John, NB	9.3	13.6	7.1	8.6	8.6	6.8	8.2	8.8
Quebec, Que...........	9.2	12.3	8.8	5.8	8.7	9.3	8.5	6.6
Montreal, Que.........	9.1	13.5	7.8	7.1	8.9	9.4	5.2	7.2
Ottawa, Ont...........	8.8	12.3	6.4	10.2	10.6	7.9	7.0	8.0
Toronto, Ont..........	9.3	12.5	6.8	11.1	10.8	10.6	6.8	7.4
Thunder Bay, Ont......	8.8	11.3	7.3	9.9	9.0	8.4	7.8	7.9
Winnipeg, Man.........	9.2	11.4	7.5	12.2	9.2	8.0	8.2	7.3
Regina, Sask.	8.4	12.2	5.9	10.4	9.1	7.5	6.8	7.1
Saskatoon, Sask.	8.9	12.4	7.3	9.5	9.1	7.0	7.0	7.3
Edmonton, Alta.	8.9	11.7	8.2	10.6	8.6	7.0	8.2	3.9
Clagary, Alta..........	8.7	12.9	7.8	10.2	7.0	8.6	6.6	5.4
Vancouver, BC........	7.7	11.8	4.6	8.1	9.1	8.8	6.7	6.4

Victoria, BC.

International Trade

Canada's merchandise exports and imports showed strong growth in both 1978 and 1979. Exports increased by 18.6 per cent to $52.8 billion in 1978 and a further 24 per cent to $65.5 billion in 1979. Imports grew 18 per cent to $49.9 billion in 1978 and 25.1 per cent to $62.5 billion in 1979.

After adjustment of these customs totals to meet the concepts and definitions used in the system of national accounts, the relative advances changed to 18.8 per cent and 24.1 per cent for exports in 1978 and 1979 respectively; with 18.5 per cent and 24.5 per cent for imports. Refinements include timing adjustments to certain exports figures, incorporation of progress payments on capital equipment, deduction of transportation charges included in some customs documents and reduction of some customs values to reflect transaction prices. On a balance-of-payments basis, Canada's surplus on merchandise trade with other countries has improved steadily since the deficit recorded in 1975. The trade balance of $1.4 billion in 1976 almost doubled to $2.7 billion in 1977; increased 24 per cent to $3.4 billion in 1978; and increased 18 per cent to $4.0 billion in 1979.

Table 6. Exports by commodities, 1977-79
(million dollars)

Commodity	1977	1978	1979
Wheat.	1,882	1,913	2,180
Animals and other edible products	2,574	3,174	3,869
Metal ores and concentrates	2,730	2,403	3,890
Crude petroleum.	1,751	1,573	2,403
Natural gas	2,028	2,190	2,889
Other crude materials	2,341	2,664	3,345
Lumber and softwood	2,387	3,229	3,911
Pulp	2,158	2,181	3,076
Newsprint	2,382	2,886	3,222
Fabricated metals	3,832	5,080	5,804
Other fabricated materials	4,168	5,530	8,352
Motor vehicles and parts (partial)	10,424	12,446	11,637
Other machinery and equipment.	3,975	5,234	7,290
Other domestic exports	1,052	1,416	2,142
Re-exports	870	923	1,317
Total exports	44,554	52,842	65,327

Exports (Customs Basis)

The United States remained Canada's most important customer in 1979, taking $43,244 million, or 67.6 per cent of domestic exports. Other leading export destinations were Japan, the United Kingdom and the Federal Republic of Germany, followed by the Benelux countries (Belgium–Netherlands–Luxembourg) and the

Deep sea terminal at Prince Rupert, BC.

USSR. Italy, Venezuela, France, the People's Republic of China and Australia have also been important export destinations. These 11 leading customers together accounted for 90 per cent of total exports in 1979.

The traditional commodities in Canada's foreign trade generally retained their standings in 1978 and 1979. At 18 per cent in 1979, motor vehicles and parts accounted for a declining share of exports down from 24 per cent in the previous year. From levels of 12.5 per cent in 1975, crude petroleum and natural gas dropped to 8.5 per cent of exports in 1977, and 7.1 per cent in 1978; followed by an increase to 8.1 per cent in 1979. The increase in the value of natural gas exports to the US outweighed the drop in petroleum shipments in 1978 and 1979. Exports of ores, refined metals and forestry products continued to expand in 1978 and 1979 in response to expanding markets abroad. Large wheat shipments in 1977, 1978 and 1979 notably to China, Japan, the USSR and the United Kingdom contributed to a recovery from the fall in exports in 1976. By stage of fabrication, the proportion of manufactured goods dropped to 32.3 per cent in 1979 from 36.1 per cent in 1978. The value of exported crude materials increased to 19.6 per cent of total exports in 1979 after falling to 17 per cent in 1978; the proportion for fabricated materials increased to 38 per cent in 1979 from 36 per cent in 1978.

Twin hoist motors, connected during manufacture at a Peterborough, Ont. plant prior to shipment to a mine in the United States.

Table 7. Domestic exports, by leading countries, 1977-79
(million dollars)

Country	1977	1978	1979
United States.	30,404	36,455	43,244
Japan.	2,513	3,052	4,081
United Kingdom	1,929	1,985	2,589
Federal Republic of Germany.	768	782	1,368
Netherlands[1]	513	563	1,080
USSR	358	567	763
Italy	498	481	729
Venezuela	568	686	698
Belgium and Luxembourg[1]	511	475	668
France	360	460	619
China	369	503	592
Australia	409	412	559
Brazil	282	417	417
Sub-total	39,482	46,838	57,407
Total domestic exports	43,684	51,919	64,010

[1] Due to tran-shipments via the Netherlands, Belgium-Luxembourg, exports to and imports from these countries tend to be overstated, whereas exports to and imports from Germany, France, and some other European destinations may be under-represented by these data.

Table 8. Imports, by commodities, 1977-79
(million dollars)

Commodity	1977	1978	1979
Meat and fish...............................	534	601	663
Fruits and vegetables	1,039	1,255	1,456
Animals and other edible products.............	1,681	1,844	2,022
Coal.......................................	618	632	864
Crude petroleum	3,215	3,471	4,430
Other crude materials.......................	1,483	1,788	2,545
Textiles....................................	890	1,074	1,384
Chemical products...........................	1,992	2,621	3,213
Fabricated metals	1,400	1,901	3,621
Other fabricated materials....................	2,711	3,197	3,844
Motor vehicles and parts (partial)..............	11,576	13,257	14,832
Other machinery and equipment	10,585	13,034	17,083
Other imports..............................	4,608	5,265	6,496
Total imports	42,332	49,938	62,453

Imports (Customs Basis)

Some $45,203 million (or 72.4 per cent) of imports entered Canada from the US in 1979, up from the share of 70.6 per cent in 1978 and 70.4 per cent in 1977. Ranking next in order of importance both in 1978 and 1979 were Japan, the United Kingdom, Venezuela, the Federal Republic of Germany, Saudi Arabia and France. Iran which dropped from seventh place in 1977 to eighth place in 1978 and to fourteenth place in 1979 has been superseded in 1979 by Italy, Taiwan, Australia, South Korea, Hong Kong and Sweden. These 14 countries accounted for 92.2 per cent of Canada's total imports in 1979.

Automotive products and other equipment and machinery continued to represent approximately half of the imports in 1978 and 1979. The share for motor vehicles and parts dropped slightly from 26.5 per cent in 1978 to 23.7 per cent in 1979, while other equipment and machinery increased to 27.4 per cent in 1979 from 26 per cent in 1978. The value of crude oil landings increased in 1978 and again in 1979; imports of coal from the United States also increased. Imports of fruits and vegetables continued to grow (40 per cent between 1977 and 1979) and imports of meat and fish also increased although at a slower rate (24 per cent between 1977 and 1979). Manufactured goods accounted for 60 per cent of all imports in 1979, down from 62 per cent in 1977 and 1978. The share for processed materials improved from 17.6 per cent in 1978 to 19 per cent in 1979 while the share for crude materials increased to 12.6 per cent in 1979 following a decline to 11.8 per cent in 1978.

Price and Volume Changes

Import prices increased faster than export prices in 1978 while export volumes were ahead of import volumes. The reverse was true in 1979. Average import prices increased 13.4 per cent in 1978 while export prices were up 8.5 per cent. In 1979

Loading potatoes in Prince Edward Island for shipment to the Caribbean.

export prices increased 20.8 per cent and import prices increased 14.2 per cent. The volume of exports rose 9.6 per cent as compared to imports which grew 3.1 per cent in 1978. In 1979 the volume of imports increased 10.6 per cent while exports grew by 2.4 per cent. Canada's terms of trade (the ratio of export to import prices) which improved marginally in 1976 to 1.123, dropped to 1.067 in 1977 and 1.022 in 1978; followed by an increase to 1.080 for 1979.

Table 9. Imports, by leading countries, 1977-79
(million dollars)

Country	1977	1978	1979
United States	29,815	35,246	45,203
Japan	1,793	2,268	2,152
United Kingdom	1,279	1,600	1,926
Venezuela	1,360	1,283	1,557
Federal Republic of Germany	967	1,244	1,538
Saudi Arabia	712	749	1,228
France	522	684	776
Italy	400	525	634
Taiwan	321	397	521
Australia	353	350	464
South Korea	323	363	462
Hong Kong	280	332	428
Sweden	260	325	383
Iran	537	594	322
Sub-total	38,922	45,960	57,594
Total imports	42,332	49,938	62,453

Finance

Public Finance

Powers and Responsibilities of the Various Levels of Government

The British North America (BNA) Act of 1867, which forms Canada's written constitution, specifies the distribution of taxing power and responsibilities between the federal Parliament and the provincial legislatures. Under Section 91 the federal Parliament is given unlimited taxing powers, while under Section 92 the provincial legislatures are granted the power of direct taxation within their provinces in order to raise revenue for provincial purposes. In addition, the BNA Act empowers the provinces to establish municipal institutions within their own territories; thus, the latter derive their powers and their fiscal and financial responsibilities from the provincial legislatures that created them.

A kraft mill on the Columbia River near Castlegar, BC.

Most major levies in Canada are direct taxes. A direct tax is generally recognized as one that is levied on the very person who should pay it; examples are personal and corporation income taxes, succession duties, social security contributions and a wide variety of provincial consumption taxes. The field of indirect taxation, which is occupied by the federal government, includes customs duties, excise levies, export charges on certain products and sales taxes levied on manufacturers. The federal government imposes both indirect taxes and direct taxes on income of individuals and corporations. The provincial governments levy only direct taxes, such as income taxes and numerous consumption taxes on sales of goods and services at the retail levels. Municipalities levy real property taxes and other imposts on places of business and specific municipal services.

Organization of Government

The organization of government is not uniform from one level to another, nor is it uniform among governments at the same level. Each government operates its affairs in the manner that it finds most convenient to its resources and most suitable to the discharge of its responsibilities. The resulting differences in the organizational

Copper Cliff smelting complex at Sudbury, Ont.

Calgary, Alta.

structures of the various governments raise problems if one seeks to compare public finance from one government to another. However, by consolidating the transactions of all levels of government to form only one governmental universe, a measure of the collective impact of government financial activities upon the general public can be obtained, as is illustrated in the first columns of Tables 1 and 2.

Intergovernment Fiscal Arrangements

Fiscal arrangements between the federal, provincial and territorial governments take various forms and are governed either by an Act of Parliament or by formal agreements between levels of government. Intergovernment transfer payments resulting from these arrangements are summarized in the following.

Statutory subsidies established by the BNA Act provide annual grants in support of provincial legislatures and annual allowances up to amounts based upon provincial populations. Under the Public Utilities Income Tax Transfer Act, the federal government remits to the provinces a certain percentage (the amount of which is established periodically by an Act of Parliament) of the income tax it collects from non-government-owned companies that generate or distribute electrical energy, gas and steam.

Federal-provincial fiscal, economic and financial relations are now governed by the Federal-Provincial Fiscal Arrangements and Established Programs Financing Act of 1977; this Act is renegotiated every five years. By virtue of the 1977 Act, the federal government pays to a province, where applicable, fiscal equalization and stabilization payments, enters with the provinces into tax collection agreements and reciprocity agreements concerning provincial taxes and fees, makes guarantee payments in relation to provincial personal income tax revenue, transfers to the provinces 20 per cent of the tax on 1971 undistributed income on hand, and contributes to the financing of established programs. Equalization payments are the most important cash transfers made under this Act, and are based on the philosophy that all Canadian citizens are entitled to a standard of public services that is fairly comparable in all the regions of the country; thus, from its revenue collected in all provinces, the federal government makes part of the nation's wealth available to provinces with incomes lower than the national average income.

In accordance with the BNA Act a government does not levy taxes on another government; for example, where a government property would normally be subject to a levy, a grant is made to the municipality, province or other local taxing

Copper mines at Murdochville, Que.

Charlottetown, PEI.

authorities in lieu of the property taxes the community must forgo because of the exempt status of the property. Due to the growing complexities of the economic and commercial transactions of governments, these constitutional provisions have become increasingly difficult to observe. To remove, or at least minimize the uncertainties and difficulties surrounding the paying of consumption taxes among governments, the federal government has entered into reciprocity agreements with the provinces concerning provincial taxes and fees. These agreements are spelled out in Part VIII of the Federal-Provincial Fiscal Arrangements and Established Programs Financing Act, 1977.

Another new feature of the 1977 Act concerns the financing of established programs such as post-secondary education, hospital insurance, medical care and extended health care services. Provisions for that financing are set out in Part VI of the Act and replace the cost-sharing provisions of the Hospital Insurance and Diagnostic Services Act and the Medical Care Act; they also deal with the arrangements pertaining to "contracting-out". Under the new financing system, the federal contributions take the form of a transfer of a share of its field of income

Primary class at Repulse Bay, NWT.

taxes and cash payments. Federal cash payments to the provinces in 1979-80, exclusive of the value of the fiscal transfers, were as follows: hospital insurance, $2,372 million; medical care insurance, $815 million; post-secondary education, $1,489 million; and extended health care services, $580 million.

Most provincial government transfer payments take the form of specific purpose transfers to local entities. Among such transfers, the largest are contributions to elementary and secondary education, which constitute a major source of funds for financing local school boards' expenditures.

Financial Transactions of the Various Levels of Government in the Fiscal Year Ended Closest to December 31, 1977

Tables 1 to 4 provide information on the revenue, expenditure, assets and liabilities of the various levels of government for the fiscal year that ended closest to December 31, 1977. The fiscal years concerned were April 1, 1977, to March 31, 1978, for the federal and provincial governments and January 1, 1977, to December 31, 1977, for most local governments.

The data are derived from the financial statements of the various governments and their agencies. Since these statements generally reflect the idiosyncratic organization of each government and hence are mutually incompatible, the data have been recast in accordance with the financial management statistical framework which identifies revenues by source and expenditures by function so that the resulting statistics are compatible among governments and the various levels of governments.

Table 1. Revenue of federal, provincial and local governments

(fiscal year ended closest to December 31, 1977)

Source of revenue	All governments consolidated $'000	Federal government Amount $'000	Federal government Share of total revenue %	Provincial governments Amount $'000	Provincial governments Share of total revenue %	Local governments Amount $'000	Local governments Share of total revenue %
Income taxes:							
Personal	22,916,775	13,562,175	34.7	9,354,600	21.4	…	…
Corporation	7,935,488	5,827,760	14.9	2,107,728	4.8	…	…
On payments to non-residents	502,695	502,695	1.3	…	…	…	…
Sub-total — income taxes	31,354,958	19,892,630	50.9	11,462,328	26.2	…	…
Property and related taxes	7,445,998	…	…	105,439	0.2	7,340,559	37.3
Consumption taxes:							
General sales	9,392,096	4,427,013	11.3	4,955,078	11.4	10,005	—
Motive fuel	2,265,966	598,402	1.5	1,667,564	3.8	…	…
Alcoholic beverages and tobacco	1,765,382	1,271,632	3.3	493,750	1.1	…	…
Custom duties	2,312,038	2,312,038	5.9	…	…	…	…
Other	486,760	156,139	0.4	312,707	0.7	17,914	0.1
Sub-total — consumption taxes	16,222,242	8,765,224	22.4	7,429,099	17.0	27,919	0.1
Health and social insurance levies	7,791,489	4,318,813	11.1	3,472,676	7.9	…	…
Miscellaneous taxes	1,369,318	531,420	1.4	782,093	1.8	55,805	0.3
Natural resources revenue	4,380,256	29,172	—	4,351,084	10.0	…	…
Privileges, licences and permits	1,189,292	60,911	0.2	1,000,196	2.3	128,185	0.7
Other revenue from own sources	12,761,929	5,455,404	14.0	5,352,341	12.3	2,380,470	12.1
Transfer from other levels of government:							
For general purposes	…	…	…	3,315,722	7.6	1,354,650	6.9
For specific purposes	…	…	…	6,424,648	14.7	8,367,280	42.6
Sub-total — transfers	…	…	…	9,740,370	22.3	9,721,930	49.5
Total revenue	82,515,482	39,053,574	100.0	43,695,626	100.0	19,654,868	100.00

… Not applicable.
— Amounts too small to be expressed.
Source: Statistics Canada Catalogue Nos. 68-202, 68-204, 68-207 and 68-211.

Table 2. Expenditure of federal, provincial and local governments
(fiscal year ended closest to December 31, 1977)

Functions of expenditure	All governments consolidated $'000	Federal government Amount $'000	Share of total expenditure %	Provincial governments Amount $'000	Share of total expenditure %	Local governments Amount $'000	Share of total expenditure %
General services	6,403,731	2,607,234	5.7	2,861,526	6.5	934,971	4.4
Protection of persons and property[1]	7,601,475	4,573,664	9.9	1,466,996	3.4	1,560,815	7.4
Transportation and communications	7,818,037	2,836,611	6.2	2,555,585	5.8	2,425,841	11.6
Health	10,994,908	277,453	0.6	10,479,076	24.0	238,379	1.1
Social services	20,735,993	14,170,156	30.8	6,004,597	13.8	561,240	2.7
Education	13,847,851	589,569	1.3	4,256,968	9.8	9,001,314	42.9
Environment	2,490,979	265,980	0.6	376,716	0.9	1,848,283	8.8
Other expenditure	20,957,139	10,594,727	23.0	6,625,141	15.2	3,737,271	17.8
Intergovernment sales of goods and services	...	130,788	0.3	295,498	0.7	...	...
Transfers to other levels of government:							
For general purposes	...	3,477,217	7.6	1,114,312	2.6	...	...
For specific purposes:							
Transportation and communications	...	134,891	0.3	781,978	1.8	4,439	—
Health	...	2,851,466	6.2	101,358	0.2	629,972	3.0
Social welfare	...	1,472,853	3.2	378,813	0.9	33,110	0.2
Education	...	1,340,985	2.9	5,723,648	13.1	388	—
Other purposes	...	631,865	1.4	562,825	1.3	11,793	0.1
Sub-total—specific purpose transfers	...	6,432,060	14.0	7,548,622	17.3	681,150	3.3
Sub-total—transfers	...	9,909,277	21.6	8,662,934	19.9	681,150	3.3
Total expenditure	90,850,113	45,955,459	100.0	43,585,037	100.0	20,989,264	100.0

[1] Includes national defence.
... Not applicable.
— Amounts too small to be expressed.
Source: Statistics Canada Catalogue Nos. 68-202, 68-204, 68-207, 68-209 and 68-211.

Table 3. Financial assets of federal, provincial and local governments
(fiscal year ended closest to December 31, 1977)

Financial assets	Federal government		Provincial governments		Local governments	
	Amount $'000	Share of total %	Amount $'000	Share of total %	Amount $'000	Share of total %
Cash on hand or on deposit	3,037,606	6.0	3,945,728	10.5	1,414,023	18.9
Receivables	271,259	0.5	2,203,128	5.8	2,677,309	35.8
Loans and advances	27,315,154	53.9	5,425,030	14.4	725,998	9.7
Investments:						
Canadian securities	17,200,402	34.0	20,918,950	55.4	1,564,960	20.9
Foreign securities	1,177,053	2.3	...	...	...	...
Sub-total-investments	18,377,455	36.3	20,918,950	55.4	1,564,960	20.9
Other financial assets	1,671,410	3.3	5,237,097	14.9	1,098,045	14.7
Total financial assets	50,672,884	100.0	37,729,933	100.0	7,480,335	100.0

... Not applicable. Source: Statistics Canada. Catalogue Nos. 68-204, 68-209 and 68-211.

Table 4. Liabilities of federal, provincial and local governments
(fiscal year ended closest to December 31, 1977)

Financial liabilities	Federal government		Provincial governments		Local governments	
	Amount $'000	Share of total %	Amount $'000	Share of total %	Amount $'000	Share of total %
Borrowings from financial institutions	...	...	492,395	1.2	2,049,375	9.8
Payables	13,532,978	21.2	2,268,752	5.6	1,668,311	7.9
Loans and advances	...	...	2,277,471	5.6	...	...
Bonds and debentures:						
Canadian market	40,971,092	64.2	25,124,705	62.1	13,567,219	64.5
Foreign market	180,517	0.3	7,943,152	19.6	3,152,396	15.0
Sub-total-bonds and debentures	41,151,609	64.5	33,067,857	81.7	16,719,615	79.5
Other liabilities	9,154,046	14.3	2,399,327	5.9	597,104	2.8
Total liabilities	63,838,633	100.0	40,505,802	100.0	21,034,405	100.0

... Not applicable. Source: Statistics Canada. Catalogue Nos. 68-202, 68-204, 68-209 and 68-211.

Federal Government Transactions. In 1977-78 the federal government derived a revenue of $39,053,574,000 and incurred an expenditure of $45,955,459,000. Of the federal revenue 34.7 per cent was obtained from personal income tax, 14.9 per cent from corporation income tax and 11.3 per cent from general sales taxes; these three sources accounted for 60.9 per cent of the total. Social welfare, transfers to other levels of government (mostly provincial) and protection of persons and property (mainly national defence) accounted for 30.8, 21.6 and 9.9 per cent respectively (62.3 per cent collectively) of the total federal expenditure.

The financial assets of the federal government amounted to $50,672,884,000 and its liabilities to $63,838,633,000 on March 31, 1978. Of its financial assets 53.9 per cent were in the form of loans and advances and 36.3 per cent pertained to holding of securities; 64.5 per cent of its liabilities related to bonds and debentures and 21.2 per cent to payables.

Provincial Government Transactions. In the fiscal year 1977-78 the total revenue of provincial governments amounted to $43,695,626,000 and total expenditure was $43,585,037,000. Health and social insurance levies and the levies on

Ocean terminal at Halifax, NS.

Saskatoon, Sask.

personal income, general sales, motive fuel and corporation income provided 7.9, 21.4, 11.4, 3.8 and 4.8 per cent respectively (49.3 per cent collectively) of total revenue. Provincial governments also received 22.3 per cent of their revenue in the form of transfers from other governments (mainly from the federal government). Health, transfers to other levels of government, education and social welfare accounted for 24.0, 19.9, 9.8 and 13.8 per cent respectively (67.5 per cent collectively) of total expenditure.

On March 31, 1978, the total financial assets of provincial governments stood at $37,729,933,000 and their total liabilities at $40,505,802,000. Of their financial assets 55.4 per cent were in the form of securities and 14.4 per cent related to loans and advances, while 81.7 per cent of the liabilities of provincial governments were covered by bonds and debentures.

Local Government Transactions. During the fiscal year ended closest to December 31, 1977, local governments had total revenue of $19,654,868,000 and total expenditure of $20,989,264,000. Real property taxes and transfers from other levels of government (mainly from provincial governments) produced 37.3 and 49.5 per cent respectively of total revenue. Education, transportation and communications, protection of persons and property, and environment accounted for 42.9, 11.6, 7.4 and 8.8 per cent respectively (70.7 per cent collectively) of total expenditure.

Sidewalk snow removal in Toronto, Ont.

At the end of the fiscal year, 1977, the total financial assets of local governments amounted to $7,480,335,000 and total liabilities to $21,034,405,000. Most of these financial assets were in the form of receivables and securities (35.8 and 20.9 per cent respectively), while their liabilities related mostly to bonds and debentures (79.5 per cent of the total).

Highway through the Richardson Mountains, NWT.

Expanding uranium centre at Elliot Lake, Ont.

Balance of International Payments

The Canadian balance of international payments summarizes transactions between residents of Canada and those of the rest of the world. International transactions in goods, services, transfers and capital have an important effect on the Canadian economy and monetary system, so the balance of payments accounts form an integral part of the system of national accounts. Transactions in goods and services are also an important constituent and determinant of the gross national product (GNP), while the capital account of the balance of payments forms a sector in the financial flow accounts.

Sources of balance of payments data are as varied as the range of transactions included in each of the accounts. A considerable amount of the information used originates from annual, quarterly and monthly surveys carried out by the Balance of Payments Division of Statistics Canada. Other divisions of Statistics Canada, other government departments and the Bank of Canada all provide information concerning transactions between residents of Canada and non-residents.

There was a fall of $283 million in the current account deficit to $5,019 million in 1979 which reflected increases of $600 million in the merchandise trade surplus and $140 million in the balance on migrants' funds, as well as decreases of $600 million in the travel deficit and $260 million in official contributions. These changes were partly offset by increases of $820 million in net payments of interest and dividends and $550 million in other service transactions.

Loading freighter with grain from elevator at Thunder Bay, Ont.

Capital movements during 1979 produced a net inflow of $11,121 million, up $7,381 million from 1978. Net capital inflow in long-term forms at $3,210 million were virtually unchanged from 1978. Within the components, however, there were major changes. Those which tended to reduce the net inflow were lower new issues abroad (reflecting a decrease in federal government issues abroad), higher retirements and an increase in purchases of foreign equities. Offsetting movements included a swing to net inflows for foreign direct investment in Canada and sales to non-residents of Canadian outstanding securities.

Short-term capital movements led to a net inflow of $7,911 million, up $7,450 million from the previous year. Virtually all accounts contributed to this change. The offset to the borrowing by the authorities from the Canadian chartered banks accounted for $3 billion of this total change while another major contribution arose from the activities of the chartered banks which substantially increased their net liability position with non-residents in the form of both foreign currencies and Canadian dollars.

Net errors and omissions were equivalent to an outflow of $4,402 million up from $1,737 million in the previous year. In 1979, the International Monetary Fund made its first allocation of Special Drawing Rights (SDR) since 1972 with Canada's share being the equivalent of $219 million. The overall surplus in the balance of payments led to an increase in net reserve assets of $1,919 million. The increase in net official monetary assets of $1,919 million reflected a decrease in reserve assets of $847 million and an even larger drop in related liabilities of $2,766 million.

Following a drop in February 1979 to its lowest level since 1933, the value of the Canadian dollar in terms of the United States dollar closed the year at 85.72 US cents, up 1.6 per cent from the end of 1978. Declines ranging from 5 per cent to 9 per cent were recorded against major European currencies while there was a sharp appreciation against the Japanese yen.

Balance of International Indebtedness

Preliminary estimates produced on the basis of available data indicate that Canada's balance of international indebtedness totalled about $69 billion at the end of 1979, up from almost $61 billion in the preceding year. This represented the amount by which the book value of Canada's liabilities to other countries, totalling $135 billion, exceeded Canada's gross external assets of $66 billion at 1979 year end.

Canadian long-term investment abroad increased to $37 billion, with direct and portfolio investment abroad accounting for almost 70 per cent of the growth. With the inclusion of short-term claims on non-residents, Canada's assets amounted to $66 billion. The accumulated balance of net errors and omissions, which was in a net debit position, contributed significantly to the growth in short-term assets while net official monetary assets, with the repayment of short-term borrowings under standby credit facilities during 1979, rose to $4.2 billion.

Reflecting largely an inflow of portfolio capital and the growth in reinvested earnings accruing to non-residents, foreign long-term investment in Canada increased to $109 billion. With the addition of other long-term liabilities (such as non-resident equity in Canada's assets abroad and official SDR liabilities) and short-term claims by non-residents, Canadian liabilities amounted to about $135 billion.

Edmonton international airport, Alta.

Currency and Banking

Canada has a decimal currency with 100 cents to the dollar. The Bank of Canada has the sole right to issue notes for circulation in Canada and these notes, together with the coinage produced by the Royal Canadian Mint, make up the currency in circulation and are the means of payment in cash transactions.

While cash transactions still play an important role in the payments system, the widespread use of cheques and, in more recent years, of credit cards has meant that the role of currency has become less important. By far the largest proportion of the public's holdings of money is held in deposit balances at financial institutions, principally the chartered banks, where it may be drawn on for making payments. Three types of chequing accounts are offered by the chartered banks — current and personal chequing accounts, on which no interest is paid, and chequable savings accounts, on which interest is paid. There are also non-chequable savings accounts, on which the banks pay a higher rate of interest, and various types of term deposits. Other deposit-taking institutions, such as credit unions, caisses populaires and trust and mortgage loan companies, also offer various types of savings and term deposits, including chequable savings accounts.

Bank of Canada

The Bank of Canada is Canada's central bank and the agency directly responsible for monetary policy. The ability of the Bank of Canada to exercise a broad controlling influence over the growth of money and the level of interest rates in Canada, and thereby to affect levels of spending and economic activity, stems primarily from the control it has over the amount of cash reserves available to the banking system.

Under the Bank Act, which regulates the operations of Canada's chartered banks, each chartered bank is required to maintain cash reserves in the form of deposits with or notes of the Bank of Canada equal to a stipulated percentage of its Canadian dollar deposit liabilities. The amount of cash reserves supplied to the banking system relative to the required level influences the willingness of the chartered banks to purchase securities or make loans and to bid for new deposits. If the supply of cash reserves is low relative to the required amount, banks will be forced to sell securities, restrict lending and bid for new deposits in order to acquire more cash reserves. These actions by the banks will tend to push up interest rates and encourage the general public to reduce its holdings of non-interest bearing demand deposits and currency. An increase in the supply of cash reserves has the opposite effect placing downward pressure on interest rates and encouraging the public to hold more money. Various techniques are used by the Bank of Canada to alter cash reserves, but the principal means involve changes to its holdings of Government of Canada securities and the transfer of government deposits between the central bank and the chartered banks.

The aim of the Bank of Canada's cash reserve management of the chartered banking system is to influence interest rates in a manner such that the money supply (defined as currency and privately-held demand deposits at chartered banks) will grow at a rate consistent with the monetary targets set by the bank. As of December 1979, the target range for the money supply has been a trend rate of

Weighing gold bricks near Timmins, Ont.

increase of 5 per cent to 9 per cent measured from the average level in the second quarter of 1979. Since 1975 the targets for monetary expansion have been lowered on four occasions in line with the Bank of Canada's long-run objective of gradually reducing money growth to a rate which would accommodate the maximum growth of output in the economy that is consistent with stable prices.

Although management of the cash reserves of the banking system is the primary policy instrument used by the Bank of Canada, various supplementary tools are also available. The bank also has the power to require the chartered banks to hold secondary reserves consisting of excess cash reserves, treasury bills and day-to-day loans to money market dealers. It is authorized to make short-term advances to chartered banks and can change the bank rate, the minimum rate at which it is prepared to make advances. Changes in the bank rate not only influence the current level of interest rates but also serve as an indication of the bank's stance on monetary policy. Although the bank rate is ordinarily administered directly by the Bank of Canada, the bank rate was set at one-quarter of 1.0 per cent above the weekly average tender rate of 91-day treasury bills during the period from November 1, 1956 to June 24, 1962 and the period beginning March 13, 1980. However, under a floating bank rate system the bank continues to play an important role in the determination of short-term interest rates through its open-market operations and its management of the reserves of the banking system.

In addition to its responsibility for monetary policy the Bank of Canada acts as fiscal agent for the Government of Canada. In this role it undertakes the management of the public debt for the government, operates a deposit account through which flow virtually all of the government's receipts and expenditures, handles foreign exchange transactions for the government and generally acts as an adviser on economic and financial matters.

Chartered Banks

The chartered banks are the largest deposit-taking institutions in Canada and a major source of short- to medium-term financing. They are major participants in the Canadian short-term money market and it is primarily through their response to the Bank of Canada's cash management that the influence of the central bank is transmitted to the money market and to credit markets generally. They also operate the country's cheque-clearing system. In addition to their domestic activities the chartered banks have an extensive foreign currency business and maintain offices and branches in major financial centres around the world.

At present there are 11 chartered banks operating in Canada; five of them have very extensive country-wide branch systems, while one operates principally in Quebec. The other more recently established banks operate largely in one region or specialize in wholesale banking. All banks operate under charters granted by Parliament under the terms of the Bank Act and are subject to inspection.

The chartered banks have a very wide range of dealings with all parts of the community. Bank loans are a major source of financing for businesses, farmers, governments and consumers, and banks account for a major share of the consumer credit extended. Most loans are relatively short-term, but the banks also provide term loans to businesses and farmers and invest in mortgages. They also offer their customers a variety of other services, including credit cards and facilities for obtaining foreign exchange and for the safekeeping of valuables.

Other Financial Institutions

In addition to the chartered banks, a wide range of other financial institutions serves the diverse needs of the community. The growth and development of such institutions has been particularly rapid during the past two or three decades, in large part reflecting the expansion of the Canadian economy and the increasing

Edmonton, Alta.

Coils of pure nickel strip are inspected at a mill at Fort Saskatchewan, Alta. before shipment to the Canadian Mint.

complexity of financial markets. While there is a degree of specialization in the different types of institutions, there is also considerable competition. Among the more important non-bank deposit-taking institutions are the trust and mortgage loan companies, the credit unions, the caisses populaires and the Quebec savings banks. Other major institutions include the sales finance and consumer loan companies, the life insurance companies and various types of investment companies. Stockbrokers and investment dealers also play an important role in financial markets. A number of institutions, including government agencies, specialize in medium- to longer-term financing for small businesses, farmers and exporters or in particular types of lending such as leasing.

The trust and mortgage loan companies have experienced rapid growth in recent years. There are about 135 such companies in Canada, most of which have branch networks. They compete with the chartered banks for deposits, mainly through the sale of fixed-term debentures and investment certificates, and are the largest lenders in the mortgage market, holding a major share of their assets in the form of mortgages. Trust companies also administer private and corporate pension funds and the estates of individuals, manage companies in receivership and act as financial agents for municipalities and corporations. Trust and mortgage loan companies are licensed and supervised either by the federal Department of Insurance or by provincial authorities.

Credit unions and caisses populaires have grown rapidly in recent years and have become an important part of the financial system. Most of them are formed on the basis of a common bond, such as employment, or organized on community lines; they differ from other financial institutions in their co-operative nature and local

The Canadian Mint at Winnipeg, Man.

character. Shares are sold to members, but most of the funds come from deposits and their assets are held largely in the form of mortgages and personal loans to members. Credit unions operate under provincial legislation; nearly all belong to central credit unions operating within their respective provinces.

Insurance

At the end of 1978, Canadians owned over $338,000 million worth of life insurance, with an average of $43,400 in force per household. Canadians are well insured compared to people in other countries. The Canadian life insurance business consists of about 250 companies and fraternal benefit societies, over half of which are federally registered companies. The latter group of companies writes more than 93 per cent of the total business of the industry and holds assets in Canada of over $33,000 million.

In addition to life insurance, most of the companies sell policies that cover expenses resulting from illness and compensate policyholders for wages not received during illness; such insurance may be purchased from a licensed insurance salesman or through a "group" plan operated by an employer, a professional association, or a union. About 300 companies sell property, automobile, liability and other casualty lines. The federally registered companies selling such insurance have assets in Canada of over $9,000 million.

Toronto international airport, Ont.

Transportation

Transportation has shaped the history of Canada and helps mould the lives of its people today. Over the years, the form of transportation has shifted from the explorer's canoe and the settler's train to the automobile and aircraft. Dramatic changes in for-hire carriage of goods have occurred in the span of two generations. In 1930, railways earned an estimated 85 per cent of Canada's freight revenue; by 1960, their share had dropped to less than 50 per cent. For-hire trucks accounted for 2 per cent of total freight revenue in 1930 and 30 per cent in 1960. By 1976, motor vehicle freight revenues had surpassed those for railway freight.

Air Transport

Transport Canada both regulates and serves civil aviation — providing registration and licensing of aircraft and licensing of personnel. From January 1970 to December 1979, the number of civil aircraft in Canada more than doubled, from

10,772 to 22,594. Licences in force for pilots, flight navigators, air traffic controllers and flight and maintenance engineers totalled 65,719 on December 31, 1979. In addition, there were 24,847 registered student pilots at the end of 1979. The department operates airports and provides air traffic control and other navigation facilities. In 1979, the 61 airports with Transport Canada air traffic control towers handled 7.2 million landings and take-offs, up 7 per cent over 1978 and 64 per cent over 1970. Both itinerant and local movements showed substantial increases over the period.

Table 1. Distribution of itinerant movements[1] at Transport Canada tower-controlled airports, by type of power plant, 1975-78

	1975		1976		1977		1978	
	No.	%	No.	%	No.	%	No.	%
Piston............	1,833,301	61.1	1,850,500	60.9	2,004,785	62.1	2,107,432	61.8
Turbo-prop........	246,825	8.3	249,911	8.2	287,841	8.9	295,919	8.7
Jet...............	781,390	26.1	786,097	25.9	771,114	23.9	805,344	23.6
Helicopter........	127,471	4.3	148,530	4.9	158,704	4.9	192,578	5.7
Glider............	4,412	0.2	3,233	0.1	5,203	0.2	6,951	0.2
Total.............	2,993,399	100.0	3,038,271	100.0	3,227,647	100.0	3,408,224	100.0

[1] A landing or take-off of an aircraft that is arriving from one airport or departing to another.

Table 2. Scheduled air passenger origin and destination journeys, top 10[1] city pairs, 1972-78

(thousands of passengers)

City pair	1972	1973	1974	1975	1976	1977	1978
Montreal, Que. — Toronto, Ont.	758.6	915.6	965.7	962.8	948.4	924.1	948.7
Calgary, Alta. — Edmonton, Alta................	275.3	332.2	372.4	412.5	429.4	478.8	551.3
Ottawa, Ont. — Toronto, Ont.	347.6	432.5	493.8	495.9	479.8	487.0	513.1
Toronto, Ont. — Vancouver, BC................	206.0	271.4	302.0	301.8	287.2	288.7	347.4
Calgary, Alta. — Vancouver, BC................	201.9	247.6	275.1	291.3	291.9	278.8	319.7
Edmonton, Alta. — Vancouver, BC................	170.1	217.3	246.7	253.8	265.7	247.7	277.6
Toronto, Ont. — Winnipeg, Man................	179.2	210.5	234.2	238.3	233.5	231.4	251.5
Calgary, Alta. — Toronto, Ont.	104.3	128.7	156.7	174.2	184.9	193.2	240.7
Edmonton, Alta. — Toronto, Ont.	88.7	111.3	124.1	138.7	150.5	153.3	195.7
Halifax, NS — Toronto, Ont.	113.5	147.3	158.6	168.4	168.6	156.6	176.7

[1] Ranked on 1978 figures.

The Canadian Transport Commission licenses and regulates commercial air carriers. The scheduled international routes of four Canadian air carriers — Air Canada, CP Air, Pacific Western Airlines and Nordair — form a vast network connecting Canada to every major continent. Canadian airlines also fly charters to destinations around the world. In addition to providing air transport, Canadian air carriers perform many varied services including crop dusting, forest fire patrol, pipeline inspection and aerial surveying.

In 1978, the 748 licensed Canadian air carriers reported operating revenues of $2,679 million; comparable figures for 1977 were $2,358 million. Expenditures, shown at $2,214 million in 1977, were estimated at $2,514 million for 1978. In 1977, these carriers transported 16.1 million passengers domestically and 6.2 million on international services; in 1978 they carried 17.0 million domestic passengers and 6.6 million international passengers, an increase of 5.8 per cent over the 1977 total of 22.3 million passengers.

Trends in domestic travel are illustrated by scheduled air passenger origin and destination data. From 1977 to 1978, figures for air journey origins and destinations showed increases for all 10 top city pairs (Table 2). While 1978 figures for Montreal–Toronto were still 1.8 per cent below the 1974 peak, Calgary–Edmonton passenger totals grew by 15.1 per cent between 1977 and 1978, and by 48.0 per cent between 1974 and 1978.

Table 3. Operations, operating revenue and expenses and fuel consumption, commercial air services, 1977 and 1978

(thousands)

	Transcontinental and regional air carriers[1]		All other air carriers		Total, all air carriers	
	1977[r]	1978	1977[r]	1978	1977[r]	1978
Operations						
Passengers	18,886	20,063	3,432	3,586	22,318	23,649
Passenger-kilometres........	31 874 885	34 277 446	3 671 595	3 940 979	35 546 480	38 218 425
Goods tonne-kilometres........	758 300	791 923	27 812	35 441	786 112	827 364
Flight departures....	363	389	824	816	1,207	1,205
Hours flown........	556	570	1,944	2,008	2,500	2,578
Operating revenues and expenses						
Total operating revenues ($)......	1,914,056	2,167,779	444,238	511,738	2,358,294	2,679,517
Total operating expenses ($)......	1,789,201	2,017,023	425,249	497,090	2,214,450	2,514,113
Fuel consumption						
Turbo fuel (litres) ...	2 993 207	3 031 784	290 725	341 193	3 283 932	3 372 977
Gasoline (litres).....	1 787	1 571	81 389	79 808	83 176	81 379

[1]Air Canada, CP Air, Eastern Provincial Airways, Quebecair, Nordair, Transair and Pacific Western Airlines.
[r]Revised.

VIA passenger train in southern Ontario.

Railways

Historically, railways have played a central role in the political integration, settlement and economic development of Canada. In 1850 there were 106 km (kilometres) of railway in all of British North America; 80 years later Canada had 91 065 km of track in operation. From 1930, growth was slow, reaching 96 958 km by 1974; by 1978, length of track in use had decreased to 94 085 km. Two continent-wide railways, Canadian National and Canadian Pacific, spanned 7 000 km from

Railway near Bathurst, NB.

Sawmill near Matagami, Que.

Atlantic to Pacific over vast stretches of rock and muskeg, flat prairie and mountain ranges to make possible the settlement of Western Canada. Today, these railways offer multi-modal transportation services, with emphasis on quick, cheap and efficient long-distance movement of bulk commodities and containers.

Canadian Pacific is a private company, while Canadian National Railways is operated by the federal government. Provincially operated railways include the British Columbia Railway, British Columbia Hydro's railway, Ontario Northland and GO Transit.

In 1978, revenue freight carried by rail decreased 3.4 per cent to 238 800 000 t (tonnes) from the 1977 total of 247 200 000 t. The number of passengers carried in 1978 remained at 23.9 million, almost unchanged from 1977. The number of employees needed to transport these people and goods in 1978 was 110,221, down slightly from 110,578 employees in 1977.

Scenic Western Canada.

Motor Vehicle Transportation

The principal means of passenger transportation remains the motor vehicle, with its associated high levels of fuel usage. Registrations of all road motor vehicle types for 1978 totalled 13.0 million. Of this figure, 75 per cent, or 9.7 million, were passenger automobiles. Truck and bus registrations were 2.8 million, or 21 per cent. Net sales of fuel to operate such vehicles amounted to 32 273 000 000 L (litres) of gasoline and 4 800 000 000 L of diesel fuel.

Network of roads near Edmonton, Alta.

Table 4. Motor carrier industry, 1978

	Motor carriers-freight[1]	Household goods movers[1]	Urban transit	Intercity passenger bus	Other passenger bus service[2]
Establishments reporting (No.)	3,589	370	78	62	1,704
Operating revenues ($ millions)	4,021	237	848	229	387
Operating expenses ($ millions)	3,855	227	810	212	354
Average number of employees including working owners (thousands).....	97	8	31	6	26
Pieces of revenue equipment operated (thousands)...............	130	6	12	2	22

[1] Excluding establishments reporting gross annual revenues of less than $100,000 for the previous year.
[2] Establishments engaged in limousine service to airports or stations, sightseeing, charter, tour and school bus service.

The annual survey of motor carriers freight covers establishments reporting annual operating revenues of $100,000 or more in the previous year. The 3,959 carriers in 1978, including 370 household goods movers, earned revenues of $4.3 billion, a 23 per cent increase over 1977 earnings of $3.5 billion reported by 3,193 carriers. The surveyed industry had 105,000 employees and 136,000 pieces of equipment in 1978, compared with an average of 90,000 employees and 123,000 pieces of equipment in 1977.

Canadian Coast Guard air cushion rescue craft patrolling the Strait of Georgia.

Motor carriers providing passenger services are classified into three basic divisions according to principal service, although a variety of services may be offered by a single operator. Of the 1,844 carriers surveyed in 1978, 78 were mainly engaged in urban transit and reported $848.4 million or 58 per cent of total operating revenues of $1,465.1 million. The 62 operating intercity passenger bus services accounted for 16 per cent of the revenue. Carriers providing such services as school bus, charter, tour and sightseeing, as well as limousine services to airports and stations, numbering 1,704, accounted for 26 per cent of the operating revenue.

Water Transport

Water transportation during 1977 generated revenues of $1.4 billion for 569 Canadian domiciled for-hire, private, government and sightseeing carriers; a 5 per cent increase in the number of carriers from 1976; and an 11 per cent increase in total water transportation revenue. The largest portion of the total revenue, $920.6

Marine lift for boats on the Severn River at Big Chute, Ont.

Digby, NS.

million, was generated by 412 carriers representing the for-hire water transportation industry. The 66 for-hire carriers reporting total water transportation operating revenue of $1 million or more from water transport accounted for $845.3 million, 92 per cent of the industry total of $920.6 million or 60 per cent of the total water transportation activity revenue of $1.4 billion. Water transportation operations, with 82 private carriers reporting, accounted for $230.0 million; 41 government carriers earned $259.8 million; and 34 water sightseeing establishments accounted for a total of $4.4 million.

Of the $1.4 billion gross revenue reported from water transport in 1977, 43 per cent of the total derived from domestic transport. In 1977, revenue of Canadian based companies having operations with foreign ports represented 28 per cent; movements between Canada and the United States accounted for 15 per cent. The remainder originated from revenue with no specific operating area.

During the 1978 shipping season, international freight handled at Canadian ports reached 178 300 000 t, a 2 per cent decline from 178 700 000 t in 1977. Related vessel arrivals and departures totalled 47,087 in 1978.

Domestic shipping at Canadian ports during 1978 increased 4 per cent to 121 300 000 t from the 1977 figure of 116 600 000 t. Related vessel arrivals and departures in domestic shipping in 1978 totalled 89,163 (83,328 in 1977).

Governments
and Their Services

Government

Canada is a federal state, established in 1867. In that year, at the request of three separate colonies (Canada, Nova Scotia and New Brunswick), the British Parliament passed the British North America (BNA) Act, which "federally united" the three "to form...one Dominion under the name of Canada". The Act merely embodied, with one modification (providing for the appointment of extra Senators to break a deadlock between the two Houses of Parliament), the decisions that delegates from the colonies, the "Fathers of Confederation", had themselves arrived at.

The Act divided the new nation into four provinces. The pre-Confederation "province of Canada" became the provinces of Ontario and Quebec, while Nova Scotia and New Brunswick retained their former limits. In 1870 the Parliament of Canada created Manitoba; British Columbia entered the federation in 1871 and Prince Edward Island in 1873. In 1905 the Parliament of Canada created Saskatchewan and Alberta and in 1949 Newfoundland joined.

The BNA Act gave Canada complete internal self-government and the country gradually acquired full control over external affairs as well. Canada is now a fully sovereign state, although a few very important parts of the Constitution can be changed only by Act of the British Parliament. This limitation, however, is purely nominal, as the British Parliament invariably passes any amendment requested by the Canadian; the only reason the full power of amendment has not been transferred to Canada is that Canadians have not been able to agree on an amending formula.

The BNA Act gives the Canadian Parliament power to "make laws for the peace, order and good government of Canada in relation to all matters...not...assigned exclusively to the Legislatures of the provinces". The Act added a list of examples of this general power, which includes: defence; raising money by any kind of taxation; regulation of trade and commerce; navigation and shipping; fisheries; currency and banking; bankruptcy and insolvency; interest; patents and copyrights; marriage and divorce; criminal law and criminal procedure; penitentiaries; interprovincial and international steamships, ferries, railways, canals and telegraphs; and any "works" declared by Parliament to be "for the general advantage of Canada". Amendments have added unemployment insurance and amendment of the Constitution, except in regard to the division of powers between Parliament and the provincial legislatures, the rights guaranteed to the English and French languages, the constitutional rights of certain religious denominations in education, the requirements of an annual session of Parliament and the maximum duration of Parliament.

The Act of 1867 gave Parliament and the provincial legislatures concurrent power over agriculture and immigration, with the federal law prevailing over the provincial in case of conflict. Amendments have since provided for concurrent jurisdiction over pensions, but with provincial law prevailing in case of conflict.

The BNA Act also established a limited official bilingualism. In debates in both Houses of Parliament members may use either English or French, the records and journals of both Houses must be kept in both languages, Acts of Parliament must be published in both languages and either language may be used in any pleading or process in courts set up by Parliament; the same provisions were made for the legislature and courts of Quebec. In 1969 Parliament adopted the Official Languages Act, which declares that English and French enjoy equal status and are the official languages of Canada for all purposes of the Parliament and Government of Canada.

Except for limited official bilingualism and certain educational rights for some religious minorities, the British North America Act provides no specific protection for fundamental rights like freedom of worship, of the press and of assembly. Therefore, the Parliament of Canada adopted a Bill of Rights in 1960 and has now adopted human rights legislation prohibiting discrimination in areas of federal jurisdiction.

Each provincial legislature has exclusive power over: the amendment of the provincial Constitution (except as regards the office of Lieutenant Governor, the legal head of the provincial executive); natural resources; direct taxation for provincial purposes; prisons; hospitals; asylums and charities; municipal institutions; licences for provincial or municipal revenue; local works and undertakings; incorporation of provincial companies; solemnization of marriage; property and civil rights; administration of justice (including the establishment of civil and criminal courts and civil procedure); matters of a merely local or private nature; and education, subject to certain safeguards for denominational schools in Newfoundland and Protestant or Roman Catholic schools in the other provinces. Judicial

Recent constitutional talks.

decisions have given "property and civil rights" a very wide scope, including most labour legislation and much of social security.

The Canadian Constitution

The BNA Act and its amendments provide only a skeleton framework of government, which is filled out by judicial interpretation, by various Acts of Parliament and of the legislatures and, most of all, by custom or "convention".

The Sovereign's powers are exercised, as the Fathers of Confederation put it, "according to the well understood principles of the British Constitution" — that is, according to the usages and understandings that gradually transformed the British monarchy into a parliamentary democracy. Canada has inherited and elaborated on these conventions to suit our own needs.

The Government of Canada

The Executive

By free and deliberate choice of the Fathers of Confederation, Canada is a constitutional monarchy. The executive government "is vested in the Queen" of Canada, who is also Queen of Britain, Australia and New Zealand. In strict law the powers of the Crown are very great. In fact they are exercised on the advice of a Cabinet responsible to the House of Commons, which is elected by the people. The Crown is represented by the Governor General (now always a Canadian), whom the Queen appoints on the advice of the Prime Minister.

The Queen Mother celebrated her 80th birthday on August 4, 1980.

Except in extraordinary circumstances, the Governor General or the Queen must act on the advice of ministers. On the advice of the Prime Minister the Governor General appoints the ministers and the members of the Senate. The Prime Minister decides when Parliament shall meet and normally decides when a new Parliament shall be elected, although there must be a general election at least once every five years. The Governor General appoints judges of the superior, district and county courts, the Lieutenant Governors of the provinces, deputy ministers and other senior appointees on the advice of the ministers.

The Cabinet and the Prime Minister are part of the convention rather than the law of the Constitution. The BNA Act provides only for a "Queen's Privy Council for Canada" appointed by the Governor General to "aid and advise" him; membership in the Privy Council is for life. It consists of all Cabinet ministers, all former ministers and various distinguished individuals appointed as a mark of honour. It is to some extent an honorific body, its practical importance being that membership in it is an essential requirement for holding ministerial office, and that only Privy Councillors currently holding ministerial office may advise the Governor General through orders-in-council.

The Cabinet is an informal body composed of those Privy Councillors currently holding ministerial office and is presided over by the Prime Minister. In April 1980 the Cabinet had 33 members, including the Prime Minister. By convention all ministers must be members of Parliament and most ministers are members of the House of Commons (at times only the Leader of the Government in the Senate is a Senator). It is customary, insofar as representation in Parliament permits, for the Cabinet to include at least one minister from every province, with the more populous provinces receiving greater representation.

The members of the Cabinet must speak as one on all questions of government policy; a minister who cannot support that policy must resign. Each minister of a department is answerable to the House of Commons for that department and the Cabinet as a whole is answerable to the House for government policy and administration generally.

If the government is defeated in the House on a motion of want of confidence, it must either resign office, at which point the Governor General calls on the Leader of the Opposition to form a new government, or seek dissolution of Parliament, which leads to a general election; the latter procedure is generally followed nowadays. Defeat of a major government bill is ordinarily considered a vote of want of confidence, leading to the same consequences, but the government can choose to consider any such defeat not decisive. The House then has the option of voting on a motion of want of confidence.

Only the government can introduce bills for the raising or spending of public money. Ordinary members of the House of Commons can move to reduce proposed taxes or expenditures, but not to raise them. The rules of the House allot most of its time to government business and nearly all legislation now comes from the government. Ministers have the sole power to move closure, cutting off debate, and if the other parties fail to agree ministers can move to fix a timetable for the various stages of a bill. But the rules are careful also to provide abundant opportunity for the Opposition to question, criticize and attack. Twenty-five days of each parliamentary year are specifically allotted to the Opposition to debate any subject it pleases and on six of those days it can move want of confidence.

A toast at the Tokyo summit in 1979.

The Legislature

Parliament. Parliament consists of the Queen, the Senate and the House of Commons. The Senate has 104 seats with the following distribution: 24 from Ontario, 24 from Quebec, 24 from the Maritime provinces (10 each from Nova Scotia and New Brunswick and 4 from Prince Edward Island), 24 from the western provinces (6 each), 6 from Newfoundland, one from the Yukon and one from the Northwest Territories. Senators are appointed by the Governor General on the advice of the Prime Minister. They retire at age 75.

The BNA Act gives the Senate the same legal powers as the House of Commons, except that money bills must originate in the Commons. The Senate can reject any bill, but rarely does. It does most of the work on private bills (such as incorporation of companies) and, like the House of Commons, subjects general legislation to careful scrutiny in committee; it makes particular use of special ad hoc committees to examine questions of major public importance. In April 1980 the Senate had 70 Liberals, 1 Independent Liberal, 27 Progressive Conservatives, 1 Social Credit, 2 Independents and 3 vacancies.

Burial services for the former Prime Minister Diefenbaker in Saskatchewan in 1979.

Parliament buildings in Ottawa, Ont.

The House of Commons has 282 seats: 7 from Newfoundland, 11 from Nova Scotia, 10 from New Brunswick, 4 from Prince Edward Island, 75 from Quebec, 95 from Ontario, 14 each from Manitoba and Saskatchewan, 21 from Alberta, 28 from British Columbia, one from the Yukon and two from the Northwest Territories. Members are elected by single-member constituencies, broadly speaking in proportion to the population of each province, but no province can have fewer members in the House of Commons than in the Senate. The total number of members and the representation of each province is readjusted after each decennial census according to rules set out in the British North America Act. Any adult Canadian citizen (with some exceptions, such as people in jail) can vote. In April 1980 the Liberals had 147 members, the Progressive Conservatives 103 and the New Democratic Party 32.

In the House of Commons, all bills pass through three stages known as "readings". The first, at which time the bill is tabled, is purely formal. On the second, the House gives the bill consideration in principle and, if satisfied, refers it to a committee, where it is dealt with clause by clause. Supply and budget bills and such others as the House thinks fit are referred to the Committee of the Whole, which is the whole House sitting under special rules facilitating detailed discussion. All other bills are sent to one of the 20 "Standing Committees" (12 to 30 members each), each of which specializes in a certain subject or subjects. The appropriate committee then reports the bill to the House, with or without amendments, and at this stage any member may propose amendments, which are debatable. Then comes a third reading. If the bill passes this it is sent to the Senate, where it goes through much the same procedure, following which it receives Royal Assent and thereby completes the process by which legislation is enacted by the Crown in Parliament.

The Canadian Constitution would be unworkable without political parties. Yet parties are almost unknown to Canadian law (an exception being the Election Expenses Act), a notable example of the conventions of the Constitution. The parties make possible a stable government, capable of carrying its policies into effect. They provide continuous organized criticism of that government. They make possible an orderly transfer of power from one government to another. They help to educate the electorate on public affairs and reconcile divergent elements and interests from different parts of the country.

The Liberal Party has its roots in the pre-Confederation Reform parties that struggled for the establishment of parliamentary responsible government in the 1840s. The Progressive Conservative Party goes back to a coalition of moderate Conservatives and moderate Reformers in the province of Canada in 1854, six years after responsible government had been won. It was broadened into a national party in 1867 when Sir John A. Macdonald, the first national Prime Minister, formed a Cabinet of eight Conservatives and five Liberals or Reformers, whose followers soon came to be known as "Liberal-Conservatives"; the present name was adopted in 1942. The New Democratic Party dates from 1961 when the major trade union federation (the Canadian Labour Congress) and the Co-operative Commonwealth Federation (CCF) joined forces to launch a new party; the CCF had been founded in 1932 by a group of farmer and labour parties in the western provinces.

Provincial and Territorial Government

In each province the machinery of government is substantially the same as that of the central government, except that no province has an upper house.

All of Northern Canada west of Hudson Bay and many islands northeast of Hudson Bay constitute two territories, the Yukon and the Northwest Territories, which come directly under the Government and Parliament of Canada but enjoy a growing degree of self-government.

The Yukon is administered by a commissioner, appointed by the Government of Canada, and an elected Council of 16 from which an Executive Council is appointed. This Council is responsible to the elected Council in much the same way as a provincial Ministry is responsible to a provincial legislature. The Commissioner in Council can pass laws dealing with direct taxation for local purposes, establishment

City Hall in Ottawa, Ont.

of territorial offices, sale of liquor, preservation of game, municipal institutions, licences, incorporation of local companies, property and civil rights, solemnization of marriage and matters of a local and private nature.

The Northwest Territories is administered by a commissioner, appointed by the Government of Canada, and an elected Council of 22, with an executive committee composed of a commissioner, deputy commissioner and up to five members of the elected Council who are nominated by the Council. The Commissioner in Council has substantially the same powers as in the Yukon.

Municipal Government

Municipal government, being a matter of provincial jurisdiction, varies considerably. All municipalities (cities, towns, villages and rural municipalities) are governed by elected councils. In Ontario and Quebec there are also counties, which group smaller municipal units for certain purposes, and both these provinces have set up regional municipalities for metropolitan areas.

In general, the municipalities are responsible for police and fire protection, local jails, roads and hospitals, water supply and sanitation, and schools (often administered by distinct boards elected for the purpose). They get their revenues mainly from taxes on real estate, fees for permits and licences and grants from the provinces. The total number of municipalities is now about 4,500.

The Legal System

The legal system is an important element in Canadian government. Since the British North America (BNA) Act established Canada as a federal state, the Canadian legal system is somewhat complex.

The Law and Law-making

The law in Canada consists of statutes and judicial decisions. Statutes are enacted by Parliament and the provincial legislatures and are written statements of legal rules in fairly precise and detailed form.

There is also a large body of case law that comes mainly from English common law and consists of legal principles evolved by the decisions of the superior courts over a period of centuries. The English common law came to Canada with the early English settlers and is the basis of much of the federal, provincial and territorial law. The province of Quebec, however, was originally settled by French inhabitants who brought with them civil law derived from French sources. Thus civil law principles govern such matters as personal, family and property relations in Quebec; the province has developed its own Civil Code and Code of Civil Procedure governing these and other matters and has, in effect, adapted the French civil law to meet Quebec's needs.

In addition to the statutes of the federal Parliament and provincial legislatures, there is a vast body of law contained in regulations adopted by appropriate authorities and in bylaws made by municipalities. This subordinate legislation, as it is called, is issued under authority conferred by either Parliament or the provincial legislatures.

Statutes enacted by the federal Parliament apply throughout the country; those enacted by provincial legislatures apply only within the territorial limits of the provinces. Hence, variations may exist from province to province in the legal rules regulating an activity governed by provincial law.

The main body of Canadian criminal law, being federal, is uniform throughout the country. Although Parliament has exclusive authority under the BNA Act to enact criminal law, the provincial legislatures have the power to impose fines or punishments for breaches of provincial laws. This gives rise to provincial offences — for example, the infraction of a provincial statute regulating the speed of automobiles travelling on the highways.

Most Canadian criminal law is contained in the Criminal Code, which is derived almost exclusively from English sources. Criminal offences are classified under the code as indictable offences, which are subject to a severe sentence, or summary conviction offences, to which a less severe sentence applies. However, the totality of statutory federal criminal law is not contained in the Criminal Code of Canada. Other federal statutes provide for the punishment of offences committed thereunder by fine or imprisonment or both. In any event, whether an offence be serious or minor, it is a fundamental principle of Canadian criminal law that no person may be convicted unless it has been proved beyond all reasonable doubt to the satisfaction of either a judge or a jury that he is guilty of the offence.

RCMP headquarters at Fredericton, NB.

Law Reform

As society changes, as its needs and even its standards change, the law has to reflect these changes. Therefore, many of the provinces now have law reform commissions that inquire into matters relating to law reform and make recommendations for this purpose. At the federal level, the Law Reform Commission of Canada carries out this activity by studying and reviewing federal law with a view to making recommendations for its reform.

The Courts and the Judiciary

The legal system includes courts, which play a key role in the process of government. Acting through an independent judiciary, the courts declare what the law is and apply it to resolve conflicting claims between individuals, between individuals and the state and between the constituent parts of the Canadian federation.

The Judiciary

Because of the special function performed by judges in Canada the BNA Act guarantees the independence of the judiciary of superior courts. This means that judges are not answerable to Parliament or to the executive branch of the government for decisions rendered. A federally appointed judge holds office during good behaviour but is removable from office by the Governor-in-Council on the address of the Senate and House of Commons; in any event, he or she ceases to hold office upon attaining the age of 75 years. The tenure of judges appointed by provinces to inferior courts is determined by the applicable provincial laws. No judge, whether federally or provincially appointed, may be subjected to legal proceedings for any acts done or words spoken in a judicial capacity in a court of justice.

The appointment and payment of judges reflect the interlocking of the divided powers found in the Canadian constitutional system. The federal government appoints and pays all judges of the federal, provincial superior and county courts, while judges of provincial inferior courts are appointed and paid by the provincial governments.

The Courts

In Canada, the power to create courts is divided. Some courts are created by Parliament (for example, the Supreme Court of Canada) and others by provincial legislatures (for example, superior courts, county courts and many lesser provincial courts). However, the Supreme Court of Canada and the provincial courts are part of an integrated whole; thus, appeals may be made from the highest courts of the provinces to the Supreme Court. Generally speaking, federal and provincial courts are not necessarily given separate mandates as to the laws that they administer. For instance, although criminal law is made by the Parliament of Canada, it is administered mainly in provincial courts.

Federal Courts. Federal courts in Canada include the Supreme Court of Canada, the Federal Court of Canada and various specialized tribunals such as the Tax Review Board, the Court Martial Appeal Court and the Immigration Appeal Board. These courts and tribunals are created by Parliament.

The Supreme Court, established in 1875, is the highest appeal court of Canada in civil and criminal matters. It consists of nine judges, of whom three at least must come from Quebec, a requirement added because of the special character of Quebec civil law. The conditions under which it hears appeals are determined by the statute law of Parliament. The Supreme Court entertains appeals from the provincial courts of appeal and from the Federal Court. It also gives advisory opinions to the federal government when asked under a special reference procedure. Five judges normally sit together to hear a case, although on important matters it is customary for all judges of the court to sit.

The Federal Court of Canada was created in its present form in 1970; its predecessor, the Exchequer Court of Canada, was originally created in 1875. This court deals with: taxation cases; claims involving the federal government (for instance, claims against the federal government for damage caused by its employees); cases involving trademarks, copyrights and patents; admiralty law cases; and aeronautics cases. It has two divisions, a Trial Division and an Appeal Division; the Appeal Division hears appeals from decisions rendered by the Trial Division and by many federal boards and agencies.

Provincial Courts. Provincial courts are established by provincial legislation and thus their names vary from province to province; nevertheless, their structures are roughly the same.

Provincial courts exist at three levels. Each province has inferior courts, such as family courts, juvenile courts, magistrates' courts and small debts courts; these deal

RCMP member performing airport security duties.

with minor civil and criminal matters and the great majority of cases originate and are decided in them. With the exception of the province of Quebec all provinces also have systems of county or district courts. These courts have intermediate jurisdiction and decide cases involving claims beyond the jurisdiction of the small debts courts, although they do not have unlimited monetary jurisdiction; they also hear criminal cases, except those of the most serious type. In addition to being trial courts, county and district courts have a limited jurisdiction to hear appeals from decisions of magistrates' courts. The highest courts in a province are its superior courts, which hear civil cases involving large sums of money and criminal cases involving serious offences. Superior courts have both trial and appeal levels; the appeal courts, with some exceptions, hear appeals from all the trial courts in the province and may also be called upon to give opinions on matters put to them under a special reference procedure by their respective provincial governments.

The Legal Profession

In common law jurisdictions in Canada, practising lawyers are both called as barristers and admitted as solicitors. In Quebec the legal profession is divided into the separate branches of advocate and notary. In all cases admission to practice is a provincial matter.

Legal Aid

In recent years all provincial governments have established publicly funded legal aid programs to assist persons of limited means in obtaining legal assistance in a number of civil and criminal matters, either at no cost or at a modest cost, depending on the individual's financial circumstances. These programs vary from province to province. Some are set up by legislative enactment, while others exist and operate by way of informal agreements between the provincial government and the provincial law society. Some provide fairly comprehensive coverage in both civil and criminal matters, while others encompass only criminal offences. In some cases federal funds are made available for development or expansion of the programs. The purpose of all such programs is to ensure that everyone gets adequate legal representation regardless of his or her financial circumstances.

The Police

The BNA Act assigns to the provinces the responsibility for judicial administration within their boundaries, but police forces have nevertheless been created by federal, provincial and municipal governments. Where municipal police forces exist it is their responsibility to provide general police services in that area. A municipality that has not created its own police force uses either the federal or the provincial police force.

Ontario and Quebec have created provincial forces that police areas of the province not served by municipal forces. Provincial police duties include providing police and traffic control over provincial highways, assisting municipal police in the investigation of serious crimes and providing a central information service about such matters as stolen and recovered property, fingerprints and criminal records.

The federal government maintains the Royal Canadian Mounted Police (RCMP). This civil force was originally created in 1873 under the name North-West Mounted Police. One of its early duties was to maintain public order in the sparsely settled Northwest Territories, which had previously been known as Rupert's Land; today the RCMP is the sole police force in the Yukon and the Northwest Territories. Eight provinces also employ the RCMP to carry out provincial policing responsibilities within their borders.

The RCMP enforces many federal statutes, with the greatest emphasis on the Criminal Code and the Narcotics Control Act. Force members are responsible for Canada's internal security, including the protection of government property and the safekeeping of visiting dignitaries, and the force also represents Canada in the International Criminal Police Organization (Interpol), which Canada joined in 1949.

The RCMP maintains and operates the Canadian Police Services, which include: eight crime detection laboratories strategically located across Canada; an identification service ranging from a computerized fingerprint retrieval system in Ottawa to Canada-wide field identification sections; the Canadian Police Information Centre (CPIC), which responds instantaneously to nationwide police-oriented requests; and the Canadian Police College in Ottawa, which provides advanced training courses to members of Canadian police forces and to a limited number of foreign authorities.

The RCMP is under the direction of a commissioner and on February 29, 1980, had an establishment of 19,937.

The RCMP finale of the Musical Ride at the Calgary Stampede.

Ministry of the Solicitor General

The Ministry of the Solicitor General was established by Parliament in 1966 and given responsibility for the Royal Canadian Mounted Police, the Canadian Penitentiary Service and the National Parole Board, agencies that had formerly been under the Department of Justice. The Correctional Investigator, first appointed in 1973, also reports to the Solicitor General.

A prime aim of the reorganization was the co-ordination of national programs for policing, penitentiaries and parole within the Canadian criminal justice system. The ministry plays a vital role in the maintenance of law, order and the country's internal security and has responsibility for offenders sentenced to two years or more in federal penitentiaries and for all inmates released on national parole.

The development and co-ordination of ministry policy is the responsibility of a Secretariat that reports to the Deputy Solicitor General. The Secretariat has branches responsible for policy, police and security, and programs.

The Correctional Service of Canada

The Correctional Service of Canada operates under the Penitentiary Act and is under the jurisdiction of the Solicitor General of Canada, with headquarters in Ottawa. It is responsible for all federal penitentiaries and for the care and training of persons committed to those institutions. The Commissioner of Corrections, under the direction of the Solicitor General, is responsible for control and management of the service and for related matters.

As of March 31, 1980, the Correctional Service of Canada controlled 61 institutions: 15 maximum security, 15 medium security, 14 minimum security and 17 community correctional centres. Total inmate population was 9,477. New, smaller institutions are being designed to provide more rehabilitation facilities for inmates, with indoor and outdoor recreation, and plans to phase out old institutions are being worked out.

The National Parole Board

Parole granted by the National Parole Board is a conditional release of an inmate serving a sentence in a prison under federal law; the selection is made when the inmate is eligible by law and ready. The conditional release is designed to offer protection to the community and there are specific obligations placed on the parolee. At the same time the release provides an opportunity for the inmate to become reintegrated into society.

The board has 26 members, located at its Ottawa headquarters and in five regions across Canada; the regional offices are located in Moncton, Montreal, Kingston, Saskatoon and Vancouver. Members are appointed by the Governor General in Council for a maximum of 10 years. All may be reappointed. Community representatives may be appointed to participate in any decisions made about releases of inmates serving life for murder, or sentences for an indeterminate period as habitual criminals, dangerous sexual offenders, or dangerous offenders. The board has both the exclusive jurisdiction and the absolute discretion to grant, refuse or revoke parole.

City Hall in Edmonton, Alta.

Citizenship

Acquisition of Citizenship

In 1947 Canada became the first country in the Commonwealth to adopt a distinct national citizenship. A new Citizenship Act was proclaimed in Parliament on February 15, 1977, with the intention, among others, of eliminating distinctions among applicants based on age, sex, marital status or country of previous citizenship.

The Citizenship Registration Branch of the Department of the Secretary of State provides facilities for the acquisition and proof of citizenship. To qualify for citizenship an adult alien (18 years of age or older) must have been admitted to Canada for permanent residence and have accumulated three years of residence in Canada within the four years immediately preceding application. Applicants for citizenship must also be able to speak either of the official languages, English or

Judge congratulates new Canadian citizens in Halifax, NS.

French, have a knowledge of Canada and of the responsibilities and privileges of citizenship and take the Oath of Citizenship. To become a Canadian citizen a person must apply for citizenship, appear before a Citizenship Judge for a hearing and attend a court ceremony to take the Oath of Citizenship. Requests for detailed information should be made to the nearest Citizenship Court or mailed to the Registrar of Canadian Citizenship, Department of the Secretary of State, Ottawa.

Citizenship Development

The Citizenship Sector administers a variety of programs that support participation in voluntary organizations and increase understanding among groups. Special emphasis is placed on increasing the understanding and enjoyment of fundamental human rights and reducing prejudice and discrimination related to sex, race or ethnic background.

The Women's Program Directorate encourages the complete integration of women as participating citizens in Canadian society. Through the provision of grants and other resources to women's groups it supports activities designed to increase the participation of women in all aspects of society. In 1980 one of the priorities of the program was to assist women's groups in promoting positive action by key institutions that have a particular impact on women's issues.

The Native Citizens' Program helps native people define and achieve their place in Canadian society by providing them with the resources to identify their needs and actively pursue their own development as Canadians. The program offers advice and technical and financial assistance to: friendship centres, operated by native groups in many cities across Canada, which help native people from reserves and isolated areas to adjust to city life; communications societies, which support the development and effective use of the media by native people; and native associations at the provincial, territorial and national levels, to undertake initiatives in recognition of basic human rights and improved lifestyles for their people.

The Multiculturalism Program encourages Canada's many different ethnic minority groups to maintain and develop their cultural heritage, to share it with others for greater inter-group understanding, and to achieve full participation in Canadian society as a whole.

The Citizens' Participation Program helps all citizens, through technical and financial assistance to their voluntary organizations, to participate in those decisions that affect the quality of their community life. The program endeavours to increase the understanding and acceptance of fundamental economic, social, cultural, civil and political rights; special emphasis is given to reducing inter-group tensions caused by prejudice and discrimination related to racial or ethnic background. The program also works with voluntary and other private organizations and with all levels of government and assists the human rights efforts of such international bodies as the United Nations.

The Open House Canada Program provides an opportunity for Canadian youths, 14 to 22 years of age, to explore the various regions of their own country, to become aware of interests and opinions of people in other areas of Canada, and to form new friendships. The program funds reciprocal exchanges between young people from all parts of Canada, in groups or individually.

Vietnamese refugees arriving in Vancouver in 1979.

Employment and Immigration

The Canada Employment and Immigration Commission is the federal government organization responsible for the development and utilization of manpower resources in Canada, the regulation of immigration and the administration of the Unemployment Insurance Program.

Labour Market Policies and Programs

More than 400 Canada Employment Centres across Canada help people find jobs and help employers find workers. To achieve this goal, the commission provides a recruitment service and specialized manpower planning assistance for employers, as well as job referral, occupational training, job creation, mobility assistance, vocational counselling and aptitude testing for workers. Special services are provided to persons who have experienced difficulty in entering the labour market. The commission operates extensive job creation programs, intended to reduce unemployment and assist future growth, and administers the federal government's Employment Tax Credit Program.

Immigration

Canada's immigration law regulates the admission of all people seeking to come into Canada. In addition to immigrants this includes foreign students, temporary workers, tourists, business people and other visitors to Canada.

The commission maintains 59 immigration offices in 40 countries around the world to assist people who intend to visit or immigrate to Canada. Anyone wishing to immigrate must apply at one of these offices and be selected according to

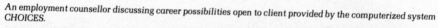

An employment counsellor discussing career possibilities open to client provided by the computerized system CHOICES.

universal standards designed to assess their ability to adapt to Canadian life and settle successfully. There are three classes of admissible immigrants — the family class sponsored by close relatives in Canada, refugees, and independent and other applicants who apply on their own initiative with or without the assistance of relatives. Similarly, visitors who wish to study or work in Canada must obtain authorizations at these offices before they travel to Canada.

In addition to its foreign offices, the commission operates a network of 107 Canada Immigration Centres at Canadian airports, sea or inland ports, and border crossings to provide landing and settlement services as well as immigration information and assistance for immigrants, visitors and residents. Officers at these centres also enforce control measures to exclude or remove individuals whose presence in Canada would threaten public safety or national security.

Under Canada's constitution, immigration is a shared responsibility, and the federal program is carried out in co-operation with provincial governments.

Unemployment Insurance

Unemployment insurance provides temporary financial assistance to workers who are out of work or are unable to work because of illness, injury, quarantine or pregnancy. About 95 per cent of Canadian workers are covered under the plan.

Following is the outline of the unemployment insurance benefit rate, qualifying weeks, insurable earnings, premiums and benefit duration.

Benefit Rate: (1) 60 per cent of average weekly insurable earnings in qualifying weeks; (2) Maximum benefit in 1980 — $174 a week; and (3) All benefits subject to income tax.

Qualifying Weeks: (1) Regular benefit for claimants applying for the first time — 10 to 14 weeks of insurable employment in the qualifying period depending on unemployment rate in area where claimant ordinarily lives; (2) Claimants applying for the second time in 52 weeks may require a maximum of six additional weeks. Recent first-time entrants into the labour force or those entering after a long absence of almost two years — 20 weeks of insurable employment; (3) Special benefit — 20 weeks in insurable employment in qualifying period; (4) Qualifying period — last 52 weeks or since last claim for unemployment insurance started, whichever is shorter.

Insurable Earnings: Maximum insurable earnings in 1980 — $290 weekly.

Premiums: (1) Basic employee premium in 1980 — $1.35 per $100 weekly insurable earnings; (2) Employer premium — 1.4 times employee rate; (3) Premiums tax deductible.

Benefit Duration: (1) Regular benefit — (a) initial phase — one week for each insurable week up to a maximum of 25 weeks; (b) labour force extended phase — one week for every two insurable weeks to a maximum of 13 weeks benefit; (c) regional extended phase — up to 32 additional weeks depending on rate of unemployment in various regions; and (d) maximum weeks of benefit — 50. (2) Special benefits — (a) illness benefit — up to 15 weeks depending on nature of illness; (b) maternity benefit — up to 15 consecutive weeks within period starting 8 weeks before birth of child to 17 weeks after; and (c) benefit paid at age 65 — one time lump sum benefit equal to 3 weeks benefit.

Labour

Labour Canada's overall objective is to promote and protect the rights of parties involved in the world of work; a working environment conducive to physical and social well-being; and a fair return for efforts in the workplace. The department is also charged with ensuring equitable access to employment opportunities. Major programs and services are aimed at meeting the objectives of Labour Canada.

Under the Canada Labour Code the Minister, in addition to other responsibilities of Labour Canada, is responsible for granting consent to refer certain complaints of unfair labour practices to the Canada Labour Relations Board and for granting consent to complainants to institute prosecution in the courts.

Although employee and employer relations in all sections of Canadian business and industry are of interest to the department, its direct concern is with enterprises within the federal jurisdiction — and their employees, numbering over 500,000.

Labour Canada is decentralized into five regions — Atlantic, St. Lawrence, Great Lakes, Central and Mountain — with headquarters in the national capital region. The department is divided into several main bodies — the Policy Co-ordination and Liaison Group; the Federal Mediation and Conciliation Service; the Executive Co-ordination, Regional Operations Group; the Women's Bureau; and Program Development and Central Operations. Administrative Policy and Services and Legal Services are also among these divisions.

An oil drilling ship undergoing refit at Esquimalt, BC, for drilling in the Beaufort Sea.

Stacking logs on Vancouver Island, BC.

The Policy Co-ordination and Liaison Group is responsible for the examination of broad issues which have a bearing on the department's programs and policies. It suggests ways to keep the department relevant to a rapidly changing economic and social environment and generates information and suggestions to appropriate centres in the department. This group is also responsible for the department's international labour activities and for managing the department's relations with the provinces, maintaining strong links with provincial departments of labour.

The Federal Mediation and Conciliation Service seeks to promote and encourage good industrial relations in federal industries governed by the Canada Labour Code through the provision of third-party conciliation and mediation assistance to labour and management in the settlement of collective bargaining and other types of industrial relations disputes. This service has offices in six centres across Canada and is composed of three branches — mediation and conciliation, planning and technical support, and arbitration services.

The Executive Co-ordination, Regional Operations Group is responsible for the decentralized segment of the department which delivers and enforces various laws, programs and services of the department. The group assumes a leading role with the regional directors in the planning and implementation of departmental programs and in development of common operational policies and procedures.

The Women's Bureau is concerned with all aspects of women's status in the workplace. In co-operation with other federal agencies the Women's Bureau has been instrumental in bringing about legislation for equal pay, maternity leave and benefits, and equal employment opportunities.

Program Development and Central Operations consists of Central Analytical Services (including Labour Data Branch, Economic Analysis Branch and Library and Legislative Analysis Branch), Occupational Safety and Health Branch, and Employment Relations and Conditions of Work Branch.

Central Analytical Services is responsible for co-ordinating analytical operations carried out in Program Development and Central Operations. Analyses of labour developments are the bases for reports that contribute to departmental and government policies concerning collective bargaining and labour affairs.

The Labour Data Branch collects, processes and distributes national labour-related information. Data are regularly provided on occupational wages and salaries; working conditions; collective agreement settlements and provisions; and strikes and lockouts.

Paper machine press section for a plant in British Columbia, being assembled at Lachine, Que.

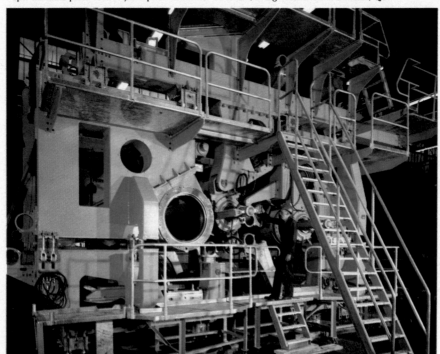

Above ground facilities of a gas storage plant. The underground storage of gas is an integral part of gas supply operations.

The Economic Analysis Branch undertakes studies dealing with wage and non-wage compensation issues and general economic conditions.

The Library and Legislative Analysis Branch provides a departmental and national information service in the fields of labour affairs and labour legislation. The library has a collection numbering more than 100,000 volumes covering all aspects of industrial relations. The legislative analysis unit undertakes research into labour laws and related administrative practices in all jurisdictions in Canada.

The Occupational Safety and Health Branch develops policies and programs to promote safe and healthy working conditions. It is also responsible for policy advice on the administration of compensation for work injuries to employees under federal jurisdiction and the administration of these benefits for seamen not covered by other compensatory legislation.

The Employment Relations and Conditions of Work Branch conducts research, designs programs and evaluates departmental policies relating to labour-management relations. It is concerned with the development and growth of constructive labour-management relations. The branch also develops policies and programs designed to improve employment standards such as hours of work, minimum wages, job security and vacation leave.

Loading a foreign ship at the wharf in Strathcona Sound, Baffin Island, NWT.

Industry, Trade and Commerce

The Department of Industry, Trade and Commerce was established on April 1, 1969, following the merger of the former Departments of Industry and of Trade and Commerce. It offers a wide variety of programs and services to the Canadian industrial and business community. The department is involved in areas of research and development, production and export marketing. The assistance provided is designed to help industry achieve increased productivity and to develop and protect markets for Canadian products both at home and abroad.

Organization and Programs

The department is organized into eight main functional groups: Industry and Commerce Development; Finance and Enterprise Development; International Trade Relations; Trade Commissioner Service and International Marketing; Economic Policy and Analysis; Tourism; and Corporate Affairs.

Industry and Commerce Development is responsible for the creation, development and maintenance of policies and programs which encourage and assist in achieving efficient and sustained growth of Canadian industrial development. The group establishes guidelines and priorities for developing a strong and internationally competitive industry. It consists of 10 industry sector branches covering the principal manufacturing, processing and service industries.

Finance and Enterprise Development is responsible for the formulation of policies and the subsequent implementation, promotion and monitoring of funded programs and services aimed at the development and maintenance of a strong and internationally competitive Canadian industry.

The International Trade Relations Section is responsible for the creation and improvement of an international trading environment favourable to Canadian trade and other economic interests. It is also responsible for policies and programs to safeguard and advance Canada's international trading interests.

The Trade Commissioner Service has 91 trade offices in 66 countries. Its primary role is to promote Canada's export trade and to represent and protect its commercial interests abroad.

Economic Policy and Analysis provides information and expertise on departmental horizontal issues. It is responsible for analysis and assessment of economic and general policy information from all sources within the federal government, provincial government, industry and labour.

The Canadian Government Office of Tourism is an agency of the department. Directly descended from the Canadian Travel Bureau, this agency was created in 1934. At present it consists of two branches, Tourism Marketing and Tourism Development.

The Small Business Secretariat performs an advocacy role on behalf of small and medium-sized business. Its functions include: research and policy development on broad issues affecting the small business community; contact with small businessmen and their organizations to aid in the resolution of problems or concerns raised; representation of a community's interests before departments whose programs impact upon it; and recommendation of changes to policy regulations or legislation which will foster the growth of small and medium-sized business.

Business Information Centres are operated, administered and funded by the Department of Industry, Trade and Commerce. Because of the number and complexity of business related policies and programs provided by all levels of government, combined with the growing program-information gap, the department opened an experimental business information centre in Ottawa in March 1978. This centre was designed to answer inquiries concerning federal government programs and services of interest to businessmen. Following a year of refining the Ottawa systems for information gathering and disseminating, a network of regional business information centres was established. Most centres are located near regional offices. Each regional centre is accessible by local phone in the centre city and the main centre by a toll-free number (ZENITH 0-3200).

Newsprint rolls being loaded onto a ship at the port of Quebec City.

Regional Economic Expansion

While Canada enjoys one of the world's highest standards of living, its history and geography have dictated a wide disparity of economic, social and cultural well-being. Centres of concentrated economic activity and population contrast with large geographic areas where levels of industry and employment, social and commercial services are far lower than national averages.

The creation of the Department of Regional Economic Expansion on April 1, 1969, was the culmination of a process which started in July of the previous year when the Prime Minister announced the government's intention of establishing a department to mount a new and comprehensive federal effort to combat regional economic disparities in Canada.

The Department of Regional Economic Expansion (DREE) works to combat regional disparities by encouraging slow-growth regions to realize their potential for contributing to the economic and social development of Canada. Accordingly, the present program approach is broadly divided into three categories: development opportunity initiatives, industrial incentives, and other programs.

Development Opportunities

Development opportunities are identified through General Development Agreements, signed separately with the provinces, and supported by other federal departments. Activities designed to exploit these development opportunities are undertaken through subsidiary agreements. Current activities in this context cover a wide range of economic sectors, including development of natural resources, manufacturing and processing, transportation and communications, tourism and northlands, and other related endeavours, varying from province to province.

Yellowknife, NWT.

Halifax, NS.

Industrial Incentives

The Regional Development Incentives Act, passed in 1969 and extended to 1981, is designed to stimulate increased manufacturing investment and employment in slow-growth regions of the country.

The Act makes grants available to encourage manufacturing and processing industries to establish, expand or modernize facilities in broad designated regions. These regions include all four Atlantic provinces, Manitoba, Saskatchewan, Yukon and the Northwest Territories, together with most of the province of Quebec and the northern portions of Ontario, Alberta and British Columbia. Under the Department of Regional Economic Expansion Act, the Montreal special area program offers incentives to selected industrial sectors in metropolitan Montreal and to industrial sectors in Montreal's satellite towns and in the Outaouais region.

Other Programs

Through the special Agricultural and Rural Development Act (ARDA) program in some western provinces and northern areas, economic and social development activities are carried out for the benefit of rural residents; particularly those of native ancestry. The 15-year Prince Edward Island comprehensive development plan, signed in 1969 under the Fund for Rural Economic Development Act, provides for development programming in a number of economic sectors. Under the Prairie Farm Rehabilitation Act, the department develops and promotes improved water supply, tree culture, farming methods and land utilization in the Prairie provinces.

Present Organization

The department is fully decentralized to enable it to respond rapidly and efficiently to local, provincial and regional needs as they arise. The present organization includes headquarters in Hull, Que., regional offices at Moncton, Montreal, Toronto and Saskatoon, a provincial office in each provincial capital and various branch offices.

Bakery research lab at Winnipeg Grain Exchange.

Consumer and Corporate Affairs

Consumer and Corporate Affairs Canada was established in December 1967 to bring together in one department many federal laws governing business and consumer transactions in the marketplace. Its legislation and policies are designed to stimulate efficiency and productivity among suppliers of goods and services and to promote fair economic treatment for all concerned in commercial transactions.

The department is organized into three key bureaus that share responsibility for achieving the department's objectives.

The Bureau of Consumer Affairs acts to ensure the fair and equitable treatment of consumers in their business transactions. It develops legislative proposals and consumer programs and provides technical guidance to field staff on consumer protection laws including those covering packaging and labelling, weights and

measures and hazardous products. The bureau monitors events and trends in the marketplace and works with organizations in business and industry to promote self-regulation for the resolution of consumer complaints. It also carries out consumer information and research programs, supports community-based consumer help offices, provides financial support to consumer advocacy programs, and, through grants to voluntary consumer organizations, fosters the development of the consumer movement in Canada.

The Bureau of Corporate Affairs seeks to provide a legal framework for the orderly conduct of business. It develops federal commercial institutions through incorporation; regulates bankruptcy proceedings for insolvent companies and individuals; and licenses and supervises trustees in bankruptcy. It also encourages invention, innovation and creativity in Canada through granting exclusive property rights for inventions (patents), trademarks, industrial design and copyright of original literary, dramatic, musical and artistic works. Ownership rights are granted so that innovators control and profit from reproduction of their creative works while making them available for the benefit of all Canadians.

During plant visits, Consumer and Corporate Affairs inspectors check labels and contents.

Market in Ottawa, Ont.

The Bureau of Competition Policy administers the Combines Investigation Act, the legislation aimed at maintaining a competitive market system. The legislation seeks to eliminate certain practices in restraint of trade and to overcome the ill effects of concentration. The director of investigation and research has authority under the Act to conduct inquiries when he has reason to believe that the Act may have been violated with respect to combines, mergers, monopolies, unfair trade practices involving price discrimination, disproportionate promotional allowances, misleading advertising, deceptive marketing practices or retail price maintenance. The results of his inquiries are sent to the Restrictive Trade Practices Commission for consideration and public report or to the Attorney General of Canada for possible legal action.

Regional and district offices are maintained in Vancouver, Winnipeg, Toronto, Montreal and Halifax; district and local offices are located in other cities. Field staff administer the department's legislation and regulations and ensure that it is uniformly applied and interpreted throughout the country. The field force includes consumer services officers, inspectors and specialists in dealing with bankruptcy and misleading marketing practices.

Veterans Affairs

The Veterans Affairs objective is to provide support for the economic, social, mental and physical well-being of veterans, certain civilians, and their dependents. Services, including pensions and war veterans' allowances, medical treatment, counselling, and educational assistance to children of the war dead, are provided by the Department of Veterans Affairs and the four agencies associated with it — the Canadian Pension Commission, the Pension Review Board, the War Veterans Allowance Board, and the Bureau of Pensions Advocates.

Veterans Affairs Program

Veterans Services. The department is responsible for the administration of federal legislation which provides benefits to veterans (and certain civilians), their dependents and survivors. These benefits include: medical and dental services; prosthetic appliances; income support programs; emergency financial assistance; counselling services for veterans, their dependents and survivors; educational

Celebrations in Halifax in July 1980 marked the 70th anniversary of the Canadian Navy.

War memorial in Ottawa, Ont.

assistance for veterans and orphans; and burial grants for veterans. Where direct assistance is not possible, a referral service to other sources of aid is provided.

Veterans Land Administration. The Veterans' Land Act was an agriculturally oriented post-war rehabilitation measure for veterans of World War II and Korea. More than 140,000 veterans were established under the various provisions of the Act before the final deadline of March 31, 1975. On March 31, 1980 more than 40,000 veterans had subsisting contracts with the director, representing a total principal indebtedness of approximately $354 million. The Veterans Land Administration also has operational responsibility for the Special Housing Assistance Program which the Department of Veterans Affairs was authorized to extend, in 1975, on behalf of modest-income veterans and to non-profit corporations who obtain

National Housing Act (NHA) loans to develop low-rental projects intended primarily, but not necessarily exclusively, for the housing of veterans.

Pensions Program

The Canadian Pension Commission administers the Pension Act, the legislation under which pensions are awarded as compensation for disability or death related to military service. This Act also provides for the payment of pensions for surviving dependents. The commission also administers: Parts I-X of the Civilian War Pensions and Allowances Act which provides for similar awards for disability or death attributable to service during World War II in certain organizations or types of employment which were closely associated with the armed forces, such as Merchant Seamen, or Auxiliary Services personnel; the Compensation for Former Prisoners of War Act which provides for the payment of compensation for former prisoners of war, evaders and escapees and their dependents, and the Halifax Relief Commission Pension Continuation Act which authorizes pension payments to certain persons injured in the Halifax explosion of 1917. As well, the commission adjudicates on pension claims under various other measures, included among these measures are the Royal Canadian Mounted Police Acts and the Flying Accidents Compensation Regulations.

The Pension Review Board serves as a final court of appeal for veterans, ex-servicemen and their dependents in all matters concerning disability pensions and the interpretation of the Pension Act. The board, although essentially an appellate body may also consider new documentary evidence, and all its sittings must be held in the national capital region.

Bureau of Pensions Advocates

The bureau provides a legal aid service for persons seeking to establish claims under the Pension Act and allied statutes and orders. The relationship between the bureau and applicant or pensioner is that of solicitor and client. Its service is highly decentralized, with advocates and support staff located in 18 cities across Canada.

War Veterans Allowance Board

The objective of the board is to ensure that qualified veterans, and certain civilians who, by reason of age or infirmity, are unable to make their way in the employment field, and widows and orphans whose entitlement flows from the veteran's service, are assisted to the full extent of the War Veterans Allowance Act and Part XI of the Civilian War Pensions and Allowances Act.

The board has the responsibility to advise the Minister generally on the legislation and specifically on the regulations; to adjudicate pursuant to specific sections of the War Veterans Allowance Act and the Civilian War Pensions and Allowances Act where the board has sole jurisdiction; to act as a court of appeal for aggrieved applicants and recipients; and, on its own motion to review decisions of the district authorities to ensure that adjudication is consistent with the intent and purview of the legislation, and that the legislation is applied uniformly throughout Canada. The board may, at any time, review and alter its own former decisions.

Children touring a flower festival in Ottawa in honour of the International Year of the Child 1979.

Health and Welfare

Health Care

Responsibility for health and welfare is distributed between the federal and the provincial governments. On the national level, the Department of National Health and Welfare is the principal federal agency for these matters. The principal objective of the department is to maintain and improve the quality of life of the Canadian people — their physical, economic and social well-being. The department aims to reduce the detrimental effects of environmental factors that are beyond an individual's control and to encourage and assist the adoption by Canadians of a way of life that enhances their well-being. Strategies for the attainment of these objectives include the development of national standards, the expansion of awareness and concern for health, economic, and social problems, and the development of new or improved systems of delivery. The department acts in conjunction with other federal agencies and with provincial and local governments. Provincial governments are directly responsible for actual administration of health and welfare services.

Federal Health Programs

The Department of National Health and Welfare includes three branches which administer federal programs dealing with health. These are the Health Protection Branch, the Medical Services Branch, and the Health Services and Promotion Branch. In addition, the Medical Research Council reports to Parliament through the Minister of National Health and Welfare.

Health Protection Branch. The Health Protection Branch carries out a wide range of activities intended to protect Canadians from hazards which may contribute to illness or death. These include efforts to guard the safety and nutritional quality of foods; to ensure the safety and effectiveness of drugs and control the availability of drugs which may be used unwisely; to reduce the presence of dangerous substances in the environment; to govern exposure to radioactivity; to control the safety and effectiveness of medical devices; to control the safety of cosmetics; to improve capabilities to diagnose diseases; and to improve public information concerning various aspects of health status.

The main legislative base of the health protection program includes: Department of National Health and Welfare Act, Food and Drugs Act, Narcotic Control Act, Radiation-Emitting Devices Act, Hazardous Products Act, atomic energy control regulations and Canada dangerous substances regulations.

Medical Services Branch. The responsibilities of the Medical Services Branch encompass a wide variety of services responding to the health needs of such varied groups of clients as the Indian and Inuit people, public servants, immigrants, residents of the Northwest Territories and Yukon, and others. The branch provides diagnosis, treatment and preventive health services including Indian and northern

Using the CAT scanner to get a diagnosis reduces the surgeon's workload.

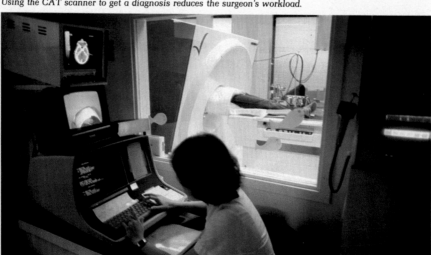

health, public service health, prosthetic services, civil aviation medicine, emergency services, quarantine and regulatory, and immigration medical services.

Health Services and Promotion Branch. This branch has two main responsibilities: to encourage and assist Canadians to adopt a way of life that enhances their physical, mental and social well-being; and to provide leadership and coordination in assisting the provinces and territories to bring their health services to national standards and maintain them at that level.

In the field of health promotion, the branch works closely with provincial governments and non-governmental organizations to develop and deliver health information and educational programs in such matters as smoking, alcohol use, nutrition, drug use, accidents, personal health care, and family and child health.

The branch is also responsible for payments with respect to provincial programs providing hospital, diagnostic, medical and extended health care services, as provided by legislation; and for monitoring provincial compliance with the program conditions associated with federal payments. Complementary branch activities include consulting services and collaboration with the provinces and professional groups in the development of standards and guidelines, in such areas as facilities

After vaccinating themselves with flu vaccine, researchers found their liver enzymes took twice as long as usual to metabolize drugs. They are conducting research into liver metabolism at Dalhousie University, Halifax, NS.

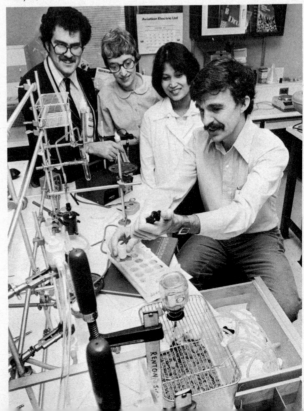

planning and design, health assessment, community health, mental health, institutional health services, health systems, and family planning. Other activities include co-ordination of planning for the training and deployment of health workers. The branch also supports extramural health research in Canada, and conducts policy and program analysis on the Canadian health system.

Health Insurance Programs

Hospital Insurance. Provincial hospital insurance programs, operating in all provinces and territories since 1961, cover 99 per cent of the population of Canada. Under the Hospital Insurance and Diagnostic Services Act of 1957, the federal government provides financial assistance to the provinces toward the cost of providing hospital services to patients insured by these programs.

Medical Care Insurance. Public medical care is provided under the Medical Care Act which was passed by Parliament in December 1966. Federal contributions to participating provinces became payable from July 1, 1968. By April 1, 1972 all provinces and territories had entered the federal program. The plan must be universally available to all eligible residents on equal terms and conditions and must cover at least 95 per cent of the total eligible provincial population. Comprehensive coverage must be provided for all medically required services rendered by a physician or surgeon.

Financing Arrangements. Until April 1977, federal contributions to the provinces for hospital and medical care services were based on the cost of insured services incurred by the provinces, with the federal government reimbursing the provinces for approximately 50 per cent of their expenditures. The Federal/Provincial Fiscal Arrangements and Established Programs Financing Act of 1977 modified the method of federal financing. Federal contributions now take the form of a transfer of tax and associated equalization to the provinces, in conjunction with equal per capita cash payments. National standards established by previous legislation are preserved. The new financing arrangements also provide additional per capita contributions toward the costs of certain extended health care services.

Provincial Health Programs

The responsibility for regulation, operation of health insurance programs, and direct provision of specialized services rests with the provincial governments. Institutional and ambulatory care for tuberculosis and mental illness is provided by agencies of the departments responsible for health. Provincial programs are giving increasing attention to preventive services. Programs related to health problems such as cancer, alcoholism and drug addiction, venereal diseases, and dental health are being developed by government agencies, often in co-operation with voluntary associations. A number of provincial programs are also being directed to meet the needs of specific population groups, such as mothers and children, the aged, the needy, and those requiring rehabilitation care.

Environmental health responsibilities, involving education, inspection, and enforcement of standards, are frequently shared by provincial health departments and other agencies.

Marathon in Montreal, Que.

Federal Welfare Programs

Health and Welfare Canada has the goal of improving and maintaining a high level of social security in Canada. The branches of the department with responsibilities primarily for social security matters are the Social Services Programs Branch and the Income Security Branch.

Social Services Programs Branch

This branch administers programs through which close to 2 million Canadians benefit from federal leadership and financial support. The financial support is provided through both cost-shared and granting programs.

Cost-shared programs include such programs as the Canada Assistance Plan which enables federal sharing with the provinces to provide assistance and welfare services such as day care, rehabilitation and homemaker services to persons who meet specified eligibility criteria. The Vocational Rehabilitation of Disabled Persons Program enables federal sharing with the provinces in costs of providing vocational rehabilitation services to the physically and mentally disabled. Total federal costs of the two programs in 1979-80 were estimated at $1.9 billion.

Granting programs encourage the development of projects which are designed to promote demonstration, research and preventive activities in social services.

The National Welfare Grants Program promotes self-help activities and improvements in welfare services. Funds are granted each year for demonstration projects, short-term research projects, program evaluation projects and social service training courses.

The objective of the New Horizons Program is to encourage groups of retired persons to initiate and participate in community projects of their own choosing, to overcome social isolation. Cash grants are distributed to groups of retired persons.

Income Security Branch

This branch has the responsibility of a wide range of publicly-funded and administered income security programs.

The Canada Pension Plan. The Canada Pension Plan is designed to provide a basic level of protection against the financial effects of retirement, disability and death. Benefits are determined by the contributor's earnings and contributions made to the plan. The plan is financed from contributions and interest on funds invested. It is accessible to salaried and self-employed persons in Canada who are between the ages of 18 and 70 and the benefits are adjusted annually to reflect full cost of living increases.

Old Age Security, Guaranteed Income Supplement and Spouse's Allowance. An Old Age Security (OAS) pension is payable to anyone who is 65 years of age and

Hand-made items of Golden Age Club members are popular at bazaars.

Day nursery at Strathcona Sound, Baffin Island, NWT.

over and who has fulfilled the residence requirements. A pensioner may receive payment indefinitely while living abroad if he or she has resided in Canada for 20 years after age 18; otherwise, payment may continue for only six months following the month of departure from Canada.

Guaranteed Income Supplement (GIS) may be added to the basic OAS pension, depending on the results of an income test. The supplement is payable for only six months outside of Canada, in addition to the month of departure.

The spouse of a pensioner may be eligible for a Spouse's Allowance (SPA) if the spouse is between 60 and 65 years of age and meets the OAS residence requirements. This allowance, like the GIS, is awarded on the basis of a test of income.

The OAS pension and the maximum SPA are adjusted quarterly to reflect increases in the consumer price index. In January 1980 the maximum SPA stood at $306.94; the monthly OAS pension at $182.42; the maximum monthly GIS for a single pensioner or a married pensioner whose spouse did not receive OAS or SPA at $149.76; and, for a married couple (both pensioners) the maximum monthly GIS was $124.52 each.

Family Allowances and Child Tax Credit. Family Allowances (FA) are paid monthly on behalf of children under the age of 18 who are resident in Canada and maintained by parents or guardians, at least one of whom must be a Canadian citizen, or a permanent resident of Canada under the Immigration Act. In the case of a person admitted to Canada under the Immigration Act as a visitor or holder of a permit, the period of admission must be for not less than one year and during that period the income of such a person must be subject to Canadian income tax. In 1980 the federal rate of Family Allowances was $21.80 a month per eligible child. Provinces may vary the rates of FA paid, provided certain conditions are met;

Quebec and Alberta have chosen this plan. Quebec has programs to supplement those of the federal government.

A federal child tax credit program became effective in January 1979. It was designed to provide additional assistance in meeting the costs of raising children in low-income to middle-income families. This lump sum benefit is in addition to the monthly Family Allowances and is normally paid to the mother. The program is administered through the income tax system. The credit for 1980 was $218 for each eligible child payable in full where the net annual family income in 1979 was less than or equal to $19,620. There is a reduction in the maximum amount payable per child at the rate of 5 per cent of family income above the basic income level. The credit and the basic income levels are escalated each year based on changes in the consumer price index.

Provincial Welfare Programs

All provinces have programs to provide social assistance and welfare services to persons who are eligible. Benefits which may be included in assistance programs are monetary benefits, items of special need and maintenance in homes for special care. Welfare services may include services such as homemaker, day care, community development, counselling, rehabilitation, and the protection and adoption of children.

International Health, Welfare and Social Security

Canada actively participates in international health, welfare and social security matters. The Department of National Health and Welfare participates on the Canadian delegation to the UNICEF Executive Board, in the World Health Organization, the Pan American Health Organization, the United Nations Commission on Narcotic Drugs and relevant United Nations seminars and conferences. The department also belongs to several international social policy-related non-governmental organizations. Bilateral health and social security agreements are negotiated where appropriate. Provincial departments and agencies are also involved in these areas.

Recycling of paper.

Environment

The Department of the Environment

The Department of the Environment officially came into being in June 1971. Created to amalgamate those elements within the federal government already involved in work related to the environment and renewable resources, the Department of the Environment is also known by the short form Environment Canada. Added to the fisheries and forestry elements to make up Environment Canada were: the Canadian Meteorological Service from the Ministry of Transport; the Air Pollution Control Division and the Public Health Engineering Division from the Department of National Health and Welfare; the Water Sector from the Department of Energy, Mines and Resources; the Canada Land Inventory from the Department of Regional Economic Expansion; and the Canadian Wildlife Service from the Department of Indian Affairs and Northern Development.

In 1980, Floralies, the international flower show was held in Montreal, Que. This was the first time in its 150 year history, that the flower show had been held outside Europe. ➡

In April 1979, the department was reorganized to form two departments, Fisheries and Oceans and the new Department of the Environment. In June 1979 Parks Canada was moved from the Department of Indian Affairs and Northern Development to become part of Environment Canada.

The primary objective of the Department of the Environment is to preserve and enhance the quality of the environment for the benefit of present and future generations of Canadians. This will lead to the achievement of the goals of safeguarding man's health and property from harmful substances and environmental changes, whether natural or man-made; protecting resource productivity, through conservation and wise use of renewable resources, for sustained economic and social benefit; safeguarding man's quality of life, based on the development of society in harmony with its environment, permitting enjoyment of the environment and its resources; and safeguarding Canada's heritage, through the protection of those places which are significant examples of Canada's natural and cultural heritage and the encouragement of public understanding, appreciation and enjoyment of this heritage, keeping it unimpaired for future generations. The

Logging scars on mountains near Revelstoke, BC will be reforested as logging companies plant seedlings to replace harvested trees.

Grand Manan, NB.

fulfilment of this commitment encompasses the functions of informing and influencing, protection and regulation, resource management and conservation, and monitoring and scientific research.

The responsibility involving the environment and its constituent resources is shared between the federal and provincial governments, with each level having jurisdiction over different aspects of the environment. The provinces have direct management responsibility for most environmental and resource matters within their borders. The federal government has responsibility for those matters which are clearly within its jurisdiction such as the territories, national parks and oceans and for matters which the provinces cannot readily or cost-effectively undertake separately such as weather services. As environmental processes transcend political boundaries, and as the same human activity can impinge on matters under both federal and provincial jurisdictions, there is a basic requirement for both levels of government to co-operate in both the formulation and the execution of their environmental policies.

In addition to activity within this overall domestic framework, the department is also dealing with international issues in a way that will protect Canada's

Kaskawulsh Glacier, Yukon. The untouched beauty of the North challenges some travellers.

environment and renewable resources and at the same time contribute mean-
ingfully to the resolution of international problems such as worldwide contaminants research, climatic change, long-range transport of air pollutants and
development in Third World countries.

The Canadian Forestry Advisory Council reports to the Minister and makes
recommendations for action in areas of federal responsibility for our renewable
forest resources. The Canadian Fisheries Advisory Council provides broad policy
advice to the Minister from outside government on areas of responsibility related to
our fisheries resources. These advisory bodies review programs, assess their impact
and provide links with organizations outside the government. The council's
members include prominent Canadians from industry, the universities and the
scientific community. The Canadian Forestry Advisory Council includes representatives from several provincial natural resources departments and the Canadian
Fisheries Advisory Council includes commercial and recreational fishermen.

Banff National Park, Alta. ➵

Winter in British Columbia

Spring in Nova Scotia

Summer in Ontario

Environmental Assessment Review

The federal environmental assessment and review process was established by Cabinet decision in 1973 to ensure that environmental matters are taken into account when projects initiated or sponsored by departments or agencies are planned and implemented, or federal funds or property are to be used. All departments and agencies are subject to the process, except proprietary Crown corporations and regulatory agencies which are invited to participate.

The process begins with a screening when a project is conceived. If the environmental consequences of it are not known or appear to be substantial, a more detailed evaluation is made. At either stage, a project may be accepted, modified or rejected. In fact, most projects need no further assessment. However, if it seems a project may have a significant effect on the environment, it is referred to the federal environmental assessment review office for a formal public review by an independent panel of experts.

An environmental impact statement is prepared by the proponent of the project following the panel's guidelines. Public meetings are held in communities near the proposed project site to hear comment on the proposal. The panel then submits a report containing recommendations on project implementation to the Minister of the Environment. Decisions on the recommendations are made by the Minister of the Environment and the Minister responsible for the project.

St. John's, Nfld.

Salmon seiner in Johnstone Strait, between Vancouver Island and the mainland.

Fisheries and Oceans

The Department of Fisheries and Oceans came into being officially in April 1979, and is responsible for a broad range of programs and services related to the living resources and aquatic environment of the oceans and inland waters.

The department's role includes overall management of Canada's ocean fisheries and certain inland fisheries; fisheries and oceanographic research contributing to the understanding, management and best use of renewable aquatic resources; developing markets for Canadian fisheries products and negotiating fisheries agreements with other countries; hydrographic surveying and charting of navigable coastal and inland waters; administration of some 2,300 small craft harbours across Canada and the co-ordination of the federal government's policies and programs in respect to the oceans.

Hauling in the catch aboard an east coast stern trawler.

National Capital Commission

The National Capital Commission (NCC) is the Crown Agency, charged under the National Capital Act (1958), with the responsibility "to prepare plans for and assist in the development, conservation and improvement of the National Capital Region in order that the nature and character of the seat of the Government of Canada may be in accordance with its national significance". The Commission is composed of a

Winterlude in Ottawa, an activity promoted by the NCC.

The Gatineau area of Quebec.

chairman and 20 commissioners, chosen from across the nation, to ensure that there will be input from all sections of the country into its policies and activities.

The NCC is responsible for acquisition, development and maintenance of federal public land in the nation's capital; it co-operates with municipalities in developing projects of benefit to both the national and local publics and it advises the Public Works Department on the siting and appearance of all federal government buildings in the National Capital Region. The NCC reports to Parliament through the Minister of Public Works.

The NCC manages Gatineau Park, the largest outdoor recreation and conservation area in the Capital Region. In addition, it promotes a wide variety of public activities on many acres of parkland, including bicycle paths, allotment gardens, cross-country and downhill ski centres and golf courses; the spring tulips and floral displays for which the region is justly famous are maintained by the NCC. The promotion of winter activities has taken on special importance with the use of the 10 km Rideau Canal ice surface, maintained as the world's longest skating rink, for the winterlude festival which features ice sculptures, horse races on the canal ice, parades and other activities designed to help residents and visitors enjoy the long Canadian winter.

The National Capital Commission has dedicated itself to the maintenance of a Capital which stands as a symbol of identity, a model of unity and a source of pride and inspiration for all Canadians, a Capital which provides a national focus representative of our values and aspirations for the future.

Farming near Victoria, PEI.

Agriculture

The responsibilities of Agriculture Canada extend from the farm to the consumer and thus affect all Canadians. The work of the department and several related agencies is carried out under the authority of 43 Acts of Parliament.

Organization

The department has eight branches. The Policy, Planning and Economics Branch advises the departmental senior management on the development of policies and programs, and on the establishment of plans and priorities. The Food Production and Inspection Branch is responsible for all production and regulatory activities of the department, including inspection, grading and veterinary services. The work of the Food and Agriculture Marketing Branch is aimed at helping to improve the marketing efficiency of Canada's agriculture industry and to increase agricultural exports and domestic use of Canadian-produced supplies. The Research Branch, with 47 establishments across Canada, conducts programs designed to solve problems of production, protection and utilization of agricultural crops and animals. Information services carries out a wide variety of programs to acquaint farmers with new knowledge from agricultural research and to keep the agriculture and food industry and the general public informed about the policies, programs and activities of the department. The Intergovernmental and International Services Branch is responsible for co-ordinating the department's domestic and international commitments relating to agriculture and the food system. It also maintains liaison with provincial and international agricultural agencies and with non-governmental organizations. Two other branches — Finance and Administration, and Personnel Administration — complete the departmental structure.

Related Agencies. The Minister of Agriculture is responsible to Parliament for the department and the following seven related agencies. The Agricultural Stabilization Board assists farmers by supporting the prices of certain food commodities. The Agricultural Products Board buys, sells or imports agricultural products to maintain a satisfactory balance of food stocks in Canada. The Canadian Dairy Commission supports the market prices of major processed dairy products. The Canadian Grain Commission licenses grain elevator operators, recommends grade specifications for Canadian grain, inspects and weighs grain, and operates a cereals and oilseeds research laboratory. The Canadian Livestock Feed Board insures the availability and price stability of feed grains. The Farm Credit

Vineyard in the Niagara area of Ontario.

Corporation makes loans to individual farmers and to syndicates of farmers. The National Farm Products Marketing Council oversees the establishment and operation of national farm commodity marketing agencies.

Programs and Policies

A major federal strategy to help the development of the Canadian horticultural industry was announced in early 1980. The goal is to help the industry expand its export markets and to replace imported fruits and vegetables with Canadian-grown produce where such replacement is efficient. About one-half of Canada's total imports of fruits and vegetables could be grown domestically. The government's role in the horticultural development strategy is to improve the infrastructure which links all segments of the horticultural food chain, from research to production and marketing.

A series of federal initiatives were also announced in 1980 to assist Canadian potato producers. The initiatives included a program to improve the quality of

Cabbages in Nova Scotia.

Potatoes in Prince Edward Island. The potato is the most important vegetable grown in Canada and the Maritime provinces are recognized as the major potato growing region of the country.

Canadian seed potatoes; funds to help producer groups build or upgrade storages; a new insurance program to protect growers against financial risks in the production, storage and marketing of seed potatoes; further federal research to improve potato production and disease control, and a market development program for seed potatoes.

Efforts to combat salmonella were strengthened in 1979-80 with the establishment of a special unit to advise the government on practical ways to reduce the incidence of the bacterial organism in poultry. The salmonella co-ordinating unit operates within Agriculture Canada's Food Production and Inspection Branch, but maintains close liaison with officers of the Department of National Health and Welfare. The unit has the mandate to make specific recommendations to meet the governmental objective of reducing the amount of salmonella, an organism that is a worldwide problem.

Tighter security has been imposed at airports by Agriculture Canada to prevent African swine fever from entry into Canada. African swine fever is a deadly swine disease for which there is no known treatment or vaccine. The disease has spread from Africa, where it originated, to the Mediterranean area and most recently to several countries in South America and the Caribbean. Because the disease organism can be carried in pork meat, imports of pork products are restricted from countries where the disease exists. Emergency measures have also been established to eradicate the disease should it appear in Canada.

The Canadian Chicken Marketing Agency was established in 1979, becoming the third agency to be created under the federal Farm Products Marketing Agencies Act. Established earlier were the Canadian Egg Marketing Agency and the Canadian Turkey Marketing Agency. The first tasks of the newest agency were to set national

Container gardening for balconies.

Farming in Saskatchewan.

chicken production targets and to develop a cost of production formula to be used to guide the pricing practices of provincial chicken marketing boards.

Prices of a variety of farm commodities were supported by means of deficiency payments to producers in 1978-79. Payments were made for yellow seed onions in Quebec, Ontario and Manitoba; white beans; sugar beets; onions in Quebec and Ontario; McIntosh apples in Quebec; winter wheat in Eastern Canada; and barley and oats grown outside the Canadian Wheat Board area.

Waste heat from thermal or nuclear power plants, oil refineries and chemical factories could become important sources of heat for greenhouses. A study funded by Agriculture Canada has identified 82 potential waste-heat sites in Canada which could provide heat for 1 100 hectares of greenhouse crops. Tomatoes and cucumbers are crops likely to be grown in such greenhouses. These could replace imports during winter, making Canada more self sufficient in horticultural production.

US President Ronald Reagan and Prime Minister Pierre Trudeau at the recent signing of the extension to the Canada–US NORAD treaty by US Secretary of State Alexander Haig and Secretary of State for External Affairs Mark MacGuigan.

External Affairs

The Department of External Affairs has three primary functions: (1) to advise the government on foreign policy matters, co-ordinate implementation of the government's foreign policy decisions, represent Canada in other countries and in international organizations, and negotiate international agreements; (2) to provide assistance to Canadians travelling or living abroad; and (3) to promote Canada and its interests abroad.

The headquarters of the department is in Ottawa. In 1980, there were 117 diplomatic and consular missions in 76 countries; many of these missions are accredited to two or more governments, thus permitting Canada to maintain diplomatic relations with an additional 81 countries. Ninety-four countries have diplomatic missions in Ottawa and 43 states have non-resident accreditation.

A Canadian diplomatic post in a Commonwealth country is designated as a high commission and is headed by a high commissioner, while a diplomatic post in a non-Commonwealth country is known as an embassy and is headed by either an ambassador or a chargé d'affaires. In countries with which Canada's trade relations or consular responsibilities are extensive, consulates have also been established in one or more cities; these are headed by consuls or consuls-general.

Canada also has missions at a number of international organizations, including: the United Nations (UN) in New York and Geneva; the European Communities (EC) and the North Atlantic Treaty Organization (NATO) in Brussels; the Organization for

Economic Co-operation and Development (OECD) and the United Nations Educational, Scientific and Cultural Organization (UNESCO) in Paris and the Organization of American States (OAS) in Washington.

Foreign Policy

A review of foreign policy published in 1970 identified six major themes of national policy at home and abroad: to foster economic growth; to safeguard sovereignty and independence; to work for peace and security; to promote social justice; to enhance the quality of life; and to ensure a harmonious natural environment. The annual review of the Department of External Affairs (which can be obtained free of charge by writing to: External Affairs, Pearson Building, Ottawa K1A 0W6) sets out the particular goals and achievements of Canadian foreign policy from country to country, from region to region and in the fields of international law, disarmament and arms control, energy and international economics.

Services to Canadians

Consular Assistance. One of the primary functions of Canada's embassies and other missions abroad is to assist the Canadian traveller or overseas resident in need of help. In any given year, consular personnel will handle close to 600,000 cases ranging from the issuance of a passport (approximately 45,000) to special services in the event of death abroad (over 400), hospitalization (in excess of 600), financial difficulties (from 2,000 to 3,000) and imprisonment due to drug-related or other offences (rarely less than 1,000).

Passports. Between 700,000 and 750,000 passports are issued every year under the authority of the Department of External Affairs. In Canada, the issuance of passports, certificates of identity, and UN refugee convention travel documents is handled through regional passport offices in Calgary, Edmonton, Halifax, Hamilton, Montreal, Quebec, St. John's, Saskatoon, Toronto, Vancouver and Winnipeg, and through the main passport office in Ottawa.

Assistance in International Legal Matters. Requests from Canadian citizens for assistance in pressing claims against or involving foreign governments are dealt with by the department's bureau of legal affairs. In the area of private international law, the bureau offers a variety of services to facilitate legal proceedings involving Canadian and foreign jurisdictions on the basis of conventions or by arranged procedures.

Canadian International Development Agency (CIDA)

CIDA is the government department that administers Canada's program of co-operation with developing countries. Canada provides assistance to more than 80 countries and in the 1979-80 fiscal year this official development assistance amounted to $1.23 billion. The goals of development assistance are to help Third World countries to meet the basic needs of their poorest populations, to support those countries' efforts to achieve self-reliance, and to ensure that the mutual interests of Canada and the recipient country are observed.

Girl in Sri Lanka tying pan, used for weaving baskets. Canada is among the countries co-operating with Sri Lanka to improve agricultural production.

The major portion of Canada's contribution to international development is made in the form of bilateral aid. In 1979-80 this amount was $598.79 million provided under agreements between Canada and the recipient governments for the financing of development projects. More than half is provided in the form of grants, and the remainder in loans which are provided under generous terms. Loans are used by developing countries to purchase materials, equipment or services for their industry and agriculture, or to gain access to the Canadian export market through lines of credit. In addition to economic assistance, bilateral grants cover such areas as food aid, which amounted to $81.8 million in 1979-80, and technical assistance, which pays the cost of sending Canadian advisers overseas and training students and trainees from developing countries. Asia remains the principal recipient of bilateral aid ($238 million in 1979-80), followed by Francophone Africa ($147 million), Commonwealth Africa ($138 million), Latin America ($35 million) and the Caribbean ($30 million).

The second channel for official development assistance to the developing world is multilateral aid ($499.92 million in 1979-80), whereby Canada and other donors provide funds to international institutions that help the Third World. Canada supports about 65 programs in all. About 56 per cent of Canada's multilateral aid is provided in the form of loans and capital subscriptions to international financial institutions — the World Bank group and the regional development banks of Asia, Africa, Latin America and the Caribbean. In addition, grants are provided to the various programs of the United Nations agencies and to international development research institutions. Food aid is also provided through multilateral channels, ($97.8 million in 1979-80), mainly the World Food Programme.

Under the third channel of development assistance CIDA provides flexible forms of assistance to the developing world through Canadian and international non-governmental organizations (NGOs) and through the Canadian business community. CIDA's support of NGOs is given through grants which can double the funds collected by the NGO and thus broaden the scope of activity. CIDA emphasizes support of efforts to build self-reliance, especially through rural development, education, training and public health. Contributions to such projects account for most of CIDA's support to NGOs, but a substantial amount ($16.5 million in 1979-80) is used to help the agencies that send volunteers (like the Canadian University Service Overseas — CUSO) or operate exchange programs (Canadian Crossroads International). In total, CIDA provided $59.5 million in 1979-80 to support the work of 195 Canadian NGOs working on 2,304 projects in 103 countries. In addition, $7.2 million was provided in support of international NGOs which stress community development, management training, and institution building and support.

Finally CIDA's industrial co-operation program ($3.9 million in 1979-80) encourages Canadian firms to establish or expand operations and to test Canadian technology in developing countries. It also assists Canadian companies to obtain a fairer share of multilaterally-funded business for development projects. Developing countries are also given assistance to create an environment conducive to industrialization. CIDA also supports the Canadian Executive Service Overseas (CESO) through its industrial co-operation program (1979-80 contribution was $1.8 million). CESO sends volunteers (often retired people) with technical, professional, or executive skills to solve short-term problems in developing countries.

Canadian Executive Service Overseas (CESO)

CESO is a private, non-profit, Canadian corporation. It was organized in 1967 by a group of Canadian business and professional people, with the support of the Canadian International Development Agency (CIDA). A board of directors determines the policy of the corporation.

The objectives of CESO include the use of qualified, experienced Canadian men and women: (1) to conduct a mutual co-operative exchange of applied professional and technical knowledge with governmental, industrial or other organizations in applicable countries; and (2) to enhance operations in projects with developing countries, through co-operative action with Canadian industry and the Canadian government.

CESO operations include three programs: (1) The overseas program operates within developing countries of the world. Applications are handled for business or

A CESO representative offers technical and programming advice for a TV station in Ecuador.

financial management and for technical and professional advice in agriculture, communications, education, fishing, lumbering, manufacturing, mining, printing, pulp and paper, pollution control, reforestation, tourism and many other areas. (2) The Canadian native program operates throughout Canada. CESO administers the program in response to requests received from the Indian bands. They can request that CESO provide consultation to assist native people in establishing effective businesses such as stores and garages or enterprises in the various fields such as tourism, lumbering and fishing. and (3) The business program includes joint ventures and trade facilitation with developing countries of the world. With increasing frequency companies in the developing countries are contacting CIDA to propose joint ventures with Canadian industry. The business program parallels an effective overseas program. CESO volunteers assist in the developing of industries in developing countries that in turn provide good products.

Canadian University Service Overseas (CUSO)

Since 1961, CUSO has sent over 6,000 volunteers of all ages and from all walks of life to fill temporary manpower requirements in developing countries.

The countries or agencies requesting help pay the volunteer's salary at local rates. CUSO, an independent, non-profit organization, pays travel, medical, orientation and insurance costs. The term of volunteer contracts is generally two years.

CUSO is also involved in funding a number of small, self-help projects overseas and in development education at home. A substantial part of the organization's finances come from the Canadian International Development Agency (CIDA), the balance being contributed by individuals, corporations, foundations, community groups and provincial governments.

A CUSO nurse in Northern Ghana using graphics to teach local people about diseases spread through water.

International Development Research Centre (IDRC)

IDRC was created by an Act of Parliament in 1970, when the need was recognized for a donor agency that had more flexibility than a government department to support research into the problems of developing countries. The objective of the centre has been to promote the economic and social development of those regions — particularly the well-being of their rural peoples — by research designed to adapt scientific and technical knowledge to their specific requirements.

This research is initiated, designed, and carried out almost entirely by scientists and technologists from the countries and regions involved, in accordance with their own priorities. The role of the centre is to help refine research proposals, recommend projects for funding, monitor their progress, and disseminate the results as widely as possible.

Research proposals are judged by such factors as: whether they fit into the priorities of developing countries; whether they are likely to have useful application beyond the country involved; whether the research will help close gaps in living standards inside these countries; whether they will make full use of local resources and people; and whether they will leave behind investments in better trained or more experienced indigenous researchers.

Within this concern for the advancement of developing countries, there is a focus on research in the following sectors: agriculture, food and nutrition sciences, communications, health sciences, information sciences and social sciences.

IDRC is financed solely by the Government of Canada; its policies, however, are set by an international Board of Governors. The chairman, vice chairman, and nine others of the 21 governors must be Canadian citizens. It has been the practice to draw the other 10 governors from outside Canada, and especially from developing countries. The centre's headquarters is in Ottawa. Regional offices are located in Africa, Asia, Latin America and the Middle East.

National Defence

The aim of Canada's defence policy is to ensure that the country remains secure and independent. To this end, Canadian forces are committed to collective security and defence arrangements with Canada's allies in the North Atlantic Treaty Organization (NATO), with the United States under a North American Air Defence (NORAD) agreement, to the United Nations in various peacekeeping and observer roles and to the maintenance of Canada's ability to function as a sovereign state within its own territory and the contiguous water areas under Canada's jurisdictional authority.

Because the main military threat to Canada lies in the possibility, however remote, of a nuclear exchange involving the United States and the Soviet Union, a major thrust of policy is to deter such an event. This involves two primary theatres, Europe and North America.

Canada's principal contribution in Europe is a contingent of more than 5,000 men with the land and air forces under Allied Command Europe. They include the

A Canadian Forces helicopter preparing to land on HMCS Ottawa during recent exercises off Halifax, NS.

Having completed his training, a Canadian Forces cook is respected widely. At the completion of the course, graduates write an additional examination to earn a certificate allowing them to practise their trade in any province.

Canadian Mechanized Brigade Group, some 3,000 men, and the 1st Canadian Air Group, operating three squadrons of CF–104 fighter and ground support planes, plus support personnel.

One of three land combat groups maintained in Canada has the task of supporting NATO deterrent forces in Norway if necessary. The group can be transported either by air or sea. Canada also has committed two squadrons of CF–5 aircraft for a close support role on NATO's northern flank. These aircraft, refuelled in flight, could be deployed quickly to any crisis area. Co-operation with United States forces, under a renewed NORAD agreement signed in 1975 and effective to 1980, is the salient feature of defence in the North American area. Canada's current contribution is three squadrons of CF–101 interceptor aircraft, 24 surveillance radars, two satellite tracking stations and participation in operation of the Distant Early Warning (DEW) radar line. This involves some 10,500 forces personnel.

Canadian maritime forces also contribute, with US forces, to operations to detect and monitor any potentially hostile maritime operations off the Atlantic and Pacific coasts. Current Canadian maritime forces include 23 destroyers, three submarines, three supply ships, three operational squadrons of long-range anti-submarine patrol aircraft and a number of shorter-range patrol planes and helicopters with anti-

The Snowbirds, Canadian Forces aerial demonstration team was created in 1971.

submarine capability. All Canada's maritime forces can be assigned to NATO in any emergency.

In support of United Nations efforts to halt hostilities through the peacekeeping and truce observation roles, Canada currently has approximately 250 military personnel serving in the Golan Heights between Syria and Israel, more than 500 in Cyprus and approximately 20 officers with the truce supervisory organization operated by the United Nations in the Middle East.

Protection of Canada as a sovereign state imposes two main roles on the Canadian Armed Forces. One concern is the possibility of challenges to Canada's right to exercise jurisdiction over her territory and its adjacent waters. With implementation of a 200-mile offshore fisheries zone, this area under Canadian jurisdiction amounts to almost half the country's land mass and has required an increase in surveillance and inspection of fishing vessels and for other civil purposes, including pollution control. A second concern is the possibility of the forces being called to the aid of the civil power in the event of a serious civil disorder. While no armed forces are maintained for this specific purpose, forces performing other tasks are trained to provide such assistance.

The forces also provide a reservoir of skills and capabilities that can be drawn on for national support and development. Examples are in such fields as search and rescue, disaster relief and assistance, construction and mapping and surveying.

Common Conversion Factors from SI Metric to Canadian Imperial Units

Length

1 mm	=	0.03937 in.
1 cm	=	0.3937 in.
1 m	=	3.28084 ft.
1 km	=	0.62137 mi.

Area

1 km²	=	0.3861 sq. mi.
1 ha	=	2.47105 acres
1 m²	=	0.000247 acres

Mass (Weight)

1 kg	=	2.204622 lbs.
1 kg	=	0.0011023 tons (short)
1 kg	=	0.000984 tons (long)
1 kg	=	32.1507 troy ounces
1 g	=	0.0321507 troy ounces
1 t	=	1.102311 tons (short)
1 t	=	0.9842065 tons (long)

Volume and Capacity

1 m³	=	220 gal.
1 m³	=	35.31466 cu. ft.
1 m³	=	423.78 board feet
1 dm³	=	0.423776 board feet
1 m³	=	6.28982 barrels
1 litre	=	0.219969 gal.
1 dm³	=	0.027496 bushels
1 m³	=	27.4962 bushels

Mass in SI Metric to Average Capacity in Canadian Imperial Units for Common Field Crops

Wheat, soybeans, potatoes, peas	1 t = 36.74 bushels
Rye, flax, corn	1 t = 39.37 bushels
Rapeseed, mustard seed	1 t = 44.09 bushels
Barley, buckwheat	1 t = 45.93 bushels
Mixed grains	1 t = 48.99 bushels
Oats	1 t = 64.84 bushels
Sunflower seed	1 t = 91.86 bushels

Temperature

9/5 temperature in °C + 32 = temperature in °F

Acknowledgements

Contributors

J. Lewis Robinson (*Regional Geography of Canada*), Professor of Geography, University of British Columbia. B.A. University of Western Ontario, 1940; M.A. Syracuse, NY, 1942; Ph.D. Clark University Worcester, Massachusetts, 1946. Author of nine books including: *The Geography of Canada* (Toronto, 1950); *The Canadian Arctic* (Ottawa, 1952) *Resources of the Canadian Shield* (Toronto, 1969); (with George Tomkins) *The Gage World Atlas: A Canadian Perspective* (Toronto, 1972); and a number of chapters in books and articles.

Charles A. Barrett (*Canada's Economic Performance, 1979-80*), Director of General Economic Analysis and Research in Marketing Divisions, the Conference Board in Canada. B.A. Toronto, 1970; M.Sc. Economics, 1971, Ph.D. Economics, 1975, London. Responsible for the Board's program of current economic analysis, for research studies in economics and marketing, and for the content of the board's program of conferences, seminars and workshops in the economics and marketing areas. Author of a number of studies and articles.

J.L. Granatstein (*History*), Professor of History, York University. B.A. Royal Military College, 1961; M.A. Toronto, 1962; Ph.D. Duke University, 1966. Author of: *The Politics of Survival: The Conservative Party of Canada 1939-45* (Toronto, 1967); (with R.D. Cuff) *Canadian-American Relations in Wartime* (Toronto, 1975, 1977); *Canada's War: The Politics of the Mackenzie King Government 1939-45* (Toronto, 1975); (with J.M. Hitsman) *Broken Promises: A History of Conscription in Canada* (Toronto, 1977); and other books and articles.

Gordon McKay (*The Climate*), Director, Meteorological Applications Branch, Fisheries and Environment Canada. B.Sc. Manitoba, 1943; M.Sc. McGill, 1953. This article is a contracted version of "Climatic Resources and Economic Activity", which appears in *Canada's Natural Environment: essays in applied geography*, edited by G.R. McBoyle and E. Sommerville (Methuen Publications, Toronto, 1976).

Photographic Credits by page number

Cover. Malak
Frontispiece. Deryk Bodington
3. Malak
4. Michael Saunders
5. Deryk Bodington
6. George Hunter
7. E. Otto/Miller Services
9. Malak
11. George Hunter
12. Louis Collis
13. Jim Merrithew
15. Mike Beedell (2)
17. Dunkin Bancroft/Photothèque
19. George Hunter
21. Malak
23. J.E. Lozanski
24. J.E. Lozanski
25. George Hunter
27. Murdoch Maclean
28. Mike Beedell
29. (1)Ted Grant/Photothèque; (2) Malak; (3) Malak
33. Malak
35. Jim Merrithew
37. Malak
38. Murdoch Maclean
43. Dunkin Bancroft/Photothèque
45. George Hunter
46. Malak
47. (1) Sig Bradshaw; (2) Malak; (3) Mike Beedell
49. Fred Bruemmer
50. Mike Beedell
51. Fred Bruemmer
53. George Hunter
57. Malak
58. Audrey Giles/Photo Source
59. Jim Merrithew
60-61. (1), (2) Malak; (3) Bodington; (4) Murdoch Maclean; (5) Malak
62. Young People's Theatre
63. Festival Lennoxville
64. Groupe Nouvelle Aire
65. Theatre Calgary
66. Les Grands Ballets Canadiens
67. The Anna Wyman Dance Theatre
68. Photo Features Ltd./The National Art Centre
70. Malak
71. The National Museum of Natural Sciences
72. The National Museum of Man
73. The National Museum of Science and Technology

75. Malak
77. Malak
79. Gilles Benoit/Photothèque
80. Barbara Johnstone
81. Sig Bradshaw
82. Les photographes Ellefsen Ltée.
83. Sig Bradshaw
84. Newfoundland Department of Education
85. Fred Bruemmer
86. Alberta Education
87. Island Information Service
89. George Hunter
90. Deryk Bodington
92. Gerry Cairns/*Winnipeg Free Press*
93. *Vancouver Sun*
95. Ontario Hydro
97. The National Research Council
98. The National Research Council
100. Deryk Bodington
101. Deryk Bodington
102. O.J. Dell/Photo Source
103. Malak
104. George Hunter
105. Ontario Hydro
107. Richard Harrington
108. Environment Canada
109. Malak
110. Fred Bruemmer
113. Dept. of Energy, Mines and Resources
114. Fred Bruemmer
115. Fred Bruemmer
116. Dept. of Communications
118. Dept. of Communications
121. Jim Merrithew
123. British Columbia Telephone Company (2)
124. *Vancouver Sun*
125. Canadian Broadcasting Corporation
126. Canadian Broadcasting Corporation
127. Canada Post
128. Alec Burns/Photo Source
129. Richard Harrington
130. Michael Saunders
131. Malak
132. Murdoch Maclean (top); Mike Beedell (bottom)
133. Jim Merrithew
134. George Hunter
135. Mike Beedell
136. George S. Zimbel
137. George Hunter
139. Mike Beedell
140. George Hunter

141. Malak
142. George Hunter/Photothèque
143. Miller Services
146. George Hunter
147. George Hunter
149. Malak
150. Deryk Bodington
151. Malak
152. Malak
154. Malak
155. Malak
156. Deryk Bodington
157. Deryk Bodington
158. George Hunter/Photothèque
160. Deryk Bodington
161. Malak (3)
162. George S. Zimbel
163. Malak
164. Bryce Flynn/Photothèque
165. Les photographes Ellefsen Ltée.
166. Reed Paper Ltd.
167. Miller Services
168. Les photographes Ellefsen Ltée.
169. Richard Harrington (2)
170. George Hunter (top); Malak (bottom)
171. *Vancouver Sun*
172. Southam Murray Printing/Consumers' Gas
173. Sulpetro Ltd.
175. Malak
177. Malak
178. George Hunter
179. Petro-Canada
180. Deryk Bodington
181. Les photographes Ellefsen Ltée.
182. Michael Saunders
183. George Hunter/Photothèque
184. Miller Services
186. Les photographes Ellefsen Ltée.
189. Sig Bradshaw
190. Miller Services
192. George Hunter
193. George Hunter
194. George Hunter
195. Deryk Bodington
196. Hawker Siddeley Canada Inc.
197. David Portigal/Indal Ltd.
200. Gulf Canada Ltd.
202. (1), (2) George Hunter/Photothèque
203. (3), (4) George Hunter/Photothèque; (5) Harold Clark/Photothèque
204. George Hunter/Photothèque
205. George Hunter

207. Canadian General Electric Co. Ltd.
209. The Steppac Group Inc./Ivaco Ltd.
210. George Hunter/Sherritt Gordon Mines Ltd.
211. Indal Ltd.
212. Malak
213. Malak
215. Malak
216. Daon Development Corp.
217. Bryce Flynn/Photothèque
219. George S. Zimbel
220. Charlie King/Photothèque
223. David Watson/Photothèque
225. George Hunter
226. Canadian General Electric Co. Ltd.
228. George S. Zimbel
229. George Hunter
230. George Hunter
231. Deryk Bodington
232. George Hunter
233. George Hunter
234. Fred Bruemmer
238. George Hunter
239. Malak
240. Audrey Giles/Photo Source (top); Jim Merrithew (bottom)
241. George Hunter
242. Murdoch Maclean
243. Ted Grant/Photothèque
245. George Hunter
246. Sig Bradshaw
247. George Hunter/Sherritt Gordon Mines Ltd.
248. George Hunter
249. George Hunter
252. Miller Services (top); George S. Zimbel (bottom)
253. George Hunter
254. Deryk Bodington (top); George Hunter/Photothèque (bottom)
255. J.E. Lozanski
256. Malak
257. Malak
261. Jim Merrithew
262. British Information Services
263. Canadian Press
264. Dept. of National Defence
265. George Hunter
267. Malak
269. Michael Saunders
271. Royal Canadian Mounted Police
273. Sig Bradshaw
274. Audrey Giles/Photo Source
275. Secretary of State
277. Vancouver Sun
278. Canadian Employment and Immigration Commission

ACKNOWLEDGEMENTS

280. J.E. Lozanski
281. George Hunter
282. Canadian General Electric Co. Ltd.
283. Southam Murray Printing/Consumers' Gas
284. George Hunter/Photothèque
285. Reed Paper Ltd.
286. George Hunter
287. George Hunter
288. George Hunter
289. Malak (bottom and top right); David Watson/Photothèque (top left)
290. Consumer and Corporate Affairs Canada.
291. Malak
292. Dept. of National Defence
293. Mike Beedell
295. Mike Beedell
296. Peter Redman/*The Financial Post*
297. Wamboldt-Waterfield
299. Jim Merrithew
300. Deryk Bodington
301. George Hunter/Photothèque
302. Bryce Flynn/Photothèque
303. O.J. Dell/Photo Source
304. Deryk Bodington
305. Malak
306. Deryk Bodington
307. George Hunter
308. Marc Poirel
309. Mike Beedell
310. Malak
311. Malak
312. Malak
313. Malak
314. Richard Harrington
315. George Hunter
316. Dept. of Fisheries and Oceans (top); Jim Merrithew (bottom)
317. Malak
318. George Hunter
319. Malak
320. Malak
321. Malak
322. Malak
323. Malak
324. Jim Merrithew/Dept. of External Affairs
326. Canadian International Development Agency
328. Canadian Executive Service Overseas
329. Canadian University Service Overseas
330. Dept. of National Defence
331. Dept. of National Defence
332. J.E. Lozanski
Please Note: Inquiries about photographs credited to Photothèque should be directed to the National Film Board of Canada.

Index